Happy Fat

Taking Up Space in a World That Wants to Shrink You

Sofie Hagen

4th ESTATE • *London*

4th Estate
An imprint of HarperCollins*Publishers*
1 London Bridge Street, London SE1 9GF
www.4thEstate.co.uk

First published in Great Britain by 4th Estate in 2019

1 3 5 7 9 8 6 4 2

A catalogue record for this book is available from the British Library

ISBN 978-0-00-829387-1

Illustrations by Mollie Cronin (Art Brat Comics).

This book contains health- or medical-related materials or discussions.
The content is the opinion of the author and is not intended to be a substitute for
professional medical advice, diagnosis, or treatment. Always seek the advice of a qualified
health provider with any questions you may have regarding a medical condition.

This book is based on the author's experiences.
Some names, identifying characteristics, dialogue and details have been
changed, reconstructed or disguised to protect the identities of those involved.

All reasonable efforts have been made by the author and the publisher
to trace the copyright holders of the images and material quoted in this book.
In the event that the author or publisher are contacted by any of the untraceable
copyright holders after the publication of this book, the author and the
publisher will endeavour to rectify the position accordingly.

Printed and bound in Great Britain by CPI Group (UK) Ltd, Croydon, CR0 4YY

MIX
Paper from
responsible sources
FSC™ C007454

This book is produced from independently certified FSC™ paper
to ensure responsible forest management

Find out more about HarperCollins and the environment at
www.harpercollins.co.uk/green

To the canaries in the coal mine

Contents

PART TWO

Introduction

Hi, I am fat. I am also thirty years old, Danish and a Scorpio. I am a person who only recently felt adult enough to buy non-plastic plants. I have owned more instruments (three) than I have learned to play (zero). My favourite colours are red and purple. I have worked in an antique bookshop, a bakery, a sex shop (where they either believed me when I said I was older than I was, or just didn't care), a video store (from which I stole sweets), a posh grocery shop, a kindergarten (from which I got fired when the children asked me to pretend to be a Sleeping Grown-up and I actually fell asleep for an hour), and various charity organisations as both a street fundraiser and a telemarketing fundraiser. That was my last normal job before I started doing stand-up comedy. I have won a few big stand-up comedy awards such as the Edinburgh Comedy Award for Best Newcomer. I have a poster on my wall of a flying llama saying '¿Que Pasa?' and I laugh every time I see it. I had my first article published when I was thirteen. It was about the pop singer P!nk and it was in a Danish teen magazine called *Vi Unge*. I had my first two-page spread published in a free newspaper called *MetroExpress* when I was fifteen. It was about *How to Be the Best Westlife Fan.* I love musical theatre and I love going to the cinema alone. I prefer dogs to cats. I also prefer dogs to most humans. I am many, many things other than my weight. I am sure you are too. I don't wish for my fatness to define me any more than I want Kindergarten Sleeper, Westlife Fan or Dog Lover to define me.

But when people see me, they see the fat. They judge and notice the fat. Despite this, they rarely say the word *fat*. That is why it's part of the title of this book. FAT. I say it as often as I can. FAT. In the hopes that the more I say it, the less scary it will seem. We all have fat on our bodies, it's only the volume of it that differs from person to person. Fat is essentially energy. Fat is protecting our organs. And fat is just a descriptive word. The negative connotations came later; hissed at us by a parent, shouted from a moving vehicle, or written in yellow all-caps letters on the front cover of a magazine as a warning.

A lot of effort is put into denying *fat*. Phrases like 'You *have* fat, you *are not* fat' and 'I am not fat, I'm just easy to see.' The intention is sweet, but it does nothing but reaffirm that *fat is bad*. This is all called fatphobia. The fear of fatness. This is a message we see constantly – from adverts on television, through fat characters in movies who either don't exist or are portrayed negatively, through your mother asking if you've gained weight with a sneer, your friends talking about their new diets, the high-street clothes shops not catering to a size bigger than 12, through the lack of fat people on the covers of magazines and the constant news stories telling us that *the obesity epidemic is coming to get us all*. Everything has the basic underlying message that it is positive to be thin and negative to be fat.

Of course, if a woman is thin, she will be wrong in other ways. She will be too thin, not the right shape of thin, not the right height, not have a large enough gap between her thighs – and she needs to smile more but not too much, because that would be slutty. She needs to laugh but not at her own jokes, preferably men's jokes. She needs to wear a dress that's not too long because then she is a prude but also not short because then she is a whore. Her breasts have to be big – but not vulgar-big and not big in length. And she most importantly has to never complain about these extreme and impossible beauty standards and society's wish to make her into an accessory.

There is a growing amount of pressure on men to look a certain way as well – but usually, they are given a slightly bigger pass than women are. Yet, even if they do get a big pass, fat men are still not allowed to be fat.* Fat is frowned upon, regardless of who embodies it and regardless of how much they embody. Trashy magazines will find even the slightest bulge on the stomach of a celebrity swimming in the ocean and plaster her all over the front

---

* You probably already know that there are more than just two genders. There are people who are **transgender** (when they were born, based on their genitals, people assumed they were the wrong gender), **agender** (people who do not identify with any gender), **bigender** (people who identify with two genders, interchangeably) and we have people who are **non-binary** or **genderqueer** (people who are 'something other than man/woman'. Often, but not always, **non-binary** people will prefer the pronouns they/them instead of he/him or she/her). **Cis** means that your actual gender fits with your 'assumed gender' – the gender you were assigned at birth. Gender is a construct and it all exists on a spectrum and gender can easily mean a different thing to different people. But regardless of which gender you subscribe to – if any at all – fatness is, in the eyes of society, not allowed.

cover of their magazine as an example of someone breaking the rules: by not staying thin.

Fat is perceived to be an exclusively negative thing. And it isn't. And it doesn't have to be.

That's the essence of this book. Fat is not an inherently negative word. Fat is, if anything, neutral. But it can be *beautiful*, it can be *loved*, it can be *absolutely magnificent*. You can be *fat and sexy, fat and healthy, fat and happy.*

I *love* my body. I love my stomach with all of its red stretch marks hanging like an impractical bum bag over my thick, fleshy thighs which spread out and drape slightly over the sides when I sit in a chair. My double and, sometimes, triple chin. The jiggly flesh on my arms where there are, in theory, somewhere deep down, triceps. There is so much fat there that I can grab a fistful of it. My body is many, many fistfuls of fat. When I wear a bra, bulges of fat pop out right above the strap under my armpits, creating side boobs. My cheeks are thick, so thick that when I smile, they almost cover my eyes completely. I smile a lot. I would tell you how much I weigh, but I don't know. I stopped weighing myself years ago.

I have never been thin and I will never be thin.

I am a fat person and I love my body. I feel lucky to be able to say that. It has never come easy. It has taken a lot of work and a lot of time to get here. I often meet people who are incredibly puzzled that I can love *this* body. Taking the world into account – how we are taught to see bodies and judge bodies – I understand the puzzlement. But I am quite sure I can explain it. I want to tell you what I have learned and how I got here.

Essentially, this book is a beginner's guide. A look into the world of being a fat person.

Introduction

More specifically, what it is like to be me – a white, pansexual,* West European person. On top of which, I come across as straight – meaning that people can't see all the internal feelings of *oh actually I want to kiss girls* and *oh actually I'd like to kiss everyone*. I am, at this moment in time, nondisabled. In the moment of writing this book, I call myself fat. There are loads of different terms you can use to describe your body, but the most commonly used ones within fat activism are big-thin, small-fat, fat, super-fat and infinity-fat.† It's hard to define. All bodies are so vastly different that you can't really make an official definition. Two people weighing the same could look completely different – and therefore be treated very differently by society. One person who is a size 28 could fit into an airplane seat whereas another person who is a size 24 could not. I am somewhere in between 'fat' and 'super-fat'. I can buy clothes in *most* online plus-size clothes shops, but I cannot fit into most seats that have armrests. Infinity-fats can definitely not do any of those things. Big-thins never have to worry about either.

This book is very much from a West European perspective and primarily deals with West European culture. It's important

---

* I'm really getting into these footnotes. Isn't this exciting? It feels less formal. Like we are at a house party and I drag you into the bathroom to have a chat about that person I fancy. Which could be a person of *any* (or no) gender, by the way, because I am pansexual. It's pretty much the same as bisexual. But some people still think that bisexuality reinforces the gender binary (the idea that there are only two genders: man and woman) because it's an old-fashioned word. So I prefer pansexual, just to make it absolutely clear that I can be sexually attracted to ab-so-lute-ly ev-er-y-on-e.

† Fat activists are people trying actively to change the world, in order to make it less fatphobic. More about this a bit later on.

for me to say this and, I guess, for you to read this, because it is worth noting that there are other viewpoints out there. It is always important to be aware of privilege – be it your own privilege or the privilege of the author whose book you're reading.*

But it is not for me to speak on behalf of others – instead, I talk about *me and my experiences*. Over the course of the last decade, I have read books and articles, studies and opinion pieces, I have watched documentaries and attended conferences, interviewed experts, scholars and highly experienced activists, all about fatphobia and its causes and its consequences. So even though my perspective is my own and as everything (hu)man-made, fundamentally subjective, the only reason I felt comfortable writing this book is that I feel like I have enough empirical knowledge to back up what I will be telling you.

Throughout the book, I have incorporated chats that I have had with people with different life experiences from my own. It's also a way of showing intersectionality at play. I have talked to Stephanie Yeboah, who is a dark-skinned black and fat woman from London, and who – just by existing – has to deal with fatphobia, racism and colourism. There is Kivan Bay, a fat, trans, queer man from Portland, US, who has to live with fatphobia, transphobia, queer- and homophobia. And Matilda Ibini, a black woman in a wheelchair from London, who has to deal with racism, colourism, body shaming and ableism. You can't separate just one 'marginalisation' on its own – which is why I urge you to not skip these chats. They are

---

* ME! AN AUTHOR! I mean, you're currently reading this book, so maybe it is not the most reassuring thing to read. Like if you overheard your doctor say 'Oh my god, can you believe they let me do this surgery?' or even worse, if you heard your hairdresser say, 'Oooh, they let me hold the scissors!'

all incredible people whom I very much enjoyed talking to. If their life experiences are not similar to your own, it is still important to include them in your journey. I'm so grateful for their input.

I also have a chat with Dina Amlund, a Danish cultural historian who focuses on fatness, who is here to fix one of our most common misconceptions within our ideas of fatness. I am very excited and proud to share her viewpoint with you.

This book is for everyone. Absolutely everyone. But I have lived as a fat woman, I relate to fat women, I relate to queer people; people who sometimes feel like they are on the outskirts of society. I have written this book for everyone, but if you are not fat, if you are a cis man, you may at times feel left out or unattended to. This is not because I am purposely leaving you out. But I have lived for thirty years now consuming art and media made by thin, white, straight cis men who have subconsciously or consciously primarily addressed other thin, white, straight, cis men, and rarely have they tried to include me or my fellow outsiders into their world, as anything but the joke or the accessory. Yet, when asked, they would probably also claim that their art was for everyone as well. So that is what I am saying to you now: this book is for everyone. If you do not relate to being fat, if you do not relate to being a woman or if you do not relate to being an outsider in any way, you should still read it. I just don't pander to you. We fatties have very little that is made by us, for us. So if you are fat, this is particularly for you. The fat, the weird, the queer, the neuroatypical,* the confused and the excluded.

---

* **Neuroatypical** is a broad umbrella term for people whose neurology doesn't fit with what most people deem 'normal'. So, anyone with a mental or behavioural disorder, depression, ADHD, anxiety, eating disorders, bipolar disorders and so on.

In this book, I am going to talk about growing up as a fat child, a fat teenager and becoming a fat adult. I am going to talk about dieting and, most importantly, failing at it. I am going to talk about the ridicule and humiliation, the ostracism and the trauma, the rejection and the heartbreak. I am going to talk about belly rolls, stretch marks and the red marks you get between your thighs when they have been rubbing together.

This is not a book about body positivity. I will mostly use the term 'Fat Liberation'. Body positivity gained momentum fairly recently – it came with TV adverts showing slightly chubby (at best) models using certain lotions or tights. It came with a lot of caveats: you can be slightly bigger than a size 10, but it's preferable if you have an hourglass figure. The fat is acceptable if it is in the right places and if there is not too much of it. Super-fat people are still not represented and there is a noticeable focus on fatties who exercise or eat salads. Another caveat: you can be fat if you at least are trying to lose weight.

It may seem like there has been a lot of progress recently, but it isn't fair to say that the progress has been made for *fat* people. We may have more adverts on TV featuring what they call 'real women' (yawn) but at the same time, clothing brands are removing their plus-size collections from their physical store and the world seems to want us to exist less and less. For example, only as recently as March 2018, Thai Airways banned fat people from using business class.[1]

Fortunately, due to social media, we can control a lot of what we see. In the back of the book, I have a list of some fat role models and fat activists who are all making a big difference. But when you look at popular media – your average TV commercial or women's magazine, or when you look at the news, the very best we can hope for is a fat person struggling to lose weight or a thin person in a fat-suit. And maybe a message from some beauty brand saying 'buy this lotion for real women' which then features a few cis women who are all a size 10–12. Maybe one of them has short hair so the brand looks super diverse. That's body positivity.

This is all so far away from what the original Fat Liberation movement stood for. By using the word 'body' instead of 'fat', we easily lose sight of what the core of the body image issue is: the hatred of fatness and fat people. By allowing the focus to rest on the 'body positivity' movement, we are allowing wealthy companies to cash in on a fight that has been fought by fat activists since the 1960s. Fat activism is very rarely about the individual's struggle with their self-esteem or feelings about their stretch marks. It is about changing the anti-fat bias, particularly the way it affects fat people politically. For example, it is still legal to discriminate against a person based on their weight in the UK,[2] 49 states in the US (the only state that has made it illegal is Michigan)[3] and a majority of countries all over the world. We are not a protected group. Fat people are, on average, paid less and have a harder time getting employed.[4] So where there is definitely a reason for also talking about the individual's self-esteem (I go fully at it in the chapter 'How to love your body', for example), it is so utterly important that we remember and understand where this whole thing started. The incredible people who fought for us and before us.

The fat-activism movement started in the US in 1967. Five hundred fat people had a 'Fat-In' in Central Park in New York, where they ate ice cream and burned diet books.[*]

---

[*] If four hundred and ninety-nine fat people would like to join me, I'll be doing this every Sunday in my nearest park from now on.

The 'National Association to Advance Fat Acceptance' was founded in America in 1969, by a guy called Bill Fabrey in response to discrimination against his wife.* Today NAAFA is seen more as a politically motivated group, but during the sixties they were much more of a social club for fat people. The San Francisco chapter of NAAFA were a bunch of wild and awesome lesbians and queer women, many of whom were Jewish, who started becoming vigilant about fat hatred in the scientific community and wanted to fix that. NAAFA considered this to be a bit too dramatic, so the San Francisco chapter splintered off and, in 1972, became the Fat Underground. They coined phrases such as, 'A diet is a cure that doesn't work, for a disease that doesn't exist.'[5]

In 1983, the Fat Underground and the New Haven Fat Liberation Front released the book *Shadow on a Tightrope*, a collection of poems, articles and essays by and about fat women and their lives and in the UK, The London Fat Women's Group was started in 1985. The terms used around this time were Fat Liberation, Fat Pride and Fat Power. The Fat Liberation movement, alongside the Fat Pride and Fat Power movement, was not too bothered with how the individual felt about their body. It was a critique and a fight directed against the structural oppression, the discrimination and the inherent fatphobia (the hatred of fat bodies) in society. The focus was not on how much you should 'love your curves'; they just wanted to be free. In 1973, two fat activists, Judy Freespirit and Aldebaran, released the Fat Liberation Manifesto, which you can read at the back of this book, and it's still as relevant today as it was back then.

---

* #RelationshipGoals

Around the same time, a lot of Fat Liberation and body-revolution politics were also being discussed by black feminists and black womanists.* Fat black women have had to fight sexism, racism and fatphobia, attacks on the colour of their skin, their perceived gender and the size of their bodies. In a 1972 edition of the American feminist magazine *Ms.*, Johnnie Tillman wrote: 'I'm a woman. I'm a black woman. I'm a poor woman. I'm a fat woman. I'm a middle-aged woman. And I'm on welfare. In this country, if you're any one of those things you count less as a human being. If you're all those things, you don't count at all. Except as a statistic.' In 1984, Guyanese-British poet Grace Nichols released the book *The Fat Black Woman's Poems*.

It is worth noting that the movement that has now been overtaken by corporations was started by women who were primarily fat, Jewish, black and queer. None of whom would be likely to feature in the adverts for lotions by these 'body positive' companies, or would be able to buy clothes in a shop using 'curvy' models to 'promote body positivity'. They took the 'fat' and replaced it with 'body' to erase the very existence of fat people and make it more palatable and sexy to consumers. They then took the searing and urgent call to arms that is the word 'liberation' and changed it to 'positivity', almost as if to say: 'Shh, sit down, don't make a fuss. Smile. Smile and be still-quite-thin.'

And we all know how women love to be told to smile.

A good thing about the body-positivity movement is that it is most likely what led you to my book. I am very much a spreader of 'love yourself' rhetorics. I use hashtags such as #HappyFat and I

---

* **Womanism** is sort of like feminism but with a focus on black women's experience. It was coined by Alice Walker (author of *The Color Purple*). It has been described as 'black feminism'.

have a chapter in this book called 'How to love your body'. I have been featured in many 'Body-Positive Babes You Must Follow on Instagram!' articles. And I would love for you to love your body, because it's a wonderful feeling. But don't get me wrong – I need you to love your body, so you can join me in the revolution. So one day you'll join me in a park for ice cream and diet-book burning like those who came before us.

But let's not focus on the far-away future right now. This is just the introduction, where I wrap you in a blanket, introduce myself and the topic of fat, and prepare you for what you are about to read. We can plan the revolution when you have finished the book.

When I set out to write this book, I wanted, first and foremost, to put into words what being fat has been like for me. In doing small, intimate readings of the initial draft to an audience, I learned that I am very much not alone with these feelings. It made me feel less alone and I sincerely hope you will feel the same way when reading this book. As I mentioned, you will find a whole chapter full of advice on *how to love your body*. What a grandiose statement. I will debunk all the damaging myths about fatness and health like many others have done before me and like so many others will have to do in years to come. I will reach out to you non-fats reading this book – you get your very own chapter. I wanted you to know how you can be a better friend to fat people. Oh, also, I wanted to refer to myself as the 'Bang Lord' at least once. And drag a lot of people who wronged me because I am vengeful, I never forget and I latch onto grudges like I am my brother twenty years after I convinced him to sell his shares in Google because it would never take off. #YahooForever. There are also lovely illustrations sprinkled all over the book by the amazing fat illustrator, Mollie Cronin.

Introduction

Before you start the book, I want you to do something that I often have had to do throughout writing it. Put your hands on your stomach – or your thighs, your upper arms, your double chin or whatever area on your body that you have struggled with the most – and close your eyes. Give yourself a nice little cuddle. Whisper, 'We are going to be okay. I love you.' Because chances are, you will have said a lot of crap to your body in your life and we are about to dig into some of that. I'd love for your body to come with you. If this is all too cutesy-wootsy and wishy-washy and it makes you roll your eyes at me, fine. I can all-too-well respect that. I am making myself a little bit sick by writing it. But just consider trying it a few times throughout the book, and maybe wonder why the very basic action of physically showing yourself and your body affection makes us cringe. We have a long way to go.

So let's go.

Welcome to my book. I hope you like it here. We are going to be okay.

PART ONE

About the reality of being fat

But it's also quite a lot about me, actually

1

My fat body

I was a child

I was a beautiful child. I tell myself that often. Depending on what mood I am in, I put the emphasis on different words. I was a *beautiful* child. I *was* a beautiful child. When I look at photos of myself as a little eight-year-old with hazel-brown hair and eyes and a big smile on my little fat face, wearing a Superman outfit, a tightened fist raised towards the sky, with little chubby cheeks and sparkly eyes, I also think of the nurse who told my mum that I needed to lose weight because 'it was dangerous'. Based on nothing but how I looked; having done no medical exams or tests. Knowing nothing about my diet or life. I can tell you now, it was not *dangerous*. I was a child. I was a beautiful *child*. My body was fine. It was still developing. More importantly, I was not feeling shame yet. She introduced that into my life.

My mother is a single mother of two children. When she told me that my dad was leaving us, I started crying. Through the tears and the snot, I said, 'Is he going to take my toys with him?' and,

19

surprised, she said, 'No. Of course not.' And like that, I stopped crying. My mum told me that anecdote. I don't remember it. This happened when I was five years old – the second time he left us. He left after my mum had given birth to me. He came back five years later, made my sister and left again. An unwanted boomerang of a man.

Food control very quickly became a thing I had to get acquainted with. My real difficulties with food started when I was five years old. My sister's birth was complicated and she ended up in an incubator for three weeks, being fed through a tube. From the beginning, she was ever so tiny and so thin. For the first ten years of her life, doctors kept telling my mother to feed her loads of full-fat foods, because she was too thin. My sister hated eating and just wanted to jump around and play. My mother was then told by other doctors that I had to stop eating junk food and I needed to start jumping around and play. I just wanted to eat.

I had to become incredibly aware of my own body and weight – the fact that I was wrong and too big. So I felt bad; and those bad feelings, I found, could be crushed by eating a lot. I would eat so much I felt numb.

✳

Once my dad left the second time, my mum was alone with two children – one too small and one too big. She had no knowledge of, or interest in, food, no money, energy or time to study it, and a lot of pressure on her shoulders to be a 'perfect single mother'. She could not figure out what to do. She tried her best: served fatty foods for my sister and salads for me. If she looked away for even a second, my sister would be running away from the table towards her toys, and I would be shovelling her fatty food into my mouth.

I always found ways of getting food. I would go to my grandparents' house and they would give me as much sugar as I wanted. I remember hearing my mother talking to them on the phone, begging them to please stick to the diet the school nurse had prescribed me. My grandmother had said to her, 'But I can't say no to her, she's my grandchild,' and from then on my mom knew she did not have a lot over control over what they gave me.

My grandparents consist of my mother's mother and my step-grandfather. Seeing as I barely knew my dad, I had little to no contact with his side of the family either. When my mother became a single mother, she moved to Søndersø – a tiny town. As I remember, there is one road, a few houses and a school. And a factory which makes crisps.

A lot of my memories from Søndersø have to do with food. The bakery sold incredibly soft sandwiches with cheese, ham and a thick layer of mayonnaise. There was a service station at the outskirts of town that sold pick 'n' mix, and their red raspberry wine gums tasted like summer. I can still hear my mother scold me, when she found out that I had been buying and eating them even though I was on a diet. At school, they sold bagels that were so soft on the inside that it felt like eating a marshmallow. I think of the food I ate when I was a child in Søndersø more fondly than might be normal – because I am not remembering the taste, I am remembering how sweet it felt to momentarily escape my own feelings by eating myself into numbness.

And a lot of my memories of my grandparents are to do with food as well. They lived only a few miles from Søndersø – in a place called Skamby.* Skamby has a population of about four hundred people. And if you live in Skamby, you know the names, occupations and relations of every single one of those people. My grandfather's favourite hobby was to sit by the window and look out onto the road. (I mean *'the* road'. The road in Skamby. There is one road in Skamby.) He would sit and look out the window and, if anyone walked past, he would comment. *Oh, is that the butcher's daughter? I thought her shift didn't end till 4 p.m. Oh, I see Gretha now. Of course. It's Tuesday. She's been at the knitting club.* He managed to do all of this without at any point catching a glimpse of his own reflection and saying: *My God, I am boring. Is this really my life?*

The emotional currency in my grandparents' house was food. They would eat six times a day. Breakfast, late-morning dessert, lunch, afternoon coffee and cake, dinner and a late-night TV snack. My grandmother would bake every day. The softest butter-buns,† cinnamon pastries, cookies and bread. I would often help her and throw myself into the bowls of leftover gooey dough and lick it all off, adding another meal to my day. Food quickly became feelings and feelings became food. Delicious food. Butter in and around and on top of everything. Juicy meat with enough salt to make you dehydrated for the rest of your life. Potatoes,

---

* If you really want to get the gist on Skamby, just look up what the words 'skam' and 'by' mean in Danish. Okay, I'll do it for you. 'Skam' means 'shame'. 'By' is 'town'. Shametown. I grew up in Shametown. That's just what I wanted to tell you. Carry on reading now.

† Fun Denmark fact: 'Tandsmør' is a Danish word which directly translated means 'tooth-butter' – it's when you put so much butter on bread that it leaves teeth marks when you take a bite. Hold on, I just have to go kiss my passport.

so many potatoes. Vegetables only if you could caramelise them. Gravy which was basically just brown cream with more butter. We had to empty our plates completely and if my grandfather said, 'Come on, have some more, your grandmother worked so hard on this food,' then you had to eat more. There was an abundance of food and you could never eat enough.

Food was how you expressed love and how you were punished, and I stopped listening to my own instincts. My grandfather would buy me pastries, sweets, cakes and ice cream and somehow make it into a declaration of love. I remember him buying me a big cake that I didn't want to eat. His face fell and he almost whimpered, 'I bought it for you because I love you.' And so I had to eat the cake. I must have been around five years old (which is an early age to start learning to ignore your appetite and disregarding your own boundaries).

We had a ritual where my grandfather would let me go with him into the basement and stand by their deep freezer and choose which ice cream I wanted. The opening of the lid was often accompanied by the sound of angels playing the harp in my head. As I remember it now, the vapour that escaped the freezer had gold specks in it. And there was so much ice cream. Cone-shaped cones, boat-shaped cones, ice lollies, big tubs full of ice cream with different flavours, mint, chocolate, vanilla, fudge, strawberry, caramel, pistachio, biscuits and all of the chocolate bars in ice cream form. I would stand on my toes and pull myself up by placing my little chubby hands on the edge of the freezer and look into this haven of ice cream.

But for my grandfather, it was not about the ice cream. It was about the fact that *he* was holding the lid, *he* had taken me into this basement and *he* was allowing me to pick and choose. I was incredibly aware, in the most childlike of ways, that I had to be very, very grateful. Even if I didn't want to eat ice cream that day, the chances of me knowing that were slim. I knew that if I said no to ice cream, my grandfather would punish me by looking at me with big, sad eyes. He would then dramatically walk into another room, where he would sit on a chair in the darkness and sigh, looking out of the window. He would not say a word for hours. My grandmother would frantically rub her hands on her apron and tell me to 'please go and speak to him and apologise' in a desperate attempt to not have this sort of drama in her husband's house. I would then have to push down the guilt of being the five-year-old who had made her grandfather sad, and apologise. And beg for the ice cream I didn't want. Until he finally smiled again and gave me the ice cream. My grandmother and I would exhale deeply out of pure relief. Disaster averted, but only slightly. The guilt would battle my appetite and win. I learned that I could not be in contact with my body and listen to its signals, *and* avoid harming the emotions of my grandfather.

I would then return home and my mother would interrogate me about the food I had just eaten. She was still just trying to follow the doctor's orders and put me on a strict diet, but she could see gravy stains on my T-shirt and butter all over my face. She was a tired single mother who probably felt like she had no authority over her own daughter. So she desperately tried to motivate me to lose the weight, to eat less, to defy my grandparents – who would retaliate by telling me that they only fed me because they loved me, insinuating that if I didn't eat any of it, I must not love them back. There were a lot of strong negative emotions at play and, fortunately, food continued to be perfect for numbing them.

At some point, food became a need. I needed food. I needed to eat so much so that I felt nothing. I was eight. I was a beautiful *child*.

At school, I found out how to borrow money from older students so I could buy cake in the cafeteria. Seeing as my mother did not want me to end up indebted as an eight-year-old, she had to give me money to give to the kids. Which I would then spend on more sweets.

My mother would buy VHS tapes called *Buns of Steel* in which a thin, white lady would do aerobics to the camera, making encouraging statements. My mother and I would move all the furniture to the side and copy her movements on the living room floor. I hated it. I hated my body and now I somehow had to collaborate with it. I just wanted it gone. I wanted to not acknowledge it. Moving it about made me very aware of its existence and how much I loathed it. The self-hatred, I killed with more eating. My mother was falling apart.

I ~~hated~~ hate PE. I dissociated from my body. My body was too big, too much, too gross. And now you want to put me in shorts and a T-shirt and I am meant to feel it move? No. No, thank you, sir. I wanted to use my words and my intelligence and basically, anything but my body, which had now become my enemy. The reason I was constantly stressed (hello, I was eight years old) and sad. I tried to get out of PE every week.* Every single week. My PE teacher was a gruesome woman.

---

* I fought against having to do PE till I left the educational system at nineteen. I won several battles against several PE teachers and various principals. I told them that if they truly believed that their need for me to attend PE was because they wanted me to exercise and *not* because they had some *fascist* desire to control children, then they should let me do the kind of exercise that I wanted to do. I won and I was allowed to either go for a walk or rehearse a dance routine alone in an unused classroom. When I got older, once I had a therapist's note saying that I was mentally unable to do PE, they let me take an arts and crafts class with younger students instead. Sofie v. PE: 3–0.

25

She refused to believe my excuses. She refused to believe I had hurt my ankle. Once, when I said I had got my period (nice work, eight-year-old me), she got me to repeat this out loud in front of the entire class. She then pulled my trousers and pants down in front of everyone and said, 'See?'

I hated showering with the other pupils. So I said I had a stiff neck. Which led her to shout at me in front of a whole dressing room full of my classmates who, at this point, had already showered and got dressed. They were all eager to leave and go to lunch break but the teacher would not allow anyone to leave until I had showered. I remember how she tore my clothes off of me in front of everyone and shoved me into the shower.

My childhood memories of PE are mostly repressed due to experiences like these. I remember little glimpses. I remember running. I remember running because I was being chased by three boys with a baseball bat. I finally gave in and crouched over, covering my head with my hands, trying not to cry, as they beat me and mocked me. I remember looking up, seeing my PE teacher laugh.

I still have fantasies about finding out where she lives and going to her house. I want to look her in the eyes and speak to her as an adult with a much more advanced vocabulary and understanding of what is right and wrong. I want to stand in front of her in the body she hated and speak on behalf of myself as a child and tell her that she was a rotten person. I would say to her, 'I was a *beautiful* child. I *was* a beautiful child. I was a beautiful *child*.'

✳

Self-loathing is such a strong feeling. Hating your entire self – both your body and your own inability to change your body –

leaves you with very little. Existence is suddenly quite difficult. Being able to pinpoint one of the causes for those negative feelings is almost freeing. It leads you to fantasise about going to old ladies' houses and screaming obscenities at them because of something that happened over twenty years ago. From a more objective and empathetic viewpoint, my old PE teacher seems to have had issues of her own. Fatphobia is prevalent in society and she was taught to hate fatness as much as my doctors, my bullies and my mother. Fatphobia is ingrained in us from the moment we are old enough to understand what happens around us. And we will continue to pass it on if it isn't challenged.

Research from Common Sense Media showed that half of girls and one third of boys as young as six to eight years old, feel that their ideal body is thinner than they are. Children as young as five are unhappy with their bodies. Five- to eight-year olds who think their mothers are dissatisfied with their bodies are more likely to feel dissatisfied with their own bodies.[1] An article in the *Journal of Applied Developmental Psychology* in 2000 stated that body size stigmatism was clearly present in three-year-olds and that 'the cultural stereotype that "fat is bad" was pervasive across gender, regardless of the child's own body build.'[2]

Teenage years

My relationship with my body only became more distorted throughout my teen years. It became a routine. I would start a new diet on a Monday and the adrenaline of thinking, *Finally, I will lose weight*, carried me through the hunger and desperation to eat for a couple of days – maybe even weeks, until I had to give up and binge-eat till I crushed the disappointment in myself. I would then wait till next Monday and start again on a new diet. With each failed diet, I would blame myself, I truly believed that my incapability of following a diet was a sign of absolute weakness, laziness and stupidity. Also, I was still fat. Which I believed to be the worst thing a person could be.

Finding a new diet was a rush. I remember finding out that Dr Phil's son Jay McGraw had a diet book on the market and punching the air. I tried the Atkins Diet, the Atkinson Diet, SlimFast (a disgusting brown powder you mixed into a drink in place of every meal), the Thinking Diet ('you will lose weight if only you THINK differently'), 5-2 Diet ('binge then starve yourself'), Weight Watchers, Slimming World, the 'just don't eat after 5 p.m.' diet, the 'only eat fruit till 2 p.m.' diet, the 'no carbs' diet and so, so many more. I found thirty-two diet books in my mother's basement recently, like a creepy shrine to thin 'health gurus' with teeth that are too white. I tried karate, swimming lessons, running, spinning, tennis, badminton, dance classes, power walking, Pilates, aerobics . . . I have owned exercise bikes, Pilates balls, step-benches and every single exercise VHS ever made. When I was sixteen, exhausted from always being either starving or numbingly full, I tried throwing up after I ate. I purposely tried to trigger bulimia, knowing full well that this was a terribly dangerous illness. I reached *that point*. Where, even though I knew full well that eating disorders can have awful consequences, often resulting in bodies that will never be able to have children, which will always struggle with health issues and food, and which sometimes just die – all of this seemed like a better option than staying fat.

I started going to the gym four times a week. I got up at 4 a.m. to be at the gym at 6 a.m., exercise for an hour and then go to school at 8 a.m. On the way there, I would feel so faint from my breakfast apple that I went by the bakery and bought myself a huge cinnamon bun and a chocolate milk. I would spend the rest of the day sleeping through maths class dreaming about the pizza that I would definitely have to binge afterwards.

The irony of me attempting to get an eating disorder is not lost on me. When I was eighteen, I learned about binge eating disorder. The reason that no one knew about it was that it was not officially registered as an eating disorder in Denmark at this point. I was mostly just relieved. There was a word for it. There was a word for me stuffing my face with carbs and sugar on a daily basis. Knowing the word didn't stop me though. It just made me feel less guilty. I continued bingeing and I continued dieting.

Throughout my teens, I was angry but my anger was misplaced. I hated beautiful people. The self-hatred, the hatred of my body and how it existed in the world had turned so strong that I needed to project it elsewhere, or I would suffocate. So I turned my anger towards thin and conventionally beautiful people. I could just about forgive someone for being thin and beautiful – but not unless they were really ashamed of this. Ideally, every thin person at my school should have to walk up to me every morning and apologise for being handed better cards than me. They could at least pity me and acknowledge that I was trying really hard to look like them.

When I was seventeen, for Danish class, we had to analyse *Sleeping Beauty*. I unleashed all of my fury onto this fairy tale. I wrote about Sleeping Beauty and how she – and all other thin, beauty-privileged, empty skin-vessels – could just go suck on a massive ham and shut up. I wrote something along the lines of, 'Beautiful people can apparently just be sleeping and still get more attention than ugly people – what have we got to do, learn to juggle?* The end.'

Their pain was nothing, nothing, I tell you. I was punished with an extra assignment to write an essay. 'The Disadvantage of Beauty'. I nearly spat in the teacher's face when she assigned it.

I was furious. I stomped my feet when I left the classroom. Slammed the door. 'The Disadvantage of Beauty'. I was prepared to write the word 'NON-EXISTENT' three thousand times on a piece of paper and hand it in. But if there was anything I hated more than beautiful women, it was getting a poor grade.

I sat down and opened MSN Messenger.† I messaged all the beautiful people I knew. Sandy, who was a model. She was my age and once told me she wanted to be my girlfriend. I had laughed in her face. Great joke, Sandy. Have you not seen how I look next to you? She would be the first of quite a few models I would reject because I felt unworthy of their genitals touching mine.‡§ I messaged someone I knew from an internet forum. A guy with sturdy cheekbones. A few more.

'What is the disadvantage of being beautiful?' I asked all of them. And waited. They were surprisingly reluctant to reply, but none of them claimed not to be beautiful.

'The worst thing,' one of the beautiful people on my MSN

---

* Or start doing comedy?

† Hi kids, MSN Messenger was a chat programme, sort of like Facebook Messenger but without the entire social platform. You got to choose your own screen name, so you could be called something like °°¤ø,,,ø¤°°˘°°¤ø westℓife ro¢ks°°¤ø,,,ø¤°°˘°°¤ø. It was pretty awesome.

‡ Two. That is technically QUITE a few.

§ Note to self: consider renaming book *The Models I Have Rejected*.

Messenger chat list wrote to me, 'is that women never become my friends just to be my friends. They always end up falling in love with me. And then I have to hurt them. I know it sounds ridiculous, but it's really painful. I just love these women but not like that. And that hurts them.'

I wanted to object, but he had answered with such vulnerability and sincerity that I couldn't help sympathising with him. Had he burst through my front door with a sign that said 'pity me' and had told me the same story, I probably would have wanted to push him out of a window. But I had begged him to share his feelings on the topic. These were not thoughts he ever shared with anyone. He knew how it sounded.

'People always assume I am unintelligent. I am not taken seriously,' someone else said.

'I am never more than my looks.' Another message popped up on my desktop.

'I can never make real friends. If I laugh at someone's boyfriend's joke, they immediately accuse me of trying to steal him away from them. If I am polite, I am being fake. If I am mean, I am stuck-up. People tell me to my face that they hate me. They feel like they can, like I owe them something. I never chose to look like this,' wrote another girl.

I assembled it all into an essay which I guiltily handed in the following day. I was left with a feeling of hollowness. I had a whole handful of resentment and nowhere to put it. Surely, someone was to blame for the way I felt. At this point, the best thing that could have happened was being forced by a teacher to write an additional essay on capitalism and beauty standards. But no one opened my eyes to that till years later. And it was hard to shake, this completely irrational and unfair hatred of beautiful people.

Jealousy of beautiful people is understandable. Privilege comes with what society perceives to be beautiful.

Beauty is a tricky one – because you can't blame someone for being beautiful, but you *can* blame the culture that created the idea of 'ideal beauty'. It has been decided that beauty is having a symmetrical face, straight, white teeth and white skin. Your eyes can be *too far* apart or *too far* into your head. Your ears can be the *wrong* angle. This is the Western idea of 'beauty'. Of course, you must also be thin and nondisabled and definitely feminine if you are perceived to be a woman, and masculine if you are perceived to be a man. There are definitely icky racist, ableist, sexist, queerphobic and fatphobic connotations connected to ideas of what beauty is and what it is not. Class plays a role too: beauty can often be bought. Plastic surgery, teeth whitening, braces, contact lenses, and just a general ability to at least make your life look beautiful on social media. That fancy cup of coffee in that fancy coffee place with just the right filter.

Beauty is so subjective. It is laughable that we have somehow been tricked into thinking we all should find the same thing pretty. But we are frail and easily influenced. So we can't deny that the lie that says *beauty is objective* means that some people who do not live up to those standards will be discriminated against. (Maybe this is why we, as a society, tend to love it when beautiful people struggle. We like to laugh at models falling on catwalks or the 'dumb blonde' trope in Hollywood films.)

Funnily, very beautiful people and fat people have something in common. Such as people being surprised when we accomplish things. It will stem from very different assumptions. If I ran a marathon, people would look at me with raised eyebrows and open mouths. Wow. For a fatty, she sure can run. I would be praised. If a really beautiful person gets a degree in law, they make movies about it. Wow. *But why can she think? She doesn't need to.*

The idea that there is an objective beauty is soul-destroying, and it begins to feel like currency.

There is a scene in the movie *Seven* where a fat man is used to symbolise gluttony. He is also, surprise surprise, seemingly mentally ill, definitely poor, definitely unhygienic. Four traits that are always mushed together in Hollywood as if they are interchangeable. In another scene, the murderer has disfigured a supermodel and given her a choice: to keep on living, being 'ugly' for the rest of her life – or kill herself. Spoiler alert: she kills herself. This is not even that far from the truth. A study conducted by the Department of Psychiatry at the University of Florida in 1991 shows that out of a group of formerly fat people, given the choice between becoming fat again or going completely blind, 89 per cent will choose going blind.[3] In another 2006 survey conducted by the Rudd Center for Food Policy and Obesity at Yale, almost half of those asked indicated that they would happily give up a year of their lives if it meant they were not fat.[4]

I never believed that I could be found attractive. Part of me loathed the boys and girls who liked me, because surely they were either lying or horrible people themselves. Why would they want *me*, when they could get *someone better*? Someone *thinner*?

I remember a desperate boyfriend hissing into my face, 'If only you could see yourself the way I see you,' and me rolling my eyes at him saying, 'You *have* to say that.' And I laughed when he eventually cheated on me with a thin woman, because the joy of being proven right was more powerful than the pain of being cheated on.

Another boyfriend joined the military and had to be gone for long periods of time. I was so scared of being alone, of not being validated, that I joined yet another gym and started working out. Within a day, my entire world went back to revolving around weight loss. I started starving myself, counting calories, skipping school, so I could spend upwards of six hours in the gym, weighing myself four times a day and losing weight rapidly. By the time my boyfriend finally came home to see me for a weekend, I was angry at him for interrupting my stride. I blamed him for accepting me as I was, so I stopped feeling the need to exercise. As soon as he came back for a weekend, I started binge-eating again, gaining all the weight back and then some. I blamed him for that. I would not let him in. I would let no one in. I would let no one love me. Because I refused to believe it was a possibility. I was fat.

Looking back, I was in a fairly fortunate position. I was fat, but I was a small-fat. I was just about excluded from being able to buy clothes in straight-sized stores. I was 'Aw, you're not *that* fat'-fat. At the same time I had stumbled into a group of friends who cared about me and who had forced me out of my shell. It's important to note that a lot of fat teens are pretty secluded and isolated – a consequence of bullying and having internalised the fatphobia they've experienced and witnessed. I talk flippantly about my teen years and the dramatic stories of love and sex, but I do so with the knowledge that not all fat people have had this experience. I especially feel this as I have grown older and fatter and my anxiety has risen. Being able to date and fool around is not a given for everybody.

I am not even sure you know how horrible it is being a teenager before you're an adult. When you are a teenager, your hormones take full control of your every move. When I was a teenager and I fell in love, I *loved more than anyone had ever loved before in the history of the world and I would die, simply die a violent death* for a person with whom I had never even spoken. It's truly a matter of swaying between all the extreme versions of every emotion to the sound of a hundred adults asking you to figure out who you are and what you want to be. And you are both scared and at the same time, convinced that you definitely know better than these *adults*. Your teen years are also full of warnings. All the monsters that you thought were under your bed when you were a child are suddenly real – and they are not under your bed where you can see and contain them. They are the reason you are asked to never leave your drink out of sight, the reason you don't walk home alone, and the reason you have to learn how to say no if there is something you don't want to do. Yet, fairly often, we are not warned about the monsters that we can see – the people controlling everything that we consume. The people targeting marketing campaigns at teenagers' fragile self-esteem, confirming their worst fears: that they are not okay, that they should be prettier and thinner and better. Basically shaking the groundwork for the person they are to become. *You don't know who you are or who to be? We will tell you. Be thin and pretty. How? By using our products.* Daddy, is there a monster under my bed? *Yes, actually, and he is holding a Slimming World brochure.*

One day, when I was single and in my late teens, in the first week of my new job, I met a man who openly declared that he liked fat women. It was not directed at me, it was not to get me into bed, so I trusted it, weirdly. He told us, after a shift when we were getting drunk in the pub next to the office, that his father used to say to him: 'Get yourself a woman with curves. They're the best ones.'

He told me this with pride. I disregarded the problematic nature of that sentence because suddenly, I wanted to be the woman that he 'got himself'. Hey, fuck feminism, this guy with sandy blond hair and wide shoulders who smokes a pipe despite being only twenty-one just told me he might fancy my fat stomach. Feminism can wait. Sure, Emily Davison threw herself under a horse to get me the vote, but I was not willing to challenge this man now – because there was the faint shadow of a promise of a kiss within his *charming* anecdote.

A year later, I found myself wishing that his father had told him, 'Son, go get yourself a woman who is wilfully obsessed with you and who will write and send you poetry and always be so close to you that you can smell her breath,' because then maybe, I would have had a chance. Instead he moved to the Danish island furthest away from Denmark. I take no responsibility for that.

Some people have fathers who do positive PR for fat women from an early age. I remember falling in love with him for just this reason. It was hard to believe that other people like that existed. Most people will have parents who tell them to 'never get fat', who will pinch their own stomach fat and say 'eww' and who will point at fat people in the shops and say words like 'lazy', 'stupid' or 'gross'. The negative attitude towards weight is so all-encompassing that the chances are that whoever you meet has been taught to hate fatness, long before they even had a chance to make up their own minds about what it is they like and don't like.

So I spent all of my teenage years hating myself, hating fatness and hating women and hating thin women, hating people who loved me and hating myself. I wasted so much time. I wasted so much money on attempting to make my body smaller.

When I was seventeen, I applied for part-time jobs. There was a plus-size clothing store selling everything from tent-like ponchos for fat people, to tent-like ponchos for fat people – with tassels. I had circled the shop a few times before I gathered the courage to go inside and apply. A large, older woman with a smile on her face took my application, looked me up and down and led me into her office. After a bit of chit-chat, she told me that she'd love to hire me. I said, as confidently as I could manage, 'Just so you know, I am going to lose this weight soon.'

The woman's face burst into a huge grin as she laughed and said, 'Oh, sure!'

Today, I like her. Back then, I detested her and the shop and I never, ever wanted to work there. I stormed out, furious that she did not believe me because I *would* lose the weight, I *would* lose all the weight and I *would* be thin. The alternative did not even bear thinking of.

Sometimes you need to meet the right people at the right time. She was the right person at the wrong time. It wasn't till years later that I met another person like her – and this time, the time was right. Let me tell you about Andrea.

Early twenties

I found stand-up comedy a few years after I finished school. Comedy was an amazing way of turning the self-hatred into a strength. I would stand on stage and tell the fat jokes that I had heard my whole life, but suddenly, I was controlling the laughter. It was liberating, standing on stage, saying: *Hey! I am so fat and so lazy! And I am aware of it!*

And hearing people laugh.

There is an annual comedy gala party in Denmark. All the comedians get drunk, horrifically drunk, and lose their already virtually non-existent inhibitions. A comic once got so upset that he lost an award that he threw his shoes into the harbour. And someone once gave a blowjob to another comedian who stopped her halfway through and said, 'Let's just be colleagues.'

That was me. Hello.

That evening, I was wearing a beautiful gala dress. I had come from a television set, so I was wearing television make-up – which is like normal make-up but with extra layers and done by a person tutting over the state of your skin. (Or like that one make-up artist who tried to wrap me in a giant scarf because my chest was 'so ugly'.)

So I fell asleep with the grim taste of 'just a colleague' in my mouth, in full gala dress, fake eyelashes draped down my cheek, next to a mediocre comedian. I woke up and realised that I had forgotten to set my alarm. I had twenty minutes before I had to get to Copenhagen University for the first day of what was going to be three years of Russian Studies. I was about to miss first day of uni. I jumped out of bed, half-heartedly brushed my teeth, pulled the fake eyelashes all the way off and got up on my bike. I became aware that I was still drunk when I was sitting amongst the rest of the new students in my gala dress, reeking of alcohol, realising that I had not locked my bike outside. The other students were dressed, well, the way you should be dressed when attending university on the first day. They had showered and everything. I was wearing one earring and torn tights. Eyeliner was everywhere apart from along my eyelids. I am not sure if I looked like someone who took university too seriously or not seriously enough. Then I saw Andrea.

Meeting Andrea changed everything. She had unapologetically hairy armpits, a mullet and an obvious disdain for the entire system. If anyone was to ever 'stick it to the man', it was Andrea, and she was going to stick it to him hard. I am not sure if she saw me before she smelled me, but either way, we got talking.

Это дома. That's all the Russian I picked up from my year at University of Copenhagen. It means 'he is home'. Or 'they are home'. Maybe it means 'someone is home' or 'is someone home?'. Either way, I can almost pronounce it perfectly.

I failed the first exam because I put a question mark after each answer. What was the main import in the thirteenth century? *Um . . . Corn? Potatoes?*

The professor looked at me sternly and said, 'It's not a quiz,' and I said, 'Rocks?'

I love the Russian language. I think I convinced myself that it was a legitimate possibility to study it for three years and graduate. I did believe that I could do both comedy and get a degree in Russian. But I was doing comedy at the same time and always prioritised that. It fulfils me in a way that vodka and babushka dolls never could. So I very rarely went to class.

And when I did, I spent most of the lessons speaking to Andrea. I spoke about the various diets I was on, how I was going to lose the weight. She saw me perform comedy and heard me tell self-deprecating jokes about my fat body on stage. But Andrea also saw something else in me. She called me a Baby Fat – a potential future self-loving fatty. At first, it felt like a set-up.

'You're allowed to like your body,' she would say. I would blink a few times. It made less sense than Russian. The words would get stuck in my brain on a loop throughout the week. It had never been an option; it had never been presented as an option.

'If you trace it back,' Andrea would tell me, 'every self-hating thought, every fat-hating feeling – it stems from somewhere. An advert, a character on a TV show, a fashion magazine, a weight-loss product. It's not something you read in *The Great Book Full of Facts*. It always stems from an individual or a system. And often from an individual with a product to sell. You can see it happen – the worse you feel about yourself, the more money you throw at the problem. The more people doing this, the richer these companies will get. So they keep spreading the idea that you are not allowed to be fat, that fat is the worst thing you can be – so that you will throw even more money at them.'

I had always considered my negative view of fatness as a truth, and suddenly it became subjective. In my head, it had been simple: the Earth is round. The sun is hot. Fat is bad. ✓

Now my world view was shaken. Every single notion that had ever been flung at me – telling me that my fatness made me unattractive, lazy and unworthy – had come from someone's subjective opinion. Or – from a company with a product to sell. What Andrea explained to me was essentially capitalism. I felt like I had understood what capitalism was – in theory – but never had it applied this strongly to my very own life. *Fat does not have to be a negative.*

Wow.

Andrea introduced me to the possibility of loving fat. With the gentle sound of our Russian Studies professor in the background, I took in these ideas that seemed much more valuable to me than anything to do with Tolstoy. I was immediately both puzzled and intrigued.

Andrea would be writing the Russian alphabet in her note-book and I would lean in and whisper in her ear, 'So basically, we have all just been taught to hate our bodies when really . . . We don't have to?'

She would nod and continue writing. I would write down an oddly shaped B which I think was meant to be pronounced as an S. I would then lean in again and whisper, 'So it's all lies?'

Andrea would whisper, 'Yes.'

I would draw a little 8 on my paper, drawing circles in the

same place repeatedly till the paper evaporated and the pen started drawing 8s on the underlying piece of paper. I leaned in, 'So I can just . . . be fat?'

Andrea smiled, 'Yes.'

I would see Andrea exist, unapologetically, and she would show me fat people that did the same. I remember the first photo I saw of a fat woman being sexy. She was wearing nothing but knickers and a big, oversized, dark-red knitted jumper which was draped over one shoulder and both of her hands and part of her left thigh. She was leaning up against a high stool, her hair brown and thick, her lips slightly parted in a sexy and sultry look. And she was fat. Fat and sexy. That was just the first of many.

The internet turned out to be full of people like her. Fat people photographed from all different angles, no regard given to double chins or floppy upper arms, fat people in crop tops, fat people laughing, fat people eating. Fat people *actually loving* themselves.

The change wasn't gradual. It happened overnight. I woke up and looked in the mirror and what I saw was different. On my bike ride to uni, everything was different. The billboards attempting to sell diet plans through before-and-after photos were suddenly not preaching facts, they were preaching a harmful body image. They were using my body to sell a product.

She showed me this door to a whole community where being different – or queer[*] – was not frowned upon, but celebrated: a

---

[*] **Queer** means 'strange or odd from a conventional viewpoint'. It was used as a degrading insult about members of the LGBTQIA+ community in the beginning of the twentieth century. It is why the term might feel a bit wrong, if this is one of the first times you have heard it used outside of a 1950s movie. The community I feel like I am a part of believes that

door which had always been concealed from me. And through which, a whole new world existed, where the *rules* are not *rules*, merely guidelines.

I loved the movie *The Truman Show* when I was growing up. If you are younger than me, this may be complete news to you, so I will quickly explain. Truman, played by Jim Carrey, has a normal life – so he thinks. He gets up, kisses his wife on the cheek, goes to work, gets the newspaper, goes back home, falls asleep. What he doesn't know is that when he was born, he became part of a reality TV show. He was placed in a fake world, an enormous bubble, and now everything in his life is filmed twenty-four hours a day and broadcast to the real world. Everyone in his life, including his wife, is an actor. He is given a fear of water, meaning that he can never leave his town – not cross the bridge, not get on a boat. He is stuck in this fake world, without knowing that millions of people watch his every move.

When Truman realises what is going on, he is forced to challenge his fears and get in a boat to try and get away. He doesn't truly believe that this can be real; that his entire world, his entire life is a lie. Until his boat bumps into a wall. A blue piece of wood painted as the sky. There is a beautiful moment where Truman

---

people with fat bodies are queer, as we do not fit in with the conventions. We are also seen as 'other'. Conventions are all about 'should'. We should be thin, we should be straight, we should have some kids, women should have long hair, men should be tall. The sitcom dream come true. To me, queerness is about realising that you are free (emotionally) from all of the internal expectations and demands. You can be whoever you want to be. Obviously, it comes with a fair amount of hassle from the outside world; loss of privileges, risk of discrimination and exclusion, abuse and so on. But internally, there are no 'shoulds'.

touches the wall. And realises that it's true. That everything was fake. The voice of God – the producer – roars through the speakers, at Truman, that he should turn around and go back to his life. For at least he knows what that is. That he can stay happy if he gives in to the dream. If he just accepts this. And Truman is standing in front of a door, which was hidden before – it is painted blue like the fake sky – and he has a choice. He can turn around, get back in the boat, go back to his life which is a lie. Or he can walk out the door, not knowing anything about the outside world. He turns to the camera and smiles and walks through the door.

That is how it felt meeting Andrea. The same stages of denial: surely, this can't *all* be fake?

If this is all true, then I have lived a lie. Then every single self-loathing thought I have ever had, every opportunity missed, every failed relationship or friendship, every harsh word said to myself, every bruise, every cut, every moment I have either starved myself or felt numb, it will all have been . . . due to either an individual, an industry or a system telling me to do it. If this is all true, then that means that I have said the meanest and most cruel things to myself, to my body, for no reason. It means that my body was never the enemy, my fat was never the enemy. Perhaps I was deserving of love all along. Perhaps I was worthy all along.

If it's all true – that the beauty industry, the diet industry, the weight-loss industry and the fashion industry, all of them have created this 'perfect body image' and a world in which that is 'just the way it is' – then it is not an objective truth. It is fake. A world in which everyone is an actor and the sky is made of wood. In which case, there must be a door.

You will have to cross an ocean, petrified of water. You will have to give up this belief you had that what you see in the media is true and reflects reality. Then you have to row. And there is a storm and you feel like you might, at any second, drown. But you don't. You reach the blue wooden wall, you touch it and feel the splinters in your fingertips. Then you see the door. And you can choose to walk out.

The reason why we empathise with Truman's difficult choice is that in his fake world, at least, he was the star. He had a decent life. It was safe. So if he had got back into his boat and sailed back to his fake life, we would partly have understood his choice.

The fake world in which fat people live is not nice. It is not safe and we are not the stars. Instead we believe that we are not worthy, that we are not attractive, that we are lesser humans. That that is *just how it is*. The world is not even safe for thinner people, because it always looms over them as possible threat. What if you get fat one day? If you are a size 8, you should be a size 6. If you are a size 6, you should be a size 4. If you are a size 0, you need a bigger gap between your thighs or clear clavicles or a flatter, more toned stomach. And you need to still be able to eat burgers because you don't want to be *one of those boring girls ordering a salad for dinner*.

I fully lived in that world for twenty-three years of my life and every single person in my life did as well. Like we were all part of a cult where the main mantra was 'fat people should be ashamed' and we all hummed in agreement whenever it was being insinuated or said.

What it took was for someone to say to me, 'What if it's all a lie?'

✳

Throughout writing about my childhood, my teens and all of the self-loathing that surrounded it, I have had to take brief pauses where I held my stomach in my hands and said to myself, 'I love you, stomach. I love you, child-me. We are good, we are safe,' because the past is overwhelming. Maybe this is time for you to do the same. Place your hands on your body, the bits that you've struggled with the most and say, 'We are good, we are safe.'

✳

The biggest misunderstanding in the body-positivity movement that we see on social media is that you have to be 'confident' and 'brave'. I have spoken to fat women who dismissed the entire idea of self-love by saying, 'I am just not that confident.'

I am not a confident person. I always feel like I should be working harder or managing adult life better. But I can honestly say that most days, when I look in the mirror, I smile. I stare admiringly at my big thighs and I turn sideways to look at my butt and my stomach and I think, 'Hello hot stuff!' I am sometimes absolutely overwhelmed with how cute and beautiful my body is. But then sometimes I catch a glimpse of myself in a shop window and think, 'Ew.' I still receive compliments from people and smile and say 'thank you' but on the inside scoff and think 'what's wrong with you?' I still sometimes instinctively take positions that make me look thinner for photographs and I would hesitate before doing jumping jacks naked in front of a person I was about to have sex with. I don't always love my body. I love it more, way more, light years more, than I did a decade ago. When I go up a size in clothing, I don't cheer. My first feeling is, 'Oh . . .' and my second feeling is, 'Oh well.' I have to repeat to myself, 'I was a beautiful child,' moving the emphasis from word to word in each repetition, because I need to remind myself. That I am attractive, worthy, deserving to be alive, is never something that comes easy. It is not something I just instinctively believe. It is hard work, telling myself that I am good enough every single day.

When I write down every memory related to my weight from my childhood, it is not to figure out the source of why I became fat. People are fat for a variety of reasons. It can be biological, psychological, socioeconomic, genetic or a choice. Some people just have *those bodies*. When I talk about the reasons for my own fatness, I am not apologising for it and nor am I explaining it to you so that you feel more comfortable with it. Usually, when the reasons for a person's fatness are looked into, it is in order to find a solution to a problem. But being fat is not a problem. The reason I share my childhood with you is to remind myself that I was not brought up loving my body. I was not brought up confident. Every little thread of confidence was crushed under the heavy foot of societal pressure to be thin. Every sense of autonomy evaporated in the presence of my abusive grandfather. Bullying shattered my sense of self-worth, sadistic teachers confirmed that I was lesser. I did not start this journey as a confident person. If I had to go back and look at who I was before I started loving my body, I would say that there seemed to be nothing left to salvage.

The only thing that had never been touched – the only thing that they forget to destroy – is our sense of logic. Our intelligence. Our minds. If anything, our minds are strengthened because we spend most of our lives inside of our heads, as we are trying to escape our bodies. This means that we have an out. I believe we can use this sense of logic to our advantage. If we can grasp – deep down inside – that all the things we have been taught about how our bodies are wrong, are lies – then we can beat it. All we need to do is *unlearn*.

But now, even when I have a self-hating day, I still funda-mentally believe that fat bodies are worthy. Even when I wear large shirts to cover my stomach, I know in my heart that I am allowed to take up space. It sometimes feels contradictory, sure, that at the same time as I have words like 'ugly' and 'gross' in my head I can think, 'I am as deserving of being here as everyone else,' and, 'Fat bodies are as beautiful as other bodies because beauty is subjective and there are no rules.'*

But to me, that was the way in. Talking with Andrea allowed me to sidestep my feelings about myself and reach the centre of my brain where I understood that systematic oppression and dis-crimination can make a person internalise a lot of hatred.

When fat people say to me, 'Oh, I could never love myself, I don't have that confidence,' I tell them this. 'You don't have to have confidence, you just have to be able to understand the basic principle of maths. The more we hate our bodies, the richer these companies get. Ergo, they make us feel bad, in order to make money. Ergo, you do not hate your body because your body is wrong. You hate your body because someone lied to you.'

We believe that the objective truth is that it is a bad thing to be fat. When you realise that it is not an objective truth, but rather, someone's capitalist and very subjective stance, you can begin to let go of the self-hatred.

---

* Beauty being subjective is only one side of the coin. What I mean is: You can teach yourself, through exposure, to perceive something as beautiful. What I think is beautiful is different to what you think is beautiful. On the other hand, beauty is also a structural hierarchy within society that allows discrimination to happen. So even though beauty is, in theory, subjective and personal, it is also a way to control people. But, for each of us, when it comes to trying to relearn how we experience fatness, beauty can become whatever we want it to be.

Your confidence grows from believing this and creating your own subjectivity. If you truly believe that your body is not the enemy, then you can begin to treat it with the love it deserves. I have bad days where I am without confidence. But the good days are incredible – where I look at my stomach and feel nothing but genuine awe. Where I observe my thighs in the mirror and feel absolutely blessed and lucky to have such sexy, plump thighs. Where I think I look amazing in every single photo I take of myself, regardless of the angles. Where I strut down the street in a crop top and tiny shorts with no make-up and enough self-esteem to blow the roof off a straight-sized clothing store.* Where I actually live the life that Instagram claims I do.

I started from the lowest point possible. The confidence came with time – and it all started when I realised that fat people are worthy. Fat people are deserving of happiness and entitled to take up space. Fat people are not lesser humans.

You can be happy and fat, you deserve to be happy and fat, being happy and fat is an option.

All you need to do is believe that and then we can begin.

---

* **Straight-sized stores** are basically just *stores*. Stores *not* for fat people. If you are straight-sized, you are not plus-sized. The tendency has been to call it normal-sized, but we can see how that's super not okay – we don't want to indicate that it's somehow freakishly weird to be fat. So instead we go with: straight-sized.

2

We need a fat Disney princess, and how to actually ask for one

I like to imagine all art as a house of mirrors. Most people when coming face to face with the way popular culture reflects them might notice that it is more or less distorted. We all know that television, for example, is not an accurate portrayal of reality. Even reality TV has been oxymoronically constructed and edited, with elaborately chosen clips, background music and leading questions from the producers. We know that very few people in real life can walk away in slow motion from an explosion behind them. That if you were to murder someone detrimental to your career in crime, you would not take up valuable time explaining to them your exact plan in great detail, giving them a chance to escape.* Deep down, we know these things. Yet art is often

---

* Excuse me, but if you have duct tape on your mouth, can't you just spit

so similar to our lives in many other ways. The hero tied up and beaten in front of the villain is scared, the same way we would be if that happened to us. The woman kissed by Chris Pratt has a big smile on her face – the same way we would probably react in that situation.* How are we meant to be able to fully distinguish between the real world and the artificial reality that's been manufactured to entertain us?

If art is a house of mirrors in which you see yourself reflected, it can be hard to tell which mirror is you – and which is slightly altered by Photoshop, a TV producer, the ad company or a camera lens. If you are a white, straight, cis-gender male in your thirties, you might see yourself reflected as a 'strong and manly' man. This is quite possibly not much different from how you have been brought up. You will often see yourself fight in wars, battle criminals in a big city, climb buildings, jump out of helicopters, save the fair maiden and kiss her passionately. You will see yourself as having a multifaceted personality – you can see yourself as the angry white, straight cis-gender man, as the happy white, straight cis-gender man, you can see yourself as the evil character, the goofy, the geeky, the nerdy, the good character, the intelligent character, the funny character, the sexy, the handsome, the ugly, the hero, the villain, the king, the president, the cab driver, the lawyer, the janitor. You can be thin, muscular, chubby, young and dating a young woman, *or* old and dating a young woman.

---

and drool a lot, until it falls off? It always feels like a #majorplothole. I know that it might ruin the momentum to see Bruce Willis spit and drool down himself, but maybe he'd kill more bad guys if he wasn't so vain.

* I prefer fatter Chris Pratt, when he was in *Parks and Recreation*. Not muscly *Jurassic Park* Chris Pratt. Wait, why is he only in things with parks in them? Can someone answer me, please?

(As a white, straight cis-gender man you can even see yourself reflected back as both black, gay and transgender, and Hollywood will even trust you to portray such a character more than people who live in this identity every day.)[1]

You may not relate to all or any of the images reflected back at you, but at least you will have a choice. There is no stereotypical 'white, straight cis-gender man' in art. You can be it all. You are it all. A study has shown that among children, the only group whose self-esteem increases by watching television is white boys.[2] The other groups tested, white and black girls and black boys, all showed a decrease of self-esteem.

As soon as there is a segment of your existence that is not seen as mainstream – whether you are a woman, fat, a person of colour, visibly religious (wearing a headscarf, for example), trans, queer, someone with a disability – you find yourself limited by the representation of you. There is a lot to say – and there has been a lot said – about the stereotypes surrounding most of these labels, but I would like to dive into the representation of fat people in particular.

When a fat person walks through the house of mirrors that is art, the mirrors almost exclusively show you as a person who is unattractive, unintentionally funny, evil, lazy, unintelligent or unwanted. Ursula, the evil Sea Witch who grabs Ariel's voice, Fat Monica in Friends, Hitchcock and Scully in the otherwise inclusive show *Brooklyn 99*, who are two dum-dums who can't figure out how to do anything and just spend all day eating, Brad Pitt's character in *Friends* who used to be fat and now is 'hot' (as it's apparently impossible to be both), the fat characters in *The Simpsons* – Homer, who is unintelligent, Barney who is an uncontrollable drunk, Ralph, who is unintelligent and unlovable. And of course, in *Family Guy*, we have Peter Griffin who is unintelligent – alongside every single fat person that ever shows up in *Family Guy* only to be mocked horrendously. Like when Peter imagines that his son Chris is dating a fat woman, we see her needing to back into the garage, like a truck, after which Peter says, 'So do you prefer Fatty or Miss Boombalatty?' Or when Bryan is forced to hit on a fat girl and he does it by saying, 'Is that highlights in your hair or potato chips?' and she answers, slightly dim-wittedly, 'Highlights!' Then, in a slow voice, 'You got me sweating above and below my ass.' When she leaves his house the following morning, Stevie says that Bettina is way too fancy a name for her: she should be called 'Thud or Oof'.

In *New Girl*, there are often flashbacks to the show's hotty Schmidt being fat (where he is wearing a fat-suit). When he is fat, he is generally a whole other person. He is pathetic and sad all the time. He is clumsy and lazy. It is laughable that he used to be fat – like when the group of Friends look back at Fat Monica – where she was also a whole other person. Jolly and in no way obsessed with neatness and tidiness. It is almost as if it is impossible for television to portray a fat character with the same traits as a thin person.

We sometimes see ourselves reflected, but then the entire character will be defined by the fatness. The role of Kate as played by Chrissy Metz in *This Is Us* is exclusively built around her weight – her need to lose it is the only thing that we see in her life. Precious in the movie *Precious*, played by Gabourey Sidibe, is victimised by her class and by her fat body. Fat Amy in *Pitch Perfect* almost exclusively makes fat jokes about herself.

More often than not, we are not reflected at all. When I watch television, most of the TV shows seem to portray this science-fiction world in which all fat people have been eradicated. At some point you might be lucky to spot a fat person behind a cash register in the background and you start to feel empathy for this poor guy, who seems to have been the only one to survive the Fatpocalypse.* It is bittersweet that the upside to this is that, at least, they do not portray us negatively. We walk into the house of mirrors and when we look into the mirror, there is no reflection. It is like we do not exist.

It's called 'symbolic annihilation'. It's a term coined in 1976 by George Gerbner to describe the *absence* of representation in the media. Basically: by not being represented at all, it sends the signal that *you don't matter*. It's a method of making sure that we keep oppressing the same groups of people. If, every time we look at a television, everyone who is not a white man feels a bit worse, it helps to maintain the current system: where the white man is in charge of almost everything. Representation is directly connected to self-esteem – one of the most important traits to possess when asserting yourself in the world. It's a self-fulfilling prophecy – if you believe that you matter more than others, you will place yourself in that position. Likewise, if you feel like you don't, you will let others assert themselves over you.

In 1978, Gaye Tuchman divided symbolic annihilation into three aspects: omission, trivialisation and condemnation, saying that it's not just about *lack* of representation, it's also the ridicule and trivialising of these groups – say, when a TV show or movie

---

* The **Fatpocalypse** has been coined by my fatlicious friend Cat Pausé as a cooler and more fun name for *The Obesity Epidemic* – which she describes as the word that they use on the news for the notion that we are all becoming fat(ter) and it's going to kill us all. Cat Pausé is a Fat Studies researcher and scholar. She is academic as fuck. She has a PhD and has won awards. But when I asked her how she wanted me to introduce her in this book, she asked me to just call her 'fatlicious'. And that is essentially all you need to know about Cat Pausé.

only places a fat person in the show as the 'fat friend' (Rebel Wilson in *How To Be Single*) or when a character is temporarily (very temporarily) put in a fat-suit to signify that they're depressed (Andy in *Modern Family*, when he realises that he isn't in love with his fiancée) or that they were a loser once (Schmidt in *New Girl*, Fat Monica in *Friends*). In a lot of movies, you will often see women getting murdered or raped. It seems like Hollywood's go-to tool to get a storyline going. The woman is angry because she was once raped. The man is a bit of a bad guy, so he murders a lady. It trivialises something that is an actual issue and uses women's lives as props to add excitement to a film. There are more naked (for no apparent reason) and murdered women on television and in films than there are women with multifaceted personalities.

There are more naked and murdered women on television and in films than there are fat women.

So, when talking about reflection and representation, it feels appropriate to look at the industry I belong to.

Fat in stand-up

A few years ago, I was waiting to go on stage at a comedy club in central London. The comedian was killing it. He had the audience in the palm of his hand. At the end of his set, he roared into the microphone, the final punchline of his show, 'Fat people shouldn't compete in the Olympics. Only if there was a . . . pie-eating contest.'

I eat, sleep and breathe stand-up comedy. From the first moment I watched it on television when I was ten years old; plunged into an armchair, gasping for air, tears of laughter wetting my sleeves, frantically shouting at my grandmother to 'come quick' because someone on television was making my insides jump up and down just by talking. That was it. Someone just talking. To me, it seemed. About me.

Six years later, when I was so depressed I could not face showering, eating or being awake, I dragged myself down to the local mall, the sunlight hurting my eyes and highlighting their redness, to buy as many stand-up comedy DVDs as I could for the money I needed to spend on rent. I valued stand-up higher than a place to live because stand-up was pure survival. Ellen DeGeneres talking about waiting for lifts, Ricky Gervais talking about Noah's Ark,* Danish comedians like Tobias Dybvad and Carsten Eskelund and their hilariously relatable material about things in my everyday life.

I will watch the same comedy show six times in a row in an attempt to analyse every single technicality, every movement, every choice of words.

When I was twenty-one, I discovered the comedy scene in Denmark. Comedians I had never seen before because they had yet to release DVDs and be on television. It blew me away. It meant that on top of eating, sleeping and breathing comedy, I could now also make love to comedy. I threw myself at the comedians, a sultry comedy fan who was soon to realise that the lust was not after the artist but the art. One of the comedians

---

* I miss the time I really liked Ricky Gervais, you know, before I learned about his general personality.

gracefully suggested that I should do comedy. I don't think he meant to suggest that I did comedy instead of comedians – nevertheless, that was what made sense to me.

A comedian once left the bed straight after sex, because he had been inspired to write a joke. He sat, naked, in front of his laptop, typing furiously. I sat, naked, on the bed and watched him, and I felt like I was watching Picasso paint a picture. It was so artistic it hurt my little 21-year-old heart. And I needed more comedy. Just more and more comedy.

So when a comedian offered me a five-minute spot at an open mic, I did not dare to say no. I went home and wrote sixteen pages of what can barely be described as jokes. From then on, it was never an option not to go on stage. It sounds like a cliché and it has been overused by characters in movies who do not mean what they are saying, but: I was home.

Comedy is about trust. The audience trusts you to be funny and more importantly, you trust yourself to be funny. If you don't trust yourself to be funny, you won't be. The audience can smell fear, you learn that very quickly. I have done a joke to cheerful applause only for my next joke to fall flat on its face and for people to start booing. All because in the beginning of that joke, I stuttered a little bit.

Which is why the pie-eating-contest joke worked for this comedian. Essentially, the crowd of about four hundred people trusted that this comedian on stage was funny and, oh boy, did he trust it as well. He delivered that joke like every word could bring a person back to life. And they laughed. Soon after, he left the stage and my name was called.

We call them fat jokes. You can recognise them by the fat people being the butt of the joke. And if you are fat, chances are, you will recognise them by that knot they place in your stomach whenever you go to watch comedy. The 'oh no' feeling.

You are being ridiculed, not just by the comedian in question, but by the entirety of the audience which agrees. As a fat person, public ridicule is something you will have come to expect. All you wanted was a fun night out and now – you're reminded that you are less in the eyes of society. You wonder if people are looking at you. If they are embarrassed for you.

When people do jokes about fat people, you are not expected to *be in the room*. I have never heard a comedian tell a fat joke starting with 'you fat people'. It's *they*. *Them*. The *others*. Outside of these comedy club walls. Let's laugh at *them*. Suddenly, it is like walking into a room while someone is talking about you – except they do not go quiet, they keep talking, because you do not exist. My therapist once told me that the most dangerous thing you can do to a person is to ignore them.

Comedy has to be relatable to a certain extent, unless we are speaking about surreal, alternative comedy. There are utterly silly comedians doing whole shows about space-dogs and it is delightful and hilarious. But if you are talking about real life, you have to be on the same page as the audience. You are talking to a group of strangers, so you can only base your jokes on the 'general truth' of most people's lives. Which is why a lot of comedy plays on stereotypes: men should be manly men who never cry and are always the big spoon, lesbians are butch and hate men and always ask me on dates* and fat people are unintelligent and lazy. Stereotypes mean that you can make a joke about a group

---

* 'Lesbians always ask me on dates' is a thing I'm trying to make a stereotype. Help me with that, will you? Thank you.

of people without having to explain it. 'Fat people shouldn't compete in the Olympics . . . Unless there was a pie-eating contest. Because fat people eat a lot, that's why they're so fat' – this would not work as a joke. But it works when the punchline is implicit. For fat jokes to work, we all have to buy into the validity of the stereotypes.

I once saw a comedian get a huge laugh because he said that his son wanted to dress up as a princess. He just stated that fact – and the audience started laughing. The subtext was that men are not allowed to dress up as princesses.

But we are beginning to collectively understand now that some men do want to dress up as princesses and they should be allowed to. That lesbians are not necessarily butch and that they almost never ask me on dates and that men should probably be allowed to start feeling their feelings.

And people don't necessarily laugh because they agree. Sometimes it's an initial reaction because the rhythm automatically lends itself to a laugh. Or perhaps you laugh because you don't want to be the dry and boring mood-killer of your friend group or maybe you laugh out of pure self-defence.

When I dated a guy in the military, he once came home laughing hysterically because of a story he had heard one of his soldier friends tell. They had all been sharing stories about how they ended up in the military and this one guy had been quiet. When he finally cracked, he told them all why.

He had wanted, his entire life, to become a gynaecologist. He went to school for years, studied hard, got good grades, got the education. On his first day as a gynaecologist, his first ever patient was a fat woman. My boyfriend at the time wiped tears of laughter from his eyes when he said, 'And she had been sweating, of course,' because *of course we sweat*. The guy had finished the check-up and walked straight out of the clinic and into the military, never looking back. The joke was that he had wanted to fondle pretty women's privates and he ended up having to give a fat woman a medical check-up.

I remember laughing. I think I even found it funny. In doing so, I hoped to erase the fact that I was also fat. That my sweaty vagina is so gross that it sends grown men* directly into a war zone in the hope of a quick and painful death. Ha ha. My boyfriend told me how everyone had laughed so hard and for so long. I remember not turning up at my next gynaecologist appointment. *Maybe I will just wait till we're in a new war against a country and they need the manpower.*

A few years ago, I was sitting backstage in a comedy club watching a comedian perform. I was enthusiastically laughing at all of the new jokes he was telling that I had never heard before. He is a good comedian. Let me just speak from a comedy point of view, for a second:

Comedy is a lot of things. It takes years, sometimes decades, to learn how to do it well. Shorter words are funnier than longer words, words that begin with a hard-sounding letter are funnier than words that begin with a soft-sounding letter, the word that reveals the surprise-twist in the joke has to go at the very end of the joke, rhythm, rhythm, rhythm. A stand-up performance, if you only listened to the beats, should sound like jazz. Ba-da-da-bam. Ba-da-da-bam. Ba-da-da-da-da-bam.† You learn about timing, intonation, pitch, where you look at which points of the show, how to hold a microphone, how not to hold a microphone,

---

* Debatable.

† I don't listen to jazz but I assume this is what it sounds like.

how to cut as many words as possible from a joke, to make the shortest trip from the beginning of a set-up to the delivery of a punchline. Every single comedian who has a notable career has worked very hard for it, has died on stage in a nightclub in Plymouth for no money only to go back to a Travelodge and cry their eyes out – and yet they have driven for six hours to Leeds the next day to do the same again. Even the comedians whose jokes are hurtful.

And a comedian can be a good comedian and still be an absolute piece of trash. Jokes can be both horrendously offensive, damaging and dangerous and at the same time, be well-constructed and technically funny. Comedy is all about technique. This is not a book about how to do comedy, but I feel like this is an important point to make when I am about to criticise stand-up. And it is important for you to know when you do decide to criticise stand-up.

The comedian I was watching from the dressing room on this particular night *was* a good comedian. He knew how to write jokes. He knew his craft. And then he closed on his final joke:

'This girl was unattractive. I'm not going to say in what way, as beauty is in the eye of the beholder. So if you think brunettes are unattractive, imagine she was brunette. If you hate big noses, imagine she had a big nose. And if you're me, *imagine she's fat.*'

He left the stage and came down backstage to the sound of the audience applauding. I couldn't congratulate him on a good set. I couldn't make myself do it. The joke had worked, the crowd had laughed, but I couldn't look him in the eyes. Fortunately for me, another comedian spoke:

'You've been in the sun all day?' she asked him, as his face was bright red.

'It's because I'm a redhead and I forgot to put on sunscreen today,' he explained with a sadness in his voice. 'I don't think you guys understand how hard it is. How many comments I have to listen to every summer. From friends and strangers. You guys don't understand,' he said.

And looked *me* in the eyes. I blinked a few times, not really understanding how he couldn't see what had just happened. How he didn't feel like an absolute fraud, doing jokes about fat people being unattractive but somehow wanting sympathy for being teased himself – from a fat person. How he could be so ignorant as to what he had just done.

When pointing out that some jokes are hurtful and damaging, we always hear the same comments: 'But what about freedom of speech? Can we not say anything anymore? It's a dictatorship now. A joke is just a joke. You need to be able to laugh at yourself. Chill out.'

Freedom of speech is a good thing. Don't get me wrong. Although sometimes I daydream that we do live in a dictatorship and it is run by a strong, powerful non-man – a radical, communist, intersectional feminist, powerhouse of a non-man. We would have one day a week – say, Monday? – where men were not allowed to speak at all. That would be the day we would get things done. Then we would emerge on a six-day weekend because we would not need to work anymore. Without a man mansplaining our thoughts back to us, a man interrupting our every sentence to repeat literally what we just said, without a man needing to assert an ego or flexing his muscles, we would get shit done.

Then there would of course be all-men-are-jailed-Tuesdays. Men are allowed to talk but they can only talk to each other, because they are all in the same jail. Meanwhile, we would have a day where we did not consider the length of our skirts and where we did not need to place keys between our fingers on our way home at night. If a white van drove past us, we would just shout 'Hi Betsy' because it would probably just be Betsy in her white van again.*

But, comedy was, for me, always something free-flowing. Something that was meant to have flaws. This act of escapism where I could just make fart sounds with my mouth for ten minutes and there would be no consequences. It was something I could do without anyone telling me what I can or cannot do. There were meant to be no rules because no one could stop me.

But I now need to be more aware of every word I say. It's not a terrible tragedy that I actually have to think before I do my job. It's just a matter of, for example, not saying 'Ladies and Gentlemen' but instead saying something like 'People of the audience' since we now know that there are not just two genders. It's a simple action and after a few times of saying it, it just becomes your automatic go-to phrase. It is not hard work to make sure the words you say do not contribute to an already toxic culture.

I'm in the privileged position to be able to get up on a stage and keep an audience's attention for a certain amount of time. And it is certainly a privilege to be able to get up in front of an almost exclusively white audience and feel safe in the fact that my whiteness is relatable. But being known as a *woman* in comedy did not make things easier – the majority of the people in the audience inherently believed that I was therefore unfunny – an attitude that is slowly beginning to change. So I am not

---

* I have been advised by my lawyers to make it very clear that all of this is NOT a serious statement. I am merely having a silly daydream like the one where I'm a contestant on *Great British Bake Off* and Paul Hollywood is very disappointed in me and needs to see me in private with a spatula.

saying that getting on stage was easy. But I felt like it was easy because I felt like I could say whatever I wanted to and not get hurt. I had never considered the fact that what I said could hurt others.

Even though it is legal for you to stand on a stage and speak from the heart, it does not mean you are not hurting people. As a comedian, I have made truly awful jokes on stage. My very first television spot was three minutes long, during which I made a joke about sexual assault, ending with the words, 'Because women aren't funny.'

I did not know about rape culture or internalised misogyny because I had never heard those terms before, and nor did I particularly understand why it was all so wrong.

Now, gradually, it is different. Comedy seems to be moving into an era where we are becoming more and more aware of the potential damage our words can cause. And now I stand on a stage on a daily basis in front of a lot more people and I have a lot more time in which to speak. Because of the way my career has progressed, I am now listened to more than I was when I was a 21-year-old with mediocre comedians' spunk in my hair. I am now a professional comedian, meaning I only allow very famous comedians to spunk in my hair.* So I have had to realise that I need to be careful with what I say on stage.

An audience member told me once, after a show, that she had gone to see a show in which the male straight comedian did a homophobic joke. She said, 'I was the only one in the audience who looked queer. Everyone stared at me.' When she left the

---

* There exist approximately seven people who can attest to this not being true and they all owe me some shampoo.

show, two men in the queue to leave addressed her with a homophobic slur – with the confidence of a straight male comedian doing a homophobic joke supposedly ironically, but without the humour and the irony.

So I love comedy. I breathe, sleep, fuck and eat comedy, but my words have been harmful in the past and they will be in the future, because that is the very nature of existing. I still love comedy but I see how comedy is not a safe haven anymore where anything goes – comedy can be a weapon and you need to be careful that it is not pointed towards the wrong people.

I love comedy and I truly wish that I didn't often hear fat people tell me that they feel unsafe in comedy clubs. That they always watch comedy with the expectation to be the punchline.

The comedian who did the pie-eating-contest joke recently messaged me to ask me if I would tweet about his upcoming show in London. (It's a delicate situation, professionally. It is delicate for him to ask, and in doing so revealing to me that he was not selling a lot of tickets. And it is delicate for me to answer, because I should not create any kind of professional tension. But I decided to answer him anyway.) 'I don't think you want my followers to come. I can't really tweet about someone who does negative jokes about fat people. My audience is full of fat people who are not – and should not – be ashamed of that. I hope you understand that. I'm sure you'll sell out the show without my help.' (He didn't.)

He wrote back, 'I understand,' and I am not sure he did that either.

But I was grateful that his answer was polite. Usually, when I have called out someone for being problematic, it has not gone so well.

We need a fat Disney princess

Calling out a guy in a private message is vastly different from calling out an entire industry and therefore an entire system, especially when you do so more or less accidentally.

A few years ago, I sat down to watch a Disney film with my younger cousin. It is completely irrelevant which Disney film because what happened could have happened with any of them, literally any of them. The female lead was thin. No shocked gasps there. Classic Disney princess – eyes bigger than her mouth and nose combined (I have a fat head and it's really difficult finding glasses – I can imagine it's impossible for Disney princesses), and the circumference of her waist smaller than the one of her throat. I felt a twinge of self-hatred creeping up through my fat body. Immediately, I became annoyed that I felt that way. If an adult who prides herself on being body-confident can suddenly feel bad about herself because she is looking at a thin Disney princess, how does a little fat eight-year-old feel?

I took to Twitter. I tweeted, 'We need a fat Disney princess'* and I put the phone away to watch the rest of the movie.

A lot of people tend to see social media as nothing but a platform for teenage girls to post selfies. But even if that's the case, to me that is still inherently positive. A platform just for young

---

* Look, of course we don't need princesses in general. And the idea that little girls want to become princesses while little boys want to become soldiers is inherently toxic. When I say we need a fat Disney princess, what I'm saying is: as long as we have Disney princesses, make some of them fat. It is two different discussions: portrayals (how we write women) and representation (who we cast or draw to play those women).

women to decide exactly how the world gets to see them, instead of only seeing themselves portrayed on television mostly through the male gaze,* often as nothing but a virtually mute sex symbol. We are so used to seeing women as objects through a man's lens. When the woman holds the lens herself and directs it at her, that is powerful, regardless of filters and amounts of make-up. They use Photoshop to make us look the way they want us to look, so there is no reason why we cannot do the same.

The internet is powerful. Important movements such as #BlackLivesMatter, #ProtectTransKids, #EverydaySexism and #MeToo started on Twitter. If you grew up as a nerdy teenager in the early 2000s and probably later, the internet was where you found your peers. I had pen pals from all over the world who understood me better than anyone at my school. If you refuse to or are unable to conform, being a child can be lonely. The internet can be a better playground than the one down the park.

Saying that the internet is a trivial thing is a very privileged statement. And let us be honest – it is boring. Whenever someone takes a photo of a bunch of people on the bus all having their heads bowed down, looking at their phones with a caption mourning the loss of 'real-life' contact, or asking 'why are they not just talking to each other?' it makes me want to scream into a pillow. We live in a world where the person sitting next to us on the bus could be any kind of threat to our personal identity

---

* Mmm, the **male gaze** is such a great feminist phrase. Coined by film critic Laura Mulvey in 1975 to describe the way visual arts and literature depicts the world through a male point of view, making women the sexual objects. It's how a movie written by a woman and featuring women is called a 'chick-flick' and how a movie written by a man featuring a man is called a 'movie'.

or our safety. In an ideal world, I would react with a smile when a man talked to me on a bus, but due to a significant amount of very uncomfortable interactions with men on buses, I no longer have any interest in engaging with any of them.* I am just saying, there is a reason why people might be on their phones when they are on public transportation. There are no men trying to grope my thigh inside of my phone. Instead, I have a community full of fat, queer, social-justice activists who preach messages of self-care and a need for a revolution.

So it deserves mentioning. After having watched the Disney film, I tweeted, 'We need a fat Disney princess,' and put my phone away, like a good millennial.

The backlash lasted days. I got thousands of comments. Each time I checked my social media, the negative comments were everywhere. I say 'negative comments' but that is misleading. It sounds like these are cool-headed people decently suggesting that I am wrong. That is the furthest from the case. These people were enraged. It was hard not to imagine them frothing at the mouth, leaned in over their keyboards, typing so furiously that their fingers couldn't keep up, just spewing anger into the world wide web. This had hit them at their core.

'i want a disney princess that's a lumbering whale so i have something to relate to'

'You need yo go gym and put the cakes down you embarrassment to little girls everywhere'

---

* *Men on Buses* is a scarier film than *Snakes on a Plane*.

**'Get ready to deal with the loneliness
and isolation of your own old age'**

(This actually sounds really nice. If I end up old, alone
and isolated somewhere, I will die with a smile on my face.
The introvert dream.)

**'to be kissed fat princess will have to lose
the weight to be attractive to any self
respecting prince, effort leads 2 reward'**

> **'fat people are a stain on our society.
> they're a giant health risk, they are
> greedy, insatiable and rely on their
> emotions to get their way'**

**'Sounds like you just need a fat dick
and you'd probably chill the fuck out'**

(How can someone be both so right and so wrong at
the same time?)

> **'Lose weight fat ass'**

**'Why, so you feel better about your inability
to stop shoving lard into your cakehole? You
eat too much why would princesses do that?'**

(Uhm, that is actually incredibly believable. Princesses
do fuck-all with their time. What else should they do but
eat? They are princesses. If you cannot eat loads when
you are a princess, why even be a princess?)

> **'You're cancerous'**

**'No. Being fat is a bad thing. It's ugly
and it's unhealthy. It's sick to encourage
kids that it's ok to be fat. It's not'**

**'We should have a fat unhealthy
disney princess for our daughters to
laugh at and mock. I'm all for it.
Have her be cursed with diabetes'**

**'Or maybe you could loose weight
and be a normal princess, land whale'**

(I'm pretty sure I need to do more than just lose weight,
I'd have to also meet a prince, make him fall in love with
me, convince him not to google my name and magically
transform myself from my land whale form to human form.
I do not have time for this, thus, I need a fat Disney princess.)

None of these Twitter trolls were angry because they thought
I would actually change the sexism that so often seems to drive
the Disney corporation. They were, as these types of people often
are, furious that A Fat Woman Spoke. It doesn't even just happen
to fat women, it just happens to *women, queer people, black people*
and really, just anyone with slightly left-leaning views. On 3
January 2017, writer and fat activist Lindy West announced that
she had deactivated her Twitter account in a *Guardian* article:

**Twitter, for the past five years, has been a machine
where I put in unpaid work and tension headaches
come out. I write jokes there for free. I post political
commentary for free. I answer questions for free.
I teach feminism 101 for free. Off Twitter, these**

are all things by which I make my living – in fact,
they comprise the totality of my income. But on
Twitter, I do them pro bono and, in return, I am
micromanaged in real time by strangers; neo-Nazis
mine my personal life for vulnerabilities to exploit;
and men enjoy unfettered, direct access to my brain
so they can inform me, for the thousandth time, that
they would gladly rape me if I weren't so fat.

As with *fat women speaking*, equally furious are the trolls about
Black Women Speaking. Or actually, just *black women existing*.
In 2016, actress Leslie Jones played one of the ghostbusters in
the all-lady reboot of *Ghostbusters*. Breitbart editor and infamous
internet troll Milo Yiannopoulos led an army of trolls to send her
so much abuse that she eventually left Twitter as well.[*]

But of course, it's the internet, so no one (belonging to a marginalised group) is safe. That same year, Chelsea Cain, a Marvel
writer, was chased off Twitter by trolls. They doxxed[†] her and
sent her so much abuse on a daily basis that she eventually left.
Her crime was writing a female superhero. Sinead O'Connor, Sue
Perkins and fourteen-year-old actress Millie Bobby Brown also
all left Twitter due to large amounts of abuse.

Author Malorie Blackman (get ready to have a new idol) was
forced off Twitter temporarily in 2014 due to racist abuse but

---

[*] If you want to feel sick to your stomach, go read about some of the other
twisted things Yiannopoulos has engaged in online.

[†] **Doxxing** is this fun little thing where trolls figure out where you and
your family live, what your phone numbers are, and where you hang out,
and then they publish it to the internet and encourage people to go find
you. How fun.

returned with this message, 'Hell will freeze over before I let racists and haters silence me. In fact, they just proved to me that I was right to speak out. I only meant to take a few days break to write an article about this whole issue. Racists and haters will never make me run away. Ever!'[3]

Bow down to Malorie Blackman, bow down.

The trolls want attention. The term 'trolls' stems from the word 'trolling' which originally had nothing to do with ogres under bridges. It meant 'trolling', the fishing term, where several fishing lines with bait at the end of them are dragged through the ocean on the back of a moving boat. Because these people online are just randomly throwing out bait, hoping to catch just *anything*. Just *any* kind of attention.

Their feeling of self-worth is so low that they believe they can only get acknowledged if it is negative. I remember seeing a troll who had a screenshot as a banner. The screenshot was of musician Cher's Twitter profile and it said: This user has blocked you. He was so proud of this; Cher blocking him meant that Cher had seen him.

I am used to these attacks. Whenever I tweet about feminism, toxic masculinity or Fat Liberation, I have begun to almost expect them. Whenever I post anything to do with social politics, I have to check social media once every fifth minute, otherwise it gets too overwhelming having to delete all the comments at once. It is easier to spread it out over a few days. During some of the worst attacks, I have had to wake up several times a night just to put 1–200 accounts on mute on Twitter.

During a filming of a sitcom pilot, one of the actors on set rolled his eyes at how much I was checking my phone. When I told him that I had to routinely check for trolls, he told me I shouldn't let it bother me. So I started reading the tweets out loud to him, as they were coming in. A few times a minute, I would tell him to kill himself, that he was a piece of fat lard, that I would not rape him because he was so gross, that he would die alone. He did not last long before he asked me to stop – and I could satisfyingly tell him that he shouldn't let it bother him.

These trolls are sad people. And there are two different ways of dealing with sadness. You can create something, or you can destroy what other people have created.

I became slightly fascinated with trolls. During the latest barrage of online abuse, Twitter suddenly introduced filters, so it was possible for you to never see a single negative comment. (Which is a quite infuriating thing as it means that Twitter definitely has the possibility of sourcing all of this hatred and vitriol and so it should not be too hard for them to delete these troll accounts.)

Instead, they just make sure that they can exist in their own shithead vacuum. I am hesitant to write too much about the way social media handles women's safety online because I have the seemingly unrealistic hope that by the time you are reading this, they have somehow decided to prioritise blocking Nazis and trolls instead of protecting them.

Despite fully understanding that all the abuse I received came from sad, sad people, I was not any less inclined to try to make them sad. That is not the most empathetic approach, I am fully aware of that. Plenty of people engage in polite chats with these people. Comedian Sarah Silverman famously found out that a troll who called her a 'cunt' had back problems and ended up making sure he got the right care. This was met with an incredible amount of positivity all over the internet. 'See What Can Happen When You Respond With Kindness'. I am happy for her and I am happy for the troll's back.

Yet there is nothing revolutionary about a woman reacting to abuse with kindness. We are taught to step down, to be polite, to assist men and to make them feel better. We do not dare to say 'no' too many times because then we will be branded a 'bitch' and we apologise more frequently than men. In some ways, having a man call a woman a 'cunt' only to have the woman ask him why he is sad and proceed to crowdfund his back surgery does not smell of progress. I believe that it is important that women like Silverman exist – let's face it, having back problems does suck and can often lead to misogynistic abuse. (I once woke up with a sore shoulder and immediately told a woman to go and make me a sandwich – what can I say? That's just the way physical pain works.)

I believe that it is also important that vitriolic women exist. I refuse to feed the stereotype that we have to be nice, that we have to be quiet and that we have to be better than them. Sometimes we have to fight 'cunt-sayers' with 'cunt-saying'.

I found the website from which these attacks originated. Someone had posted my tweet and urged people to attack. At this point, a few nice people had already messaged me, offering me support so I had tweeted that I was fine – due to the new Twitter layout, I was not seeing any of the abuse. This sent the trolls into a frenzy.

One troll posted on the website, 'She has just tweeted that she isn't seeing the abuse. Can this be true?' and another commented, 'No, don't worry, she is lying, she definitely sees it', and another, 'Yeah, I promise you, she is seeing it', and the original troll, 'Okay, thank you.'

It was almost beautiful. When I was a child, my biggest dream was to be part of a gang. We are not talking motorcycles and cocaine (that is merely my current dream), I just wanted to do normal kids' stuff like solve crime. At one point, a couple of friends of mine found a car park full of abandoned and broken lorries. We managed to get into the back of a lorry, which was where we established our gang. Our first attempt at solving local crime started with us buying sweets at the gas station, then eating them, then going home, realising that no criminals had been jailed this time around. The next day we were just bored. Our gang went our separate ways after that. If only we had known back then what we know now: that if only we had all got together and started hating women and sending them abuse online, we would have felt a camaraderie beyond anything we had ever felt.

On another group, a troll suggested that people should stop sending me direct abuse – at first. Instead, they should start by asking me in a kind way, 'What do you mean?' or 'Care to elaborate?' and then, once I had wobbled into their clever trap and attempted to answer their question, they would turn around and tell me to kill myself or that they wanted to disembowel me. All this meant was that I received hundreds of tweets at the same time saying 'Care to elaborate?' from various Twitter accounts that Cher had blocked, with drawings of Pepe the Frog as avatars. One of the things I love about misogynists is that their hatred of women makes them underestimate our intelligence, which makes it easier for us to eventually win.

As I saw the notifications come in on my timeline, I awaited an emotional response. Surely, when a lot of people shout at you, you are meant to feel sad. But it was like when a villain in a superhero movie gets their superpower and the meek police force try to shoot them, but the bullets bounce off. You see their face change as they realise their immortality and superiority. I felt much like that. It was no longer about the fact that we need a fat Disney princess. We do – we definitely need a fat Disney princess, but that was never going to be my main objective. It was no longer about chubby Cinderella, plump Pocahontas, rotund Rapunzel or Ariel with a great personality. It was about something much bigger – fighting back.

So even though I was wearing slippers with rabbit ears and I had just had Coco Pops for dinner, the word-bullets bounced right off my chest. And I started typing, posting tweet after tweet with a repetition of the same six words, frothing at the mouth (half froth, half whipped cream, you know, from the Coco Pops), fuelled by not wanting to be silenced, refusing to be quiet:

We need a fat Disney princess.
We need a fat Disney princess.
We need a fat Disney princess.
We need a fat Disney princess.
We need a fat Disney princess.
We need a fat Disney princess.
We need a fat Disney princess.
We need a fat Disney princess.
We need a fat Disney princess.
We need a fat Disney princess.
We need a fat Disney princess.
We need a fat Disney princess.
We need a fat Disney princess.
We need a fat Disney princess.
We need a fat Disney princess.
We need a fat Disney princess.
We need a fat Disney princess.

Because when calling out for better representation *also* annoys trolls, it's a win-win.

Hollywood

There was a scene in Aziz Ansari's TV show *Master of None* that exasperated me. Aziz plays 'the good guy'. All he wants is love. He is confused, like a lot of us, when it comes to love, but it is important to note just how much of a 'good guy' he is. Aziz Ansari being the lead of a TV show is a great thing, in a lot of ways.* Diversity on TV is important and the show touched upon many important topics such as race, sexism, feminism, family, morality and so on. Which is probably why it hit me right in the chest when this scene happened.

Aziz's character Dev goes on ten dates with 'different kinds of women'. And boy, are they different. There is, for example, a thin, young, nondisabled, femme brown woman, a thin, young, nondisabled, femme blonde woman, a thin, young, nondisabled, femme brunette, I mean, the list goes on. It was so freeing to see Dev date all the women on the front covers of all of the magazines. It is refreshing to see just how many versions of essentially the same woman exist. And it is far from the worst example on TV. But when you zoom out – and look at the two seasons in total – there are two fat people in the entirety of the show. There is a scene where the character Dev and the woman he is on a date with see a fat person walk into a restaurant, and conclude that therefore the food must be good. And there is a three-second scene where a fat woman climbs on top of a man, who tries desperately to get out from underneath her.

---

* That is, if you look away from the later allegations that came out against Aziz, which a quick Google search will update you on.

When a show that is trying to do the right thing, trying to be diverse and inclusive, fails to include, it somehow hurts more than when an obviously oppressive show does the same.

Hollywood is so full of thin, white women that it is hard to comprehend. There are whole films I have not been able to enjoy because I found it impossible to tell the two lead women apart. Tall, thin, blonde, symmetrical faces. At least give one of them a hat or a different haircut, Hollywood.

Hollywood feels like such a closed, glamorous exclusive place that I was surprised they allowed me to go there a few years ago. I simply bought a plane ticket and when I landed, I was *in Holly-wood*. I think I had expected someone at the airport to measure my thighs and then send me to a lesser Hollywood. B-Hollywood. Paul Hollywood. But I went. To do *meetings*. Meetings, in my industry, often means meeting with people who tell you that they adore you, that they love all of your stuff and that they can't wait to work with you, after which you never hear from them again. There is a lot of networking – which is you dropping hints about *how successful you are* and *how well you are doing* but also *how you are actually pretty free at the moment to be in lots of television*. I have always been quite rubbish at this. My manager knows this so he decided to come with me to Hollywood to sit in on all of these *meetings*. We never expected anything to really come from this – so we were very surprised when we got a phone call. A production company wanted me to audition for a role in a huge new drama series by a very famous writer and director.

A few days later, we were sitting in my manager's rental car on the parking lot of the huge Fox Studios lot in America.

'This is like in the movies,' I said.

'It's because this is where they film the movies,' my manager said. I read the script over and over again.

'Uh. This is . . .'

'Yeah.' he replied. I looked over the words. 'How will I ever find a man when I look like this?' one of the lines said. In the description of the character, it was made very clear that she was fat. 'I need to lose weight,' the character exclaimed on another page.

I turned to my manager and said, 'I can't say these words. It is so wrong.'

He understood. I added, 'Also. I think I am meant to have an American accent.'

'The main difference is in the word "water",' he told me, 'Try rolling the *r* in water.'

I gave it my best. Waterrr. I sounded just nasal enough that it felt American. I kept repeating it to myself. Waterr. Waaarrrteerrr. Waterrrr.*

The situation felt so ridiculous. I felt like I was on TV, auditioning to be on TV. So I stepped out of the car and walked in to do the audition. In the midst of all of this chaos, I had seemingly forgotten one very important detail: I am not an actor.

At no point had I questioned my acting skills until I finally stood before the casting director. She looked like a casting director. Imagine a casting director. Yes, that is her. I went inside a little shed-like office and was placed in front of a white wall. I started saying the lines, tripping over the words and looking down at the script. The lady did not blink once. She kept smiling at me, intensely not wishing to squander my dream of becoming an actress. It is quite possibly one of the nicest things anyone could

---

* This is going to be so much fun in the audiobook. You eye-readers, you'll have to just imagine this bit.

have done for me, seeing as the most natural thing to do would be to ask me to stop wasting her time.

'Great! Now, can you do that one more time and this time . . . could you do an American accent? Your character is the twin of a man who is American,' she explained.

I took a deep breath and looked her straight in the eyes and said, 'Waterrr.'

'What?'

'Waterrr. Waarrrteeerrrrr.'

'Uhm. Could you do a line from the script, please?'

And I went back to reading from the script in my Danish accent. 'How am I ever going to find a man when I look like this? Tell me to lose weight, goddamnit.'

The lady's smile had now faded into something a bit more stern as she said, 'Well, thank you, that was great. We will be in touch.'

'Don't worry about it, I know I won't get it,' I said with a relieved smile. I forgot that Hollywood might not be the place in which you can successfully seem realistic about life.

'Oh, don't say that, you were great. Don't give up.' With that, she shut the door behind me. I still think of her occasionally and whether or not she thinks I am out there, saying 'water' to strangers, wanting so desperately to be an actress. I hope she knows that the situation is much more positive than that: I merely wasted her and everyone else's time.

I can now say two things that sound more impressive than they are:

1. I auditioned for a part in Hollywood.
2. Waterrr.

A year or so later, I was sent another script. This was in Danish – an accent I am much more comfortable with. The role was a 45-year-old fat woman. I was twenty-seven. The woman is meant to aggressively hit on a 'poor guy' who is visibly turned off by her.

At one point, she sexually assaults him. I had to check again that this was indeed a comedy script written by comedians. The punchline of the scene is his friends hearing him scream for help. When he sees his friends afterwards, one of them says to him, 'You smell of fish.'

In another scene, the woman asks for a car battery for her dildo.

There was absolutely no indication that the casting director of this role found it to be in any way problematic. I turned it down.

Soon after, I was offered another role. This role was likewise for a fat character* – a role I am, demonstrably, perfect for. This was a comedy sketch about a fat spinning instructor.

This fat spinning instructor just wanted a boyfriend. And she had tried internet dating – and they all wanted to date her when she had only put up her occupation but once she put up her photo, no one wanted to meet her. (The joke here is that men saw that she was a spinning instructor and assumed she was thin and therefore hot, but then when they realised she was fat, they no longer found her attractive.) And she was utterly puzzled by this (the joke is that the fat woman is too unintelligent to understand this). In the same way as she was also puzzled by being unable to lose weight, even though she had cheat days. (The joke is that she only cheats on days that end with the word -day and it's funny

---

* FUN FACT: The description for a thin character is just 'character'.

because that's EVERY DAY and also, the joke is still that she is too unintelligent to know this.)

I furiously emailed the casting director back. Denmark is one of those places where everyone pretty much knows everyone – you walk down any street of Copenhagen and you are bound to run into an old teacher, an ex-boyfriend and a cousin. And that is just *one* person.* The boy I fancied when I was fifteen now works in Danish radio. (When as a teenager I wrote the poem which included the line 'when your brown eyes tell me I can stop pretending, I let my guard down and pray for a happy ending' and sent it to him, I had not ever imagined that I one day would be writing him a professional email asking for a contact. And when he spent all night recording my poem about him as a ballad only to send it back to me, I do not think that he imagined that he would ever send me a work email asking me to do a radio show.)

I suddenly had a portal. A portal to someone who actually had the power to effect change. No one was ever going to read my tweets and change their policy, no one was ever going to give us a fat Disney princess, but this – this one person was casting a fat woman for this particularly awful sketch and I – I had been asked to do something. In a way, this could be my only chance to ever make a difference.

My email was a shorter version of this:

I would have been so sad if I had seen that show as a fifteen-year-old girl who went to spinning classes every other day and was fighting through therapy that I needed, due to years of the bullying that I

---

* This is a perfect example of a very funny joke.

had endured because of my weight. I would have
lost all desire to work out – and my love for comedy.
Comedy – the thing I ended up trusting more than
anything and anyone; the art form that ended up
being my calling and the thing to give me life. I
would have seen that on television and felt excluded.
Additionally, everyone at my fitness centre, who
would have also seen this sketch, could have seen me
on my exercise bike and made their jokes. Now that
their comedy idol had done it on television – why
could they not do the same?

I am actually sad right now – even though I
have reached a point where I am finally fine with
how I look. It even hits me now, just reading it. I
cannot imagine how many young people will see
this and how hard it will hit them too. It breaks my
heart. You are intelligent, well-educated, seemingly
empathetic people – and yet you are creating a piece
of work that will be seen by thousands of people,
which will actively damage the lives of people. I
cannot see how you can ever justify putting that on
television.

I can in no way endorse or participate in a sketch
which, to this degree, confirms a negative stereotype
in a time where body-shaming is one of the main
causes of a super high teenage suicide rate.

When you make jokes – or even just fiction –
based on stereotypes, you are upholding the status
quo. And the status quo is killing people. Be it the
way you strengthen the beliefs of people who hate
the 'others', people who commit actual hate crimes,

people who bully, exclude and kill. Or be it the
way you add to marginalised people's internalised
hatred, which makes them lead lives that are quite
possibly miserable, sad and empty.

After further investigation, I can see that your
writing staff consists exclusively of white, straight,
cis men. I suggest that when writing about women or
from the point of view of women, you will consider
hiring – and this might seem like a long shot – a
woman.

Kind regards,
Sofie

And I won.[*]

✳

Due to the negative portrayals of fat people in the media, I am
now constantly on guard. When I listen to musical-theatre sound-
tracks, if a character sounds like an outsider or someone who is
considered unintelligent, I feel a knot growing in my stomach as
I think to myself: Please, do not be a fat character.

---

[*] I absolutely did not win. The writers of the show immediately got back
to me, trying to defend themselves by saying, 'We needed a character
who could not find a boyfriend, so she could not be thin. If she was thin,
people would think that she could easily find someone who would want
her', and after a very long, furious email back to them (after which they
offered me work writing for the show – I declined), we stopped speaking.
As far as I know, the sketch was never filmed or broadcast, but I also
never watched the show. I just thought 'And I won' was a cool way to end
an anecdote.

Like when I was reading a book and a fat character popped up.[4] I immediately felt the knot and thought: Please, do not be lazy or unintelligent or the laughing stock of the book.

In this particular instance, I was taken aback. The fat character in the book was not any of the stereotypes. She was feisty, strong, intelligent and very, very desired by the protagonist of the story. Not because she was fat. He just wanted her – and also she was fat. The fact that she was fat was not mentioned other than when necessary. It never defined her. It just . . . was. Eventually, in the book, they end up sleeping together. And a line stood out to me, in the middle of the page:

He feels, with a wild joy, the weight of her on top of him.

I read it over and over again. My stomach felt like a tumble dryer full of emotions. 'Wild joy' is never a term I have heard associated with fatty sex before. Someone describing wanting a fat woman sexually, but without, in any way, fetishising it.

But another thing hit me, when I read that line.

I had never before considered how sex with me *feels*. Now, stay with me. Allow me to explain. In my lifetime, I have probably thought more about how my naked body looks to everyone than I have thought about anything else. Ever since I started finding boys cute right up till now, when I find everyone cute, it has been on my mind. When embarking on a one-night stand, the only thought on my mind has been: I wonder what this person will think of the way my body looks. And during the sex, my only thought will be: *I wonder how I look from this angle. And this. And this. Also, why is he making that face? Wrong hole, abort mission.*

I have never once thought about the physical sensation of having sex with me and how it differs from having sex with a thin(ner) person. I imagine it might be softer, more squishy, some positions will be harder to do, I will feel heavier if I am on top of someone and there is just more flesh to grab and kiss. I am considering these things neutrally. The way I would talk about feeling up a beanbag chair compared to groping a coat stand.

This blew my mind. Sex is more than looks. I started thinking about smells, tastes and sounds. In a peculiar way, I felt like I was capable of adding dimensions to my person. As if, up until this point in time, I had just been a person who looked a certain way. I was my appearance. That was all I was. In terms of sex, I had disconnected from my body and treated myself as a canvas to be observed.

These thoughts led me to see myself in a very different light. It was life changing, in a way. All from having read one sentence in one book. The only positive description I have ever read of someone having sex with a fat woman. It was the first time I truly felt – instead of just stubbornly believing – that representation matters.

Which is why, and I can't stress this enough, we need a fat Disney princess.

Don't @ me.

AN INTERVIEW WITH

Stephanie Yeboah
London

*Sofie: Hi Stephanie, thank you so much for doing this.
First I'd just like to ask you to tell me a little bit about
yourself. Who you are, what you do, how you, I guess,
identify and maybe where you are in your life?*

Stephanie: My name is Stephanie Yeboah. I identify as a, oh
gosh, a fat black cis woman. I live in London and I am a plus-
size blogger. I also work in PR. In regards to where I am in my
life, I think I would probably say, I've always had issues with
how I look, being a fat person and being someone who is also
darker-skinned fat person.

My issues stem from when I was around eleven years old,
when I started being bullied in secondary school for my weight.
It kinda developed throughout secondary school till I was a
teenager. I became very self-conscious. I had a depression when
I was fourteen, and yeah, I sort of just grew up hating my body,
hating this vessel. All it was trying to do was keep me alive.
It wasn't until the age of twenty-four when I went on holiday
to Barcelona, I realised that I had an issue. Because up until
then, I was partaking in a lot of self-harm, I was starving myself,
sorry trigger warning, I was taking substances that I shouldn't
have – things in order to lose weight. I was ordering dieting
pills online, I was eating and throwing up. I didn't see that as
a disorder at the time because – I was fat and *apparently* fat
people can't have eating disorders.

So I didn't see it as something counterproductive, I just saw it as me curbing what I eat and trying to lose weight. It wasn't until I lost four stone because I wanted to have a bikini body for the beach, that I realised that I had an issue with my attitude towards my body. I lost a lot of weight but mentally I felt absolutely awful. It really hit home to me that I was actually abusing the same body that had been trying to keep me alive. Despite everything that I had done to it, it was still here ticking along, it was the reason I was here. It was then I started proactively trying to love myself and, you know, come aboard the body-positivity train. It's been a long road. It's been fifteen years or so, and there are lots of dips in the road and there will still be times when I feel really shit about myself, or there will be times when I do wish that I was smaller. But I think it's a journey that we all go on. Even if we are body positive, self-love is such a long journey and so I think I'm at a point now where I feel a lot more confident about myself and about my skin. I feel a lot more comfortable about identifying as fat. My self-esteem is up and I'm at a place where I feel really content and happy in my skin.

Sofie: You mention 'body positivity', and to me at least, it seems to be quite white? How does it feel to be a person of colour within the movement?

Stephanie: In regards to the movement, I guess I use it as a blanket term, but to be honest I would probably associate myself with the fat-acceptance movement. The reason that is, is because the bo-po movement was a movement that has been around for absolutely ages, it's been around from since the sixties. Then it had a bit of a revival in the late nineties, and then it's come around again in this millennial era. Historically it was a movement created by fat black women and women of colour and what we see now is that body positivity has been co-opted and commercialised by white women. White, physically attractive women who sort of fluctuate between sizes 10 to 14. They are women who fit society's standards of beauty and what bo-po has done, is that it has forgotten the very root and demographic that gave it prominence in favour of 'society's ideal', and so it refuses to lift up thoughts, opinions and perspectives of black women.

And as someone who has to navigate this space as a black, fat, dark-skinned woman, I don't have any sort of privilege whatsoever. First of all, I'm fat, second of all, I'm black, third of all, I'm dark-skinned black, so along with racism and things of that nature, even within my own community, we have colourism, where dark skin is seen as disgusting. It's likened to animals and monkeys. Light skin is seen as beautiful. The lighter you are, the better you are. And so, it's very difficult to navigate my way throughout this body-positivity space as somebody with no privilege. Once upon a time I'd think that bo-po was here to serve people who look like me, women whose bodies and features fit outside the scope of what society considers beautiful, however, since it has now become a buzzword and a marketing term, it has lost all of its appeal to me, personally. For a movement that lives to celebrate our differences and to highlight our bodies and all of their fat glory; for a movement that's supposed to be championing diversity, it's not diverse at all. It's no different to straight-size fashion or straight-size modelling and things like that, where it's always the people on the bottom rung that are forgotten.

Sofie: I want to ask you about this . . . stereotype that fatness is celebrated more within the black community than it is among white people. This whole idea that it's somehow easier being a fat black woman than it is being a fat white woman. Because it doesn't really ring true with everything we know about intersectionality.

Stephanie: This whole thing is one hundred per cent fabricated. And I think this is one of the main reasons why I feel that black women aren't as celebrated within the plus-size/ body-positivity movement. Someone once told me, 'Oh but we need body positivity more than you because being fat is seen as attractive in the black community,' but I think it's a certain *type* of plus size that is celebrated – this isn't for everybody, but it's generally accepted that black women have a bit of a different shape, than anybody else. So within our community, people who have big boobs, big butts, small waists – those are the physical attributes that are celebrated within the black community. This sort of stems from African society. I guess within every sort of ethnic group or culture there is always something that is celebrated that other people might not see as beautiful. So with black people it's sort of 'the curvier you are, the better', but the thing is that it's the *type* of curvy that's celebrated. It's women like Kim Kardashian and Nicki Minaj. Big boobs, big bum, small waist, hourglass-shape. That's the sort of body type that is celebrated, not women who are just fat, really. And what a lot of people don't seem to take into consideration, is that there is a lot of misogynoir within the black community.* So it is one of these things where, even when it comes to black men, they

---

* **Misogynoir** is misogyny directed towards black women.

would prefer to go out with a white woman who is hourglass shaped as opposed to a hourglass-shaped woman with darker skin.

A lot of my abuse personally has come from my own community. The bulk of abuse and dislike for the way we look actually comes from within our own ethnic group. I don't know if it's a case of self-hate – a lot of it seems to come from colourism as well. Like I said, plus-size women who are black are absolutely seen as the bottom of the rung from our own communities. A lot of the abuse that I have encountered has been from men who look like me and who are the same colour as me. I think this whole notion of us being celebrated more is unfounded. Yes, there are communities in Africa who do celebrate plus-size women and do see it as a sign of prosperity and wealth, but it's only, like, really minor, small communities within Africa that do this. And that's amazing but unfortunately that doesn't transcend over to Europe, America and the Western world in general, where we are encouraged to look up to a specific standard of beauty that doesn't include us.

Sofie: How does the intersection between blackness and fatness work, when it comes to learning to love your body? Have you been taught to hate the colour of your skin the same way as we have all been taught to hate our bodies? And can you learn to love your body without also confronting your relationship with your skin colour?

Stephanie: I guess it is kind of difficult, because we are kind of dealing with two demographics that have no privilege whatsoever. Growing up, it was kind of double trouble for me, in the sense of, I had to adjust myself in this body that I was taught to hate from a young age. Equally I was growing up and watching all of these you know, cartoons and TV shows and movies and not seeing women who looked like me. I think in regards to which one I was getting over first, it will be the skin colour. When I was younger, I used to bleach my skin because I wanted to be lighter. I thought *you know what, if I am going to be fat, at least I'm going to be light-skin fat so I am not judged as harshly*, but then obviously I started to feel the repercussions of that, in that my skin got very dry and while I was getting lighter, my skin was just turning weird. It started going grey and it wasn't good. So I stopped when I was about fifteen. I just went on this whole journey of trying to love my skin colour; trying to love how dark it was. Around this age, fifteen to sixteen, I started to see more representation on American TV, when it came to darker-skinned women.

But still there was the issue of being plus size to deal with as well. Fortunately, we are in a society now where being plus size is a bit more popular than it was back in the day but we are still seeing instances where darker-skinned women who *are* plus size aren't being represented *at all*. It's great that we do have women within the space who are not white, however, a lot of the critical acclaim and a lot of the attention is still going to lighter-skinned or mixed-raced bloggers. There are still darker-skinned bloggers who are not getting the recognition they deserve.

I don't think that I could do one without the other. In order to love myself as a complete entity, I have to love both my body and my skin colour, because it was both part of my journey of self-love that meant loving each part of me, so I had to do it in unison. It's difficult because it's two intersections or demographics that are seen as the lowest of the low, but after a while, I got there and it turned out for the best.

Sofie: Could you tell me a bit about representation and why it matters?

Stephanie: Representation, for me, means inclusivity. It means equality. It means seeing myself valued on a wider level. It means seeing people that look like me being celebrated, it means seeing people who look like me being given the love and the respect and the dignity that they deserve. It means being seen as a person, I think that's the most important thing. It's so easy for loads of demographics to be hidden, and representation is such an important factor. It just means being seen and being acknowledged, that we are here and we deserve the same amount of respect and basic level of humanity as everyone else.

Sofie: And then . . . I guess, I want to ask: how can we do better as white people? And I know the first answer to that is probably: Stop asking people of colour, when this question has been answered a million times on the internet. But I'm just asking because I'm sure my readers would love to hear it from you.

Stephanie: It's not an annoying question. It's a valid question, it's just difficult to answer. And I've always had this view when it comes to race and things like that: the onus isn't on the oppressed people or the people that are minorities. The onus isn't on us to tell white people how to act or how to be decent human beings or how to not see us as inferior. It's not our job to do that.

We fight every day to be heard and to be seen and I guess, in a way, that's kind of leading by example. So we shouldn't have to add anything onto that. In a way it's like we want white people to see all of the work and emotional labour we're doing and just replicate it. So this can be in the form of giving ethnic minorities room to talk. To highlight and lift up minority voices. This isn't to say 'step down' or 'do not take a job' or 'say no to being part of a campaign in aid of an ethnic minority'. It's just that if you know somebody or you come across someone who is fighting for equality: amazing, lift up their voices. Unfortunately, we still live in a society where people who are not white or slim or not hourglass shapes – our voices are rarely going to be heard unless it comes from someone who is socially acceptable and that's a sad truth.

Nobody cares until somebody who fits that norm says it and then all of a sudden people care. And it shouldn't be like that, our voices should be just as important and impactful. If you come across any kind of white supremacy or fatphobia or anything that puts down another demographic, I think it's important to let your voice be heard. I know that white people sometimes feel afraid or a bit apprehensive of stepping into an argument because they feel like they don't want to talk over our voices and that's valid, but there are different ways in which you can do it, so I think it's still important. It shows a really strong sign of solidarity when you do fight for us. When you defend us and speak with us. But as long as you're not saying it in a way that comes across as . . . I guess overstepping or centralising the conversation around yourself; if you can rally with us and fight with us and debate with us without making it about you, then that's amazing but the issue is when it becomes about you.

Sofie: Like when it took for Hannibal Buress to call out Bill Cosby for being a rapist before anyone started listening to his victims?

Stephanie: Yeah. It took a man for him to be held accountable for his crimes. And for the whole thing to be taken seriously. It's like it has to be spoken through someone who has that power in society for anyone to take it seriously. It's annoying.

Sofie: Thank you for answering the allyship question. It must be tiring having to call us out all the time. I saw a hashtag recently #BlackWomenInYellow and it was glorious. I thought: This is the only reason why the colour yellow exists! So, within fatshion,* in which you're a star. I guess my question is: What did fashion begin to mean to you, when you discovered the blogging scene?

Stephanie: That hashtag is just excellent. I love it. It's beautiful. I've always been into fashion, oddly enough. I was into it since I was eleven. I was a tomboy at school and it wasn't necessarily because it was in my interest, it was because of the availability – the clothes that were available to me as a teenage fat person was all very mannish. Big flared jeans and big hoodies. Everything was just big and bulky and it looked horrible. And for the large amount of my teen years I dressed very hyper masculine because the alternative to that was going to Marks and Spencer's and getting these huge butterfly dresses, like tents – I was not about that life at all. Now we have accessibility to these trendy current clothes, so it allows for us

---

* **Fatshion** is fat fashion. Great, isn't it?

to express our creativity and our individuality on a fat canvas and I think that's the most beautiful thing. Society has a specific way that they view fat people and that is, you know, long skirts, empire lines, batwing dresses, you know, very frumpy and mumsy because that's how they expect us to dress. They expect us to be very ashamed of our bodies and want to cover it up. The gag is, we are no longer living in that society. We have access to crop tops and fishnet tights and we have access to mesh and thong bodies and short shorts and all of these amazing clothes that reveal more of our bodies and we're gonna highlight that and we are going to show that through our clothes, we are going to show that we are capable of being stylish, we are capable of being sexy, we are capable of being desired and we deserve to show our skin and our bodies in these clothes, same as you. I like showing my belly off. I like showing my boobs and bras. People deserve to see it, Sofie. (*Laughter*)

Sofie: On behalf of us all . . . Thank you for letting us see it!

Stephanie: Ha ha, you're welcome.

3

Public bathrooms and other places where fat people can get stuck

When you go to the toilet during an important meeting, you have to hurry. There was one time that I failed to do that. I blame the burrito I had for breakfast.

It was technically lunch because the meeting happened at lunchtime, but I had not had breakfast, so the spicy meat roll was the first thing I ate that day and, to be honest with you, my stomach hated me for it. Usually I have quite a good relationship with my stomach. I cuddle it and tell it that it is pretty and it digests the food I eat like a champ. But every once in a while, when I make a decision such as filling it with carbs, meat and chilli first thing in the morning, it will look at me and shrug as if to say: I gotta do what I gotta do. You're on your own here.

So I had to excuse myself from the table and run to the bathroom.

The toilet was placed in a very narrow alcove, with just enough room for backing in, sitting down and doing what needed to be done. Usually, when I go to a public bathroom, one butt cheek will be resting on a sanitary bin. In this particular toilet, there was not even room for a sanitary bin. It was wall – toilet – wall. And the wall was so close to the toilet, I pretty much had to squeeze myself in there. I allowed my body to punish me for a few minutes. I apologise for giving you this information but at the same time, if this in any way offends you, I need you to calm down. We all do it. Literally all of us. Animals too. Even fish poo. And the Queen. Fish and the Queen poo. My queen* and your queen. All the queens. Including me. Your queen 2.0.

When I was finished, I realised that there was not enough room to reach my fat hands down between my fat thighs. I could not wipe. I began to understand why people want thigh gaps. Maybe they just enjoy being able to wipe themselves clean in public toilets. I can respect that. At this moment, I was, as they say, fucked. I tried reaching behind me, but my arms are too short – or maybe my butt is too big. It could easily be both. I tried everything. Eventually, I was doing improvised acrobatics with toilet paper in one hand and my trousers down around my ankles. I smashed my elbows, head and knees into the cubicle walls, as I was trying to get enough room to reach my own bum. To the people in the other stalls, this must have sounded like someone trying to wrestle cattle.

At this point, a good ten or twelve minutes had passed. A producer was sitting nearby putting two and two together. Maybe that burrito was her breakfast, he would think to himself. Do I want to

---

* Shout out to Queen Margrethe the Second, of Denmark.

work with someone who eats spicy food for breakfast? Do I want to work with someone with explosive diarrhoea?

I eventually managed to find a position that worked for me. When I went back into the restaurant, I noticed how many fat people were eating their food. I wanted to shout at them. 'Don't go to the bathroom! It's a trap! Bring a hose or a really (really!) close friend who's not too fussy.'

I have friends larger than me who told me that they have been in situations where they just had to *not wipe*. That is a sentence that is about as beautiful as the sentiment. Sure, there were alternatives. The fat people could just have stayed at home. Cancelled on their best friend's birthday party. Not consumed food or liquid for the three days leading up to the event. Or, you know, the establishment could just have bathrooms that were *slightly larger*.

Whether or not fat people should accommodate ourselves to the world or the world should accommodate us is, unfortunately, up for discussion. I think my stance on this is fairly obvious. So, as we are discussing public space and existing as a fat person in that public space, I am going to talk from the position of someone believing that a world that is inclusive to everyone is a better world than one that is not.

Is it a bird? Is it a plane?
Yes, it's a plane, which sucks: I really
had hoped it was Superman

About a year ago, a friend of mine booked plane tickets for her and her boyfriend and I to go to Berlin. We're a little group of friends out of which I am the only fat person. We were going to spend two days in Berlin, my favourite city, and we were all quite excited. I asked her to please book me a window seat, because I have anxiety.

See, I am scared of people. Every aspect of meeting a person terrifies me. From saying hello to them and not knowing if you should shake their hand, hug them, give them a high-five or just a cool-guy nod to finding a seat in a restaurant.* Allow me to say this now: I need a corner seat. If I sit in the middle of the room, it feels like my chair is balancing on a mountain ledge and every moment can lead to my death. A waiter walking behind me will send my heart into my throat in an instant.

On public transportation, I need the window seat. Otherwise I will constantly be clutching my bag or my hands, my pulse in a frenzy, anticipating when the person next to me will get up – or when someone is going to walk past me in the aisle and bump my shoulder, in which case, I will definitely die, and that will hurt.

This gets worse on planes, because you might not know this, but planes are actually the size of those little plastic toy planes you can buy at the airport to give to your child as an apology for travelling too much and never being around. Planes are so tiny that they have to hire actual ants as members of staff. They may look like real-life, life-sized people, but actually, they are ants. Look closer the next time you are on a plane. Try holding out a crumb and you will see them fight the urge to all carry it to their queen, who I assume is the pilot.

---

* The first time I said goodbye to a very famous Danish comedian, he opened his arms and I just embraced his body. I then realised that he had just reached out for the door-handle. I think about that every time I feel confident, as if my body has an automatic 'let's not get too happy' function that sets in every time there is a danger of me actually becoming an adult person.

I prefer to be in the window seat, so I can get on the plane first and find my seat and only be a nuisance to the person next to me. I know that other fat people prefer the aisle seat, because then they can spill over into the aisle and get up every once in a while when the pain from the armrest gets too much. Each fat person to their own.

There is a group on Facebook called 'Flying While Fat', created by fat activist and illustrator Stacy Bias, in which fat people compare notes on planes. It is quite practical. Someone will upload a full-body photo of themselves and say which flight they are taking, accompanied by 'Will I fit in my seat? Any tips?'

Then a whole bunch of lovely people will share their advice. Such as: You will need an extension belt. The armrest close to the window goes up, so get a window seat. Or book two seats. Or contact the company ahead of time and ask for a spare seat next to you. Or do not expect to eat on the plane as the table will not be able to go down. Or, this plane actually has an accessible toilet, you just have to ask to use it.

It is very useful. I highly recommend it. Most people share the same fear. Fear of being ridiculed, of being thrown off the plane, of sitting next to someone who is going to take their photo or tweet about it or sigh loudly or complain to the flight attendant. All things that happen to loads of fat people all the time. People have a nasty tendency to blame *you* for the plane being too small. Plane seats are getting increasingly smaller. Thirty years ago, the average width of a plane seat would be 19–20 inches. Now it's down to 16–17 inches.[1] All in order for airlines to fit more passengers onboard and thus make (more) money. Some airlines in the USA have got a COS policy – a Customer of Size policy – where fat people can get two plane seats, free of charge. They seem to still be in business despite being accommodating to fat people. A lot of us would just be satisfied if it was possible to lift up the armrest by the window. That would easily lend us another couple of inches. If we were to play by the rules of capitalism, perhaps the plane could have a few wider seats that would cost a bit more money, to make up for the difference. I am simply desperate to have the option here.

I *try* to get on the plane first. I find my window seat – which I always try to reserve near the front, so that I do not have to squeeze past too many sighing people either throwing themselves dramatically into the middle seat as if they are afraid that I am going to dislocate their shoulder or people who absolutely refuse to move so I have to mutter, 'Sorry, sorry, sorry' as my butt or stomach slaps into them. I get into the window seat as quickly as possible – quickly check if I need an extension, if I have not brought my own.* I press myself up against the window, force the armrest down, check if the table goes down (it does not) and lodge my knees into the back of the seat in front of me. I then prepare for what will feel like forever in constant pain.†

I once spent eleven hours on a plane from South Africa with literally every joint in my body aching. The armrest was pressing itself into my skin so hard that it stopped my bloodstream to my legs. I tried lifting it slightly, but my very thin seat-neighbour kept pressing it down, into my flesh. Twice she went to the bathroom

---

* TIP: You can buy your own extension belt online. This is potentially life-changing advice, if you feel uncomfortable asking for one on the plane. I once asked for one twice and she never gave it to me, so, feeling stubborn and annoyed, I just never wore a seatbelt. I have to tell you: I have never felt more alive.

† I am talking about the lack of WiFi, am I right, Millennials? Huh? What if someone tweets something while I am in the sky? FOMO much?

and both times I desperately lifted the armrest all the way up and let myself spill into her seat. I remember crying with relief at feeling the blood back in my legs, at my shoulders opening up instead of keeping me crouched together in a classic 'I am sorry I am fat and existing' pose, at my inner thigh muscles relaxing because I no longer had to hold them together so they wouldn't touch her thin, white, probably naturally hairless legs. My seat-mate came back and I had to grab all my fat and let myself back into a partly self-made cage for the remaining seven hours of the flight. I was in so much pain that I decided to never fly again.

Another time, I sat next to a very fat man on a plane. That was equally crammed. This was a twelve-hour flight to Australia and I was squeezed into the window seat. He was overflowing into my seat and our bodies were touching so much that I almost lost my virginity. I didn't, though, and to this day I remain a good Christian.* We were both almost twice as big as our seats. It was physically uncomfortable, sure, but at the same time, I was relieved. And I would sit next to him any day rather than someone thin. I will explain.

I cannot make assumptions about what strangers sitting next to me think about me – but hey, I will give it a pretty good shot. Fatphobia is a thing, I hope we have established that by now. The person sitting next to me on a plane could have been raised in a jungle by kangaroos or something, but knowing this world and this society, there is probably a kangaroo version of SlimFast with billboards everywhere featuring kangaroos drinking powder whilst faking smiles. So I do not trust the person sitting next to

---

* Just kidding, I'm totally the atheist Bang Lord you expect me to be. I have been beating that puss and riding the purple stick since I was legal, if you know what I mean. (I'm sorry.)

me on the plane to not also have been brainwashed into thinking that fat people are less worthy than others.

Because I have never read any think piece or article or tweet or blog post where someone complained about sitting next to a muscly man. And I have been that person and can I just point out: muscly people hurt. Muscles are hard. It's the prize you win by working out a lot: if a bus hits you, the bus gets hurt. At least fat is soft and squishy. I am not saying that one is necessarily better than the other, all I am saying is: people prefer different hardness of the mattress they sleep on is all.

Because listen, it might be annoying sitting next to us on planes, but did you ever consider what it's like having to sit next to someone who hates you?

I would rather sit next to a fellow fatty than a judgemental thin person.* So I sat there on the plane to Australia, slowly losing feeling in my arms and legs, but I was content. For at least he did not have to sit next to someone loudly sighing and rolling their eyes. Like the business man who sat next to me on a plane to Denmark and poked me in the ribs with his elbow, probably believing that he was making some sort of point. As if I was capable of saying, 'Oh, you know what, you are *right*, I *am* way too big, let me just do some quick push-ups and lose some weight and you can spend the rest of the flight less uncomfortable. Oh no, that's right, you are still flying economy on a low budget airplane, so you will never be fully comfortable. On top of which you are also a spiteful human being with the need to make other people feel bad, so now that I think of it, you will never feel

---

* Let's have 'Fellow Fatty' T-shirts and badges made. Seriously, guys. Let's do it.

comfortable. At least I can get off this plane, whereas you cannot get off your shitty personality. Goodbye, sir.'*

My two friends and I got on the plane to Berlin. We had the first row. The ones where the seats are divided by a hard wall instead of liftable armrests. I managed to squeeze myself into it all right. The seatbelt was way too short so I casually asked for the extension. I have reached a point where I am not ashamed of asking. I genuinely feel like they should be ashamed for their seatbelts being too short. Asking for an extension now feels like saying, 'Bad plane, bad!' but unfortunately the flight attendants rarely feel the same. I am used to being met with slightly wide eyes and a worried wrinkle in their foreheads. Severely lowered voices that whisper 'of course', as they hand you the extension with shaky hands. Like a scared nurse in a hospital TV drama where the handsome doctor is about to perform surgery that has not been authorised.

'But Doctor—'
'I said: SCALPEL.'
'He could die!'
'He is going to die if I don't make the
**   incision. Now, SCALPEL.'**

On this particular flight, the flight attendant looked more nervous than usual. She squatted in front of me and whispered,

---

* I practise speeches a lot. In mirrors, in the shower, on the bus. Oscar thank-you speeches, wedding speeches, you-never-should-have-left-me-you-piece-of-shit ex-boyfriend speeches, but my favourite speeches are the shouting-at-white-men-in-suits speeches. They all end with GOOD-BYE, SIR, by the way. That'll teach them.

'You are in an emergency exit row, so you can't have the extension. I have to move you.'

Just for a brief second, time stood still. Then I took a breath and said, 'Okay, where do I go?' and got up. There was a full empty row a few seats back. Once a month I have a nightmare where the plane is full and I have to get off the plane. It happens. It has happened before. It is part of the package deal called 'Being Fat on a Plane'. You might not get to fly.

My friends were visibly shocked. And understandably, they felt bad for me. They tried complaining to the staff. I just wanted everyone to be quiet. *Please* do not make this a thing.

I am so used to travelling alone – and constantly adjusting my plans to my body. Getting that specific seat on the plane, turning up early, doing my regular checks once I am on board, that it now all happens automatically.

I barely notice that constant fight to force myself into a world that is not accommodating towards me.

All of this was a shock to my friends. To them, a fat person being moved to another seat because they are too fat, was not a given. Not something to almost be expected. They did not even have to say anything – their nervous, frustrated and sad energy took up the entire plane. I was desperately smiling – the way you smile to a toddler when it falls down to convince it that everything is fine and nothing hurts. Only my eyes were filling with tears which I didn't want them to see. I didn't feel humiliated or ashamed. At all. Bad plane, bad, bad plane. I felt incredibly guilty that my two innocent best friends had to see how my world looks. I wanted them to keep living in their world – a world in which people are allowed to exist and travel the way they please.

This all happened a year ago. As I am writing this, I have had to come to terms with the fact that I am now too fat to fly in a single seat in economy. This culminated when I found myself stranded in Australia, with the knowledge that there was no way I could go home with the ticket I possessed. The trip to Australia had been so painful that I had been unable to walk or sleep for days after, due to my aching back and bruised legs.

Only a few days afterwards, I was unable to fit into a seat in a theatre and I was placed on a regular chair without an arm-rest, next to a row of seats, towering over everyone else, looking like a lifeguard ready to save some lives if the comedy show ever became *too funny*.

I realised: I am now *too fat* for the world.

And I was stuck in Australia. After calling various airlines trying to find a solution, I had to cave in and order a Business Class flight home, emptying my account in the process. I am lucky to have had the amount ready. I am lucky that it did not completely debilitate me. I know many other people who would have had no choice but to either risk being thrown off the plane or who would simply have had to live in Australia forever.[*]

Getting *too fat* for the world was not something I had antici-pated. I did not know that I was growing. I do not weigh myself and I do not measure anything. I do not focus on my size when I look in the mirror. When it happened, I was momentarily frozen.

Then an unsuspected wave of relief overcame me. Alongside the intense sadness that there were now entire spaces I could not fit into and trips I could no longer afford to go on, that I would find it increasingly harder to find clothes, that the abuse would get worse, that my chances of a career would decrease, that there

---

[*] Not the worst destiny in the world, but I'm sure most people would appreciate a heads up.

would probably soon come a time where I would have to just *not wipe*, that there would be shows I couldn't attend – but all these things were just worse versions of something I was used to. What surprised me, was the relief. That I would no longer be in extreme pain when I *do* travel or go to the theatre. I am now forced to ask for a chair without armrests, go Business Class or book two seats on a plane. After years of being *too fat* but not *fat enough* to be comfortable, I felt like I had been released from a prison and I could finally breathe.

My body has made the decision for me: I am no longer capable of being uncomfortable. Uncomfortable is now too small for me. I am forced to be comfortable. Something I never felt like I deserved.

Finally.

Dina Amlund

Denmark

Dina is an activist in the Danish activist group FedFront. I saw her do a talk at the Politics of Volume conference, a fat-activism conference, in Amsterdam. It was about how fatness has been viewed throughout history. It was so interesting and something I had never heard of or even considered, so I invited her to be a guest in this book.

Sofie: Hi Dina. Talk to me about your degree and your fatness and, I guess, the combination of the two?

Dina: Hi Sofie. I have a BA in literature and a masters in cultural history. So, I graduated ten years ago and a lot has happened since, for me personally as well as the level of *wokeness* everywhere. My focus was always feminism and otherness in my studies. But I hadn't discovered fat activism yet. It wasn't until shortly after I finished my masters degree. So on my own I started looking at Western cultural history from this perspective. Once you've seen it you cannot un-see it.

Sofie: So if I say to you 'Oh, in the olden days, being fat was seen as a good thing!' what would you say?

Dina: UGH! That is one tough myth to bust! Actually, it's not that hard providing examples of fatphobia through the different eras of Western culture. But the myth is being repeated over and over and over again in ways that are both meant to be negative and positive towards fatness. So most people believe that fatphobia is a new phenomenon.

Sofie: *What's the earliest example of fatphobia you've found?*

Dina: Western history starts with ancient Greece where you immediately find the body ideal we're familiar with today – the very slender muscular man, and the equally slender woman who isn't muscular. To step out of the gender-binary language, I'll say that the *human* ideal was super slender. Historians and art historians sometimes describe the female ideal of ancient Greece as full-figured, but all the statues show slender women. You will find a striking, sort of, *absence* of fatness when looking at art from this era as well as in plays and epic poems of this time. The first recorded corset originates from Crete and various pottery from all over Greece show both men and women wearing *form-fitting* belts.

The slender body ideal from the antiquity has ruled all the way up till today. Through the early, high, and late Middle Ages 500–1500 we don't see *any* sign of fatness being celebrated. People who were fat were considered gluttonous, and gluttony was one of the seven deadly sins which were taken very seriously.

Sofie: *Oh! Yeah!*

Dina: Right? The fashion of the medieval period included bones and wooden slats which were sewn into garments to shape the body in some parts of Europe. The body was hidden away much more during the three Middle Ages than it was earlier and later in history. Because the body was seen as extremely sinful in medieval times – but even though the body was not so much on display fatness was held in with bandages under the long outfits.

Through the Renaissance – which has an overlap with the late Middle Ages and runs from the fourteenth to the seventeenth century – during this time ancient Greece and Rome were rediscovered with their body ideals and love of nude bodies in art. And this is when the 'cotte' appears. The cotte is like a prequel to a corset. Which is used to make the torso cone shaped.

Sofie: Ouch? This is how academic I can get: Ouch. It sounds ouch.

Dina: Yeah, ouch! And during the 1500s thick waists were *actually* forbidden at the French court. And then it takes a terrible course where bodies are made to fit into clothes and not clothes made to fit onto bodies. They kind of did, but with bone and wood sewn into them to shape them. In England, the Tudor corset was made of iron to make the upper body completely flat.

Sofie: Wait, IRON?

Dina: IRON. Actual iron. It was expected to be worn by the aristocracy and wealthy people. There was highly unpleasant shape-wear for both men and women. In this era you can see fatphobic images in art and literature, the same way you still can.

In the baroque era, from 1600–1750, corsets were made from linen and bone to make the waist smaller. The first novel was published in this time, and it is of course utterly fatphobic: Cervantes' *Don Quixote*, about a man who lost his mind and travelled with his gullible, ill-smelling fat helper, who believes everything Quixote says. It takes a fat person to fill that role of the unpleasant, unintelligent force that takes the story where it goes. And it takes a person who lost his mind to want to travel with a disgusting and gullible fat person.

From the second half of the eighteenth century through the 1800s up to the middle of the twentieth century we see corsets of silk and muslin, which create the infamous hourglass shape with the very narrow waist in focus. There are also corsets for men during different eras but they are harder to come by in fashion records.

During all these times slenderness is a virtue of whichever ruling idea at the time – whether it is God, aesthetics, morality, social status and so on.

Sofie: But we have words such as 'Rubenesque' which sounds like a happy fatty old-time term?

Dina: I cannot count how many times I've heard that fatness was acceptable in 'the old days'. That at times when food was scarce and most people worked really hard in the fields, being fat was the ideal way to have a body.

Thinness with slightly different size variations, from small-thin to big-thin, has reigned the claim of aesthetics, health, intelligence, morality, and worthiness in the entire history of Western culture. With *no* time period exceptions.

So, Peter Paul Rubens is the origin of the term 'Rubenesque'.

But if you look at his models – most of them are slender and some a little bit bigger than that, small-fat women, very small-fat. Rubenesque in the language of our time is used about fat women. But that does not mean that you and me would have been accepted, let alone celebrated for our looks, back in the 'good old days'.

Sofie: This changes my time-travel fantasy quite drastically.

Dina: Yeah, mine too! The women in the paintings are slender and have very little fat. It is also worth mentioning that the women in the paintings didn't portray the height of beauty anyway. Because women as 'the fairer sex' is a social construct which only appeared over a hundred years after Rubens died. In the era of Rubens, and painters like him, men were the most beautiful because they were created in the image of God. Rubens painted mostly slender men (and Jesus, who was obviously the most beautiful of all men, was always very slender and muscular like an ancient Greek statue. And white).

Sofie: The **Venus of Willendorf, The Crouching Aphrodite, The Birth of Venus** *and the* **Rape of the Daughters of Leucippus?** *You know, the 'fat-positive art' that proves that we loved fat people in the olden days? (Just to be very clear, I just did a quick Google, I have never heard of any of these before. My idea of art is whatever is on Netflix.)*

Dina: I'm glad you googled! Those are some of the pieces that people do normally talk about as 'fat-positive art'. The *Venus of Willendorf* is a very interesting piece. But it doesn't belong to Western culture. Though it was found in what we today call Austria, we must keep in mind that since it is 25,000 years old it does not belong in what we call Western culture or Western civilisation that began with the age of antiquity, which started 5,000 years ago. And it is interesting that *Venus of Willendorf*, the image of a fat person, has been thin-washed by modern Western views who wanted her to be a pregnant woman – when really she is fat. If she is pregnant, she is a fat pregnant person.

The *Crouching Aphrodite* is a very good example of art from the age of antiquity that we are told is a fat woman – but look at her. You see a few rolls, because she is crouching, but she is *not fat*.

The Birth of Venus is just a thin person. I don't even understand how people ever speak of her as fat. But they do.

The Rape of the Daughters of Leucippus is a perfect example of Rubens' art. Women who are big-thin – small-fat at best – whom we are told are so very fat but when look at it we see that they are not. They are a little softer looking than women portrayed in later periods but that does not make them fat. Perhaps just a little less skinny.

Sofie: Is art a fair portrayal of the culture? If they hated or loved fat people in art, can we assume that reflected onto actual everyday life?

Dina: Art, as well as fashion, is very much a thermometer that shows us the ideal of the time. As you can tell from the history of shape-wear – it has been there all through Western culture – the body has always been maintained and policed for different reasons perhaps, but always from a fatphobic angle. Trying to make the body thinner. Though fashion and art has changed over time, it always shows the height of sophistication and all that is good. So the absence of fat bodies, the mockery of fat bodies, the worshipping of thin bodies are all ever present in Western cultural history.

Sofie: So, are there not any actually fat people portrayed in art at all?

Dina: Oh, there are plenty of caricatures in painting and writing throughout the entire Western history. Shakespeare is full of fatphobia; fatness is used as comic relief in his tragedies and is significant in his comedies. An example of fatphobia used as comic relief in a tragedy is *King Henry IV*: Falstaff says, 'There live not three good men unhanged in England, and one of them is fat . . .' So not really a man or a person. Falstaff was a fan favourite: he was written into other tragedies and in the comedy *The Merry Wives of Windsor*. Falstaff himself is a fat character and brings on fatphobic jokes, just like watching the few fat characters in Hollywood films today.

In the 1800s, Doctor Banting, a British doctor, described how fat people were being mocked and ridiculed in social gatherings, and he encouraged fat people to lose weight to gain more social status.

It really is not a new phenomenon that society discriminates against fat people for various reasons, aesthetics, status or, as we see today, with a normative description of health.

Sofie: Well. Wow. So, why do you think we feel the need to say that 'in the olden days, it was different', if it wasn't?

Dina: Well, as I see it, there are two aspects to repeating that fatness was endured or even celebrated in the old days:

There is the fatphobic repetition that fatness is an outdated phenomenon from when common sense didn't rule, back in the times when people believed all sorts of strange and illogical things, and this adds another layer of inhumanity to fat people. In this light, we are seen as ghosts of the past, alongside other curiosities and abominations that people are thankful to be without in these modern days, or that they *should* be without in our times of enlightenment, knowledge and common sense.

The fat-positive repetition which states that in better times, before the world went astray, fatness was accepted in Western culture and even celebrated in a humane way, like, *damn I was born in the wrong century*, creates a false notion of fatphobia as a new phenomenon. By doing so our awareness *of fat as othered* in Western culture is belittled. And so is the work we have in front of us when decoding fatphobia.

Sofie: Wow. Thank you, Dina.

4

Clothes
and why it's okay to
dress almost exclusively
in orange

As a fat person, I never found my 'style'. It was never an option. I had to wear whatever was available – be it my aunt's old clothes or whatever was lying in a big pile of maternity clothes on sale at the local low-budget supermarket. We lived in a small town – we could not even get near the big malls to look for more options and, even if we could, my mother would have no interest in doing so. To her, clothes never mattered and she could not imagine why they would matter to me. So they didn't.

I was a thirteen-year-old wearing my aunt's oversized T-shirts and jeans in different colours. On my feet, I wore clogs, which gave me the nickname 'Farm Fashion', because children are creative geniuses. The nicknames did not really bother me – clothes meant nothing to me.

I proceeded to wear black. Always black. Black and baggy. Whatever was *flattering*, meaning 'whatever hid my body'. I had a few brightly coloured dresses in my cupboard – they were for whenever I would lose all the weight. Something so fancy and pretty belonged to Thin Sofie. In the same way as you would not bother washing an old, dirty car that you were going to replace soon anyway, I made sure that all my money and energy went into Thin Sofie. I felt like I was utterly unworthy of bothering with clothes because I felt like I was living in a temporary shell.

Eventually, I became obsessed with skater dresses. That is when the dress is tight around the chest and then cuts off right under the breasts – only to fall freely over your stomach. It placed the focus on my boobs and it hid my stomach – which I understood was a good thing. There would be no real pattern in what I wore. I went on the few plus-size websites I knew and bought whatever seemed to be able to cover my body the best. At this point I did not care if the dresses were covered in skulls and fire or flowers and puppies. It was just a matter of waking up and getting dressed without having to think too hard.

One night I complained half-heartedly to a friend, 'I envy people who have a style. People who wake up and know they are jeans-and-a-T-shirt guy or a yellow-dresses woman.'

I told my friend about the Orange Lady. A co-worker once set me up on a date with her housemate – a charming man who studied anthropology. For reasons unknown to everyone, we ended up having our date in *the* lesbian bar in Copenhagen. The music was ridiculously loud and we struggled to hear what each other was saying – which turned out to be a positive, seeing as we had absolutely nothing to say to each other. The long-drawn-out, painful silences were only interrupted by one of us getting up to get more, much-needed, drinks. Until I saw the Orange Lady. She was dressed completely in orange. She had orange hair, an orange dress, orange tights, orange glasses, an orange hat, orange earrings, orange shoes, bag, make-up, everything. To fill the silence, I shouted at my date, 'Look at the Orange Lady!' and he smiled back at me. Whenever she passed, I said to him, 'Look at her, she is completely orange,' and eventually it became the only thing I said.

The next morning, I called my co-worker to tell her about the catastrophe that was our date. Eventually, as I would be doing with great joy for weeks to come, I told her about the Orange Lady. 'Oh!' she exclaimed. 'That makes so much sense! He came home and said you had shouted "orange lady" at him for hours and he had been desperately trying to find out if it was a drink request or a question.'

'He never saw the Orange Lady?' I asked.

'No,' she answered. Oh. There was no second date. And I started questioning if the Orange Lady even existed. Maybe I had made her up due to being too bored in the presence of my date or perhaps she was a ghost – the ghost of Bad Dates. Months later, I started university. During a lecture, the woman next to me asked if she could show me a photo of her girlfriend. On her phone, the Orange Lady showed up and I squealed, 'It's the Orange Lady! It's her!' and I learned two things: a whole classroom full of people staring at you for shouting 'Orange Lady' is worse than one cute anthropologist-to-be doing so. And the Orange Lady is a real lady and she has a nice girlfriend. And she really, really loves the colour orange.

I told my friend about the Orange Lady. How I had been obsessed with her. I envied that she had found her *thing*. Her *style*. And that she did not seem to give a fuck about conventions. To me, she was a powerhouse of a woman who just decided that she liked the colour orange so why not wear nothing but orange forever?

Meanwhile, I felt like a mess of a human. I would wear over-sized masculine vests from the men's department, flowery dresses, dungarees with cute dogs on them, T-shirt dresses with skulls and blood on them. I just wanted to find my orange.

'What do you like wearing?' my friend asked. I stared at him for what felt like forever. I had no answer. No one had ever asked me and I had never thought about it before. I had never bought the clothes *I wanted to wear* or the clothes *I liked*. I had bought the clothes that fit me. I had never even allowed myself to express myself through fashion.

It sent me into a many-months-long spiral. I dived into my phone's photo album. I looked at myself in all the photos and asked myself: Is this me? Does this feel like me and look like me?

There were so many dresses I actively disliked. That, when I thought about them, almost made me feel sick. Dresses I had worn for years. I realised how often I wore the bra that hurt and wounded my skin. Realised that I really, really do not like the colour green, yet I so often wore green. It felt like I had spent my entire life functioning as a head only, my body being a necessary means to walk around. There had not been much thought about how my body felt or about who I felt I was as a person.

I bought my first pair of trousers and something clicked. At the age of twenty-eight, I started listening to my body and, finally, started exploring my identity through clothes.

✳

When you have felt 'too big' for normal everyday stuff like seats or T-shirts that are already labelled X-LARGE, suddenly being 'too small' for something is an exhilarating feeling. The first time I discovered plus-size clothing, the first thing I did was purchase the largest size, so I knew what it felt like to wear something bigger than my body instead of something I had to squeeze myself into.

A few years ago, I was doing a TV show – and it was just fancy enough that I was assigned a woman to buy clothes for me. This has happened once in my life and it's safe to say, I learned a lesson.

She was a lovely woman, the costume designer. I was introduced to her by the production company and I immediately started listing the two or three websites that have dresses in my size. I quickly added that she had to order them quickly because it took a while for them to be sent to Denmark, but she interrupted me and said, confidently, 'Don't worry, this is my job.'

I continued to warn her, tell her that it was very hard to find clothes in my si— but she interrupted me with a, 'Honey, I do this for a living.'

So I reluctantly trusted her. Maybe there are big warehouses full of plus-sized clothes where only costume designers can go and find clothes for the two fat women on Danish TV.* When she returned a few weeks later with three small bags, she seemed frantic. The warehouse was but a dream, it turned out.

'I didn't know it would be so hard to find a black dress,' she said apologetically, and pulled out three black dresses. Actually, that's an exaggeration. She pulled out two black dresses and a black, oversized T-shirt from H&M. One of them fit. Almost. She pinned needles everywhere and assured me that she would make it look better.

---

* I have not actually counted but this seems like a fair shot.

'I cannot believe how hard it was finding a dress. I went into every shop,' she kept repeating.

I know. I knew. I've known since I started buying my own clothes at the age of thirteen. When my friends would empty a shop for clothes and I would take some size 10s and try them on, even though I knew they wouldn't fit. Afterwards I'd claim the colour was wrong.

I was suddenly very into accessories, so that I could also buy something I could fit. Earrings are thankfully not fatphobic in their sizes. Bracelets, headbands, nail polish. Scarves. I still own a lot of scarves. I know how hard it is. I had known when she had said she was just going to go into central Copenhagen to find a dress. When I tried to warn her, she had looked at me with a facial expression which told me that she knew most about this topic. That was now the look I was giving her.

'I bet you've never had to find anything for someone my size?' I asked. She widened her eyes and started telling me what I've heard so many times before. That oh, I'm not *that* big and either way, it suits *me* and it's *not* the *first* thing people notice. I stopped her to let her know that I'm okay with it. We discussed shoes and tights and hugged goodbye.

I didn't give it much thought, but then it finally hit me. I was relieved. I was relieved that I didn't have to be the one to tell yet another person what it's like being a fat person. She didn't even get the full experience – of having clerks look at you with narrowed eyes, followed by them looking up and down your body and finally looking into the ground saying, 'Sorry, we don't carry your size.'

She just had to experience her job becoming harder and almost impossible to do – because I am a size 26–28. Instead of walking a mile in my shoes, she walked a mile in my oversized H&M T-shirt.

I want to acknowledge the importance that clothes and fashion can have, and at the same time I want to make it clear that I do not believe it should matter.

Fat women are not allowed to wear trousers

Before a concert, I was still trying to find my style. Out of sheer habit, I put on a dress. I looked in the mirror and I was not looking at me. I put all of my dresses into a black bag and made a mental note to donate it to FatSwap later.* I put on a pair of dark red trousers and an oversized 'men's' vest in grey. Looking in the mirror, I said to myself, very quietly, 'There you are.'

I had never considered trousers, because fat women are not allowed to wear trousers. It seems like it is expected of us to attempt to obtain ultimate femininity to make up for how desexual we automatically become just from being fat.†

---

* **FatSwap** is an amazing event that takes place all over the UK (and I know that other cities all over Europe and probably USA are starting to do it as well) where fat people bring all the clothes they no longer want or need and put them on long tables, in their size group and then you are just free to grab whatever you want. You donate a bit to the cause at the entrance, but other than that it is free for all. It is glorious and wonderful and fat people are supporting each other and complimenting each other right, left and centre. Go to a FatSwap or set up one in your local area. It is the best.

† When someone is **desexualised**, their sexual appeal is removed from them. A desexual person is not considered sexy. Whereas an asexual

We also want to be seen 'making an effort'. A few years ago, the whole messy-haired, come-to-bed look became a thing. Mostly thin, white women with blonde hair would rock a pair of pyjamas in public and go make-up free.* That is thin, white privilege in a nutshell. A thin, white woman can dress like a lazy person because she would never be perceived as lazy, whereas there is a pressure on fat women (and people of colour) to dress up, to negate this 'lazy stereotype'. The more time we have spent getting ready, the less slouchy we seem. The more feminine we are, the more we are apologising for being unfuckable fatties. There is a reason why plus-size clothes are 99 per cent flowery. It is cute and unthreatening. What says 'sorry' more than a shit-load of flowers?

I started wearing trousers and, immediately, I felt like I was losing fuckability. Whether or not I actually did is irrelevant. Shortly thereafter I cut my hair shorter. The same fear of being unfuckable crept in, but I liked the look. Through my own lens and not the general male gaze through which I had spent my life looking.

Alongside every single dress in my cupboard, I also threw out everything that was too small. It is the ultimate acknowledgement of the fact that I will probably never get smaller. I deserve to have a wardrobe full of clothes that both fit me and which I want

person is just a person with a lack of sexual feelings. Basically, desexual is how the world views you or how the world makes you appear, and asexual is how a person feels on the inside.

* I once told my friend that I considered going make-up free and she said, 'I know how to do that. You just have to use a lot of foundation to make it look like you're not wearing make-up,' and that turns out to be the trick. What a world.

to wear. It is a privilege I never thought I would have. I never thought I could have.

It gets increasingly harder to find clothes that fit, the bigger you are. I am currently in the 26–28 range, and so I have a much harder time finding clothes than people who are a size 20–22. I am still quite fortunate compared to infinity-fats, people who are 32+, for whom it is near impossible to find clothes. If you are much bigger than a size 40, it is straight up impossible. A lot of clothing brands are now recognising that there is great commercial value in seeming to back up around the body-positivity movement, so they announce their plus-size ranges using size 12 models in their adverts. But when you go to the physical shops, the clothes are shoved into a tiny corner and the range is almost non-existent and only in a few chosen shops. Often, the sizes only go up to a 24 or 26. And there is a big chance it *won't* be the same clothes as in the straight-sized department. It will be more baggy, more black, more flowers or weirdly have holes in the shoulders. Or peplum. They love to put fat people in peplum. They will often brand themselves with the phrases 'We now cater to ALL BODIES' or 'We now have ALL SIZES' yet they keep excluding anyone above a size 24. Even the most popular plus-size brands like ASOS, Navabi, SimplyBe, River Island Plus or New Look Curves struggle to produce many clothes above a size 32–34. So what do people do, who are larger than that?

The options are then to have clothes custom-made, which very few plus-size brands do offer to do. (In the UK, I only currently know of PlusEquals which, to be fair, is a pretty awesome brand making pretty great clothes.) But this is understandably expensive and not something that everyone has the ability to do. Engaging with fashion in itself is very much a thing for privileged people already, as it costs money and time. If you are bigger than a size 18, shopping in physical shops becomes close to impossible and you are stuck with online shopping only. You cannot try on the clothes before you buy them, you have to be home to receive a parcel that never shows up, and the models the websites use are often a size 12, so you have no realistic way of knowing how the outfit is going to look on you.

If you add the difficulty of finding clothes to the deep general feeling of shame and worthlessness that fat people tend to feel, fashion does not seem like a thing for many fat people to even start caring about.

But I believe in self-expression. I believe in selfies and looking in the mirror and *doing you*. As self-indulgent and boring as it may seem, I have to believe that it is a good place to start. If you have money to spend on yourself without big financial consequences, it is worth doing.* If nothing else, to prove to yourself that you are worth spending money on. You deserve to wear something that feels nice on your skin as much as anyone. There is no reason why this fictional future you, who might never happen, gets to wear all the cool outfits. Clothes can be self-expression as much as self-reflection.

The extent to which I care about fashion ends at actual fashion. I couldn't care less about what is in fashion at the moment. I have never seen myself represented on a catwalk. I don't think

---

* All right, so this is a tricky one. The saying goes, 'There is no ethical consumption under capitalism,' and I am someone who has not just flirted with the communist ideology, I have full-on snogged it behind a skip at a private party and later texted to it, 'U up?' So I feel weird saying something as capitalist as, 'Yeah, spend your money on stuff you don't essentially need.' But we do live under capitalism and we are all consumers. So if you can, try to be aware of where the stuff you buy comes from.

that there should be any rules in fashion. Whenever I hear anyone judge someone's clothing, be it because it's a skirt they feel is too short or because it's a man who wears socks and sandals, I switch off immediately. If you want to wear a short skirt, have socks in your sandals or wear an outfit that is exclusively orange, you are allowed to do so without anyone mocking that choice. If you are one of these judgy types: Why? What gives you the right? And what do you get out of it?

The first time I ever wore high heels was also the last. I went shopping with some of my friends when I was sixteen and I found a pair of high heels in my size. It is rare. I have big feet. I bought them. I had struggled with what I perceived as my own lack of femininity and 'not being a real girl' and definitely not being 'a real adult' and I was in that Britney Spears-esque era of being not yet a girl, not yet a woman, and sort of wanting to shave my head. I was terrified when I put them on at the station as we were waiting for our train home. I took exactly three steps before my friends behind me broke down laughing. I had no patience and no room for laughing at myself, so the shoes went into a bag and later into the bin. God, imagine if – and this goes for not just all people during your teenage years but essentially for all people in the world – imagine if people were just nice to each other.

Fashion can be used for a myriad of things. Some people may use it to express their gender identity, to regain or simply gain confidence in their bodies after a long, insufferable period of dark thoughts; some people wear what they wear out of religious beliefs or to make a political statement that means a lot to them, and some people just do not care. When you ask for someone's opinion, that is when they should give it. Unless it's a positive and encouraging (and absolutely a non-creepy or non-patronising) comment, then people need to shut up.

I was sitting in the back of a cab in the spring of 2016, when I saw the Gold Man. He emerged from the shadows to cross the road in front of us, all dressed in . . . gold. An old-timey suit as well as a waistcoat, a tie, a pocket watch and, on his head, a mysterious and old-fashioned pilot's helmet. All in gold. He was crossing slowly but proudly, using a gold cane (of course). I was one big smile when the cab driver said, 'What a mental case! Look at him!'

And as we drove past him, I exploded, 'What if that is what makes him happy? Why would he not wear that? I wish more people dared to wear what they wanted to wear!' and as we passed a group of young children all wearing school uniforms, something snapped in my head and I pointed at them and said, 'See! This is why you feel this way! Because it is indoctrinated into our brains that we are all meant to look the same and dress the same, thus killing all originality, creativity and personality!'*

The cab driver did not speak again.

If any great leaders before me have already said this, feel free to use their quotes instead, but if not, allow me to introduce this inspirational quote into your life: Get the fuck out of people's wardrobes.

And if you are a socks-and-sandals wearer, a fatty in a crop top, a woman wearing only orange or a man wearing only gold, you can use this retort that I coined when I was a thirteen-year-old wearing a red T-shirt, red jeans that were too big for me, no bra but definitely already-a-bit-saggy breasts, and clogs – with

---

* Never point at kids as you are shouting inside a cab, it sends a wrong signal. It could look like you are shouting, 'Let me out and let me get those little fuckers!' and no one wants that.

socks in them, and the local bullies shouting at me on my way home from school:

'So what? So fucking what?'*

or on better days, 'Thanks for noticing.'

Ah, summer

Summer can be the best friend of your mental health and the mortal enemy of your fat body.

I love the summer – in theory. The winter makes me depressed. It drains me of energy and I hate layers. Taking big woollen coats and scarves on and off continuously from October till March is my idea of hell. My skin feels like it is suffocating, my eyelids feel constantly heavy and I can almost taste the lack of vitamins in my mouth. I trip once a day if there is ice on the roads because my legs are incapable of communicating with the rest of my body, and my lips go so dry that they could be used as a nail file – although I would not recommend it.

Around January, I am desperate for sun. That is when I start to buy extra-bright light bulbs and all the vitamin C, B, D and whatever else I can find. I go to travel websites just to look at planes and hotels in some sunny resort. Then finally, summer arrives. And with summer, a whole other definition of hell.

'Bikini-body ready' is a phrase that can take itself and fuck off. It is nothing but a sassy way of saying, 'Do not dare show your fat body in a bikini, you lard monster,' but you know, with a bright yellow background and a photo of a thin woman in a bikini,

---

* Note to self: Figure out how to patent 'So what?' as an expression.

advocating for some powder drink to replace actual food, some fitness centre or some skin-tightening lotion or whatever the new thing is this year.* Unless you are talking about putting a bikini on your body, then you should never use the term 'bikini body'. And even then, you should only ever use it if that is just how you always speak. If you put on a jacket and exclaim, 'Jacket body!' or if you squeal 'Pyjamas body!' right before you go to bed. And no one does that. If you do, call me, I want to be your friend. But if you are using 'bikini body' to refer to a body you are trying to obtain through weight loss, you need to stop.

The idea that fat people are not allowed to wear bikinis or that they should not do so means that beaches and poolsides particularly become places that feel unsafe. The outside world can already feel like a challenge most days. A world full of potential verbal and physical attacks, both direct and subtle. It can take a lot of courage to acknowledge that a big part of the world would

---

* Remember when it was the bleaching of assholes? People would bleach. their. assholes. so. that. they. were. pink. instead. of. brown. BLEACH. THEIR. ASSHOLES. This might even still be a thing. I just did a quick google and it turns out the official word for it is 'anal bleaching' and I stumbled upon an article called 'How to Bleach Your Anus' and also an article called 'What You Need to Know Before You Whiten your Butthole'. When I tried to find out why this is a thing, an article suggested that it is a 'safe and effective way to increase your confidence', which is bullshit shat from a bleached asshole. Another article suggested that this started happening because people started bleaching their genitals and at this point, I just shut down the entire computer, burned it, burned the world to the ground and now, we are all dead because we do not deserve to live in this world anymore. I mean, you do you, but also, stop bleaching your genitals. If anything, having a white asshole only makes the stains more visible? Same reason I never wear white. Kind regards, Sofie, thirty years old, asshole unbleached.

rather not look at you at all, and then to decide to chuck on a tiny bikini and venture into it. We do not need more bias thrust upon us.

Most of us have body issues, whether or not we are fat – and I understand it is different for men, but not that much. I am basing most of my research on the man who was standing in front of me when I sat by a poolside. He was a muscular man who looked like he spent a lot of time in the gym. He had one of those cheese-grater chests, also called an eight-pack. He had the energy of a Manly Man. The patriarchy really hit this guy hard. He had not smiled once. He went for a swim in the pool and was suddenly faced with a big challenge: sun lotion. He held the bottle in his hand for a bit, just staring it down as if he hoped that it would get scared of his many muscles and just apply itself. The bottle out-alpha'ed him, it seemed, because he poured it into the palm of his hand. He obviously couldn't make himself smear it all over his body, no, that would be too feminine for this guy. His eyes lit up. He figured it out. He started to smack it into his skin. He absolutely beat himself up with the sun lotion. Flat hands just spanking himself all over with the sun lotion splattering all over him. He was punching himself, like only a real masculine manly man would. I conclude that men also have unrealistic standards to live up to. The pain is absolutely real.

But back to us fat people. It makes sense that anything that requires us to undress – like the sun, the beach, the pool – makes us anxious. Showing off a body that many have deemed diseased or unworthy is, at best, challenging. I still remember seeing a meme on the internet – a fat woman in a bikini lying on a beach with a text alluding to her being a stranded whale. No one wants to be that woman. Yet, we do – who would not want to be a woman in a bikini on the beach?

The warm sun on your skin, a light breeze, the smells and sounds of the ocean. In 2016 I went on vacation to a place where I had a private pool – a fact I will never stop sharing because it was the best week of my life – and I swam naked. Yes, of course I now have a lot of diseases inside my vagina* probably, but the sensation was incredible.

When I was eight years old, I took swimming lessons in my local swimming pool in the south of Denmark. I would get special permission to wear shorts and a T-shirt because I would not subject myself to the comments from the other kids if they saw my actual body.

Cut to twenty years later and I am nude and splashing around in a pool. Splashing around because I never actually really learned to swim – the shyness and shame got to me and I quit the lessons. Swimming naked with your gloriously fat body almost felt like the manifestation of an oxymoron. You are taught to cover up and you are taught to never approach a pool or a beach. And here you are – boobs floating to the surface, stomach floating to the surface, you floating to the surface, you are light and you are free.

Because of terms like 'bikini body', because of memes that mock fat people showing skin, and because of the real difficulty of finding bathing suits and bikinis if you are over a size 18, we are given the idea that we are not welcome outside if it is hot.

Sometimes it feels like even our own bodies are against the concept of outside. Chafing is when skin repeatedly rubs against skin and creates a 'friction burn' or – a chub rub. Your skin gets irritated and red. It hurts. I can only speak for my body – and

---

* unbleached.

for me, it is mainly an inner thigh problem. I cannot just have my bare legs out in the open and go for a walk because, within a few minutes, I will feel a burn between my legs and not the good 'Hey, is that Fat Chris Pratt on TV again?' kind. When that happens, all you want to do is ride a horse made of ice till the pain subsides. I bet you that the most searched phrase by fat people during the summer is 'How to prevent chafing' followed by 'Hats for big heads'. I have yet to find an answer to the latter, but the chafing has a few solutions. If you are a big-thighed person, here are some suggestions as to what you can do:

1 Shorts. I know this is barely a solution and more of a 'fuck you', if your intention is to be bare-legged. However, bicycle shorts and short leggings can work wonders under a dress or a skirt and the lower part of your legs will still be out in the open.

2 Antiperspirant deodorant stick. Reapply every two hours. Some people say it works – it has not worked for me, but it might work for you.

3 Talcum powder. If you know a baby, that baby might have some talcum powder. And I hear that those little fuckers are easy to steal from. Then whack it on your inner thighs and you should be good to go.

4 Bandelettes. They look like the top of a sexy stocking but without the stocking part. They are a bit weird and supposedly feel weird but they also supposedly work.

5 Various anti-chafing lotions. There are loads and it might be worth checking out your local pharmacy or preferred online shop.

The only product that has helped me has been shorts. As sad and disheartening as that sounds, it is true. However – we all have different bodies, different skin and different sized thighs. Find your own way. Just never let society's conventions keep your fat, beautiful legs from feeling the warmth of the sun.

Summer can be exhausting if you are in the stage of your fat life where you hate your body – or even just certain areas of your body. For many, the upper arms are an absolutely no-go zone.

Till I was twenty-five years old, I wore T-shirts or long sleeves, regardless of the weather. Yet, the shame I felt about my arms was nothing compared to the shame I felt about my stomach. The very idea of wearing something tight – like a bathing suit – or of not wearing anything at all to cover it up, made me want to be sick. It would not matter how hot it was, I would prioritise covering up my body over being comfortable in the heat. Of course, then there was the shame over the vast amounts of sweat – like my body kept telling on me, revealing to the world that I am fat and overheated; and it felt like betrayal. When it came down to it, it would often just be safer to stay at home.

I have glimpses of memories of pool parties and beach-barbecue parties and me being the only fully clothed teenager amongst a large group of bikini-clad classmates. My heart was constantly in my throat because I knew that inevitably someone would ask, 'Why are you not getting in the water?' and I had to come up with some excuse. Very rarely, as a teenager, do you have the courage and insight to say, 'I am not taking off my clothes because I am fat and I am the only fat person here because the other fat person from our school had the intelligence to stay away from this nightmare of a scenario,' because you would ruin the atmosphere immediately and you would no longer be invited to the barbecue.

So I want to talk about staying inside. There is an odd morality surrounding 'going outside'. Since we were children, we were either encouraged or directly forced to go outside during playtime or break-time. I am not sure if I hated being forced to do something more than I hated going outside, but nevertheless I spent many break-times sitting in the principal's office because I had done something bad purely so I could stay inside. At one point, age nine, I started a small movement in my classroom.

I got three other kids on board, luring them with my logic: that we should not be forced outside. I remember arguing that inside were books and knowledge, outside was just trees and boys who bullied. My three friends and I did a sit-in protest until we were sent to the principal's office – again – and we managed to stay inside yet another day. Even as adults, we are urged to be outside. 'Go for a walk', 'Get some fresh air', or, 'At least open a goddamn window, Sofie.' It is somehow better reading a book in a park than reading a book in bed, even though grass is notoriously never used as a mattress when people wish to lie down comfortably. The beach is supposedly 'fun' even though no one voluntarily shoves gallons of sand into their buttholes* just for fun.†

I do not judge anyone who likes the outside – but I judge people who judge people for staying inside. Sometimes, if you are fat, staying inside is a means of self-care. Keeping yourself from potential abuse shouted at you is self-preservation. You do not have to go to the parties. You do not have to go to the beach. It is not a morally superior act to go outside. Of course there are probably loads of benefits to going outside – you get a bit

---

* unbleached or bleached.

† Maybe some people do this and I am not one to judge. I am very sex-positive. If you get off on shoving gallons of sand into your asshole, then I respect you for it. Godspeed.

of vitamin D* and I am sure nature has a calming effect on a lot of people.

But vitamins come in jars now and lots of people have allergies. Saying that going outside is the 'right thing to do' is only something you can say with accuracy if a building is on fire. Kill that voice in your head that says, 'Why are you sitting inside when it is such good weather outside?' or, 'A good, long walk makes you feel better,' which will almost certainly be the voice of a parent, a teacher or some sort of health guru. Even if they are right, it is not up to them what you do with your body. It might be physically beneficial to be outside, but walking around all fat and wobbly during the summer when everyone is outside could quite potentially lead to someone telling you that you are a fat whale and in that situation, would the psychological damage not negate the potential physical benefits?

Let people decide for themselves what they do with their bodies, and allow yourself to do what feels best on any given day.

This being said – if you want to go outside and flaunt your fatness, I am all on board with that.

Eventually, when I turned twenty-five, I joined a gym close to where I lived, in order to use the pool. I had recently visited my brother in Dubai and on the way there, I promised myself that I would try swimming. Day after day, I went to the pool in his building and just sat there, watching all the thin model-looking people get in the pool. I would go back to my brother's flat and take off my dry bathing suit and exhale. Next day I would get back down.

---

* Hehe. (I have been asked by my editor to clarify why this is funny. It's because 'vitamin D' also means 'dick'. Vitamin Dick. But in this particular instance, I did mean the actual vitamin. But then it reminded me of the dick. Hehe. Dick.)

There was no way I was going to undress and get into a pool in front of those people. *Those people*. The people for whom this pool was made. I felt like I was invading their space. And I have no doubt that some of them felt like I was too.

One evening, I managed to sneak into the pool area after hours. It was late in the evening and no one was around because, well, they were not allowed to be. Shaking, I took off my dress and just stood there in my bathing suit. I lowered myself into the pool. It was the first time I had been surrounded by water in a bathing suit since I was a small child. It was extraordinary. I almost full-on wept in the pool as I splashed around, trying to remember the basic swimming moves. It sounds like a cliché, but I felt alive. Things are clichés for a reason. When I came back to London, I joined a gym.

I stood in the tiny changing booth for a good forty-five minutes before I dared to go out. My heart was racing. As I entered the swimming pool area, I was met by thirty screaming children and I legged it back to the changing booth and stood there for another length of time, till I was certain they had left. Then I went back out.

The walk to the stairs leading into the pool is the worst bit – you are sort of a show pony on display and you expect each person in the pool to suddenly each show you a sign with a number between one and ten, but in the lower end, probably, because this is your nightmare. I held my breath and walked to the steps. I got into the water. I felt a bit safer under the water but there were still people everywhere. Muscly people, thin people, fit people. A swimming pool in a gym, like most places that deal with what society perceives as being 'healthy', attracts people whom society perceives as 'healthy'. It makes sense. Gyms are for thin people, staying home eating chips is for fat people. When I first turned up at the gym, I was sure they were going to greet me with a, 'It's so nice to meet you in person, Before. We've only ever seen photos.'

So I splashed around a bit – not only feeling scared and self-conscious about my body, but now also about my inability to swim properly. I took a deep breath and decided that I would have to do a few lanes before I got back out. I had already impressed myself with coming this far. I tried to ignore the people around me. And how they looked at me.

Then a woman walked into the area – she was also fat. She looked as scared as I had felt. I saw the other people in the pool look at her and then look at me as if they assumed that we must know each other. I wish we had and I felt like we did. I noticed her face change when she spotted me. I imagined how I would have felt if I had seen a fat person when I walked in, and I assumed that that was how she felt. She got in the pool and we swam close to each other for a bit before we both got back up. I never exchanged a word with her but I love her.

5

Love, friendship and fat fucking

I always wear headphones when I leave my house. I like music more than I like people. My anxiety sometimes means that a lot of noises – say from traffic and people and music from shops – stress me out to a certain extent. But more importantly, I get shouted at in the street. It does not happen every day. But it does happen. Enough that I feel safer with my headphones on.

I stay away from nightclubs. Again, I am not a fan of people or loud, fast music. It is not a big sacrifice that I have made, cutting out nightclubs. Even if I were not fat, I probably would have stayed away from them. But I had a period of trying to fit in when I went to them quite a bit. I was of the opinion – or hope – that if only I didn't think about being fat, maybe people could not see that I was. Maybe all those people who said, 'No, you're not fat,' were actually right. Maybe I could trick more people.

Allow me to introduce to you the normalisation of the abuse and violence against fat people in the form of 'fun party games'.

Two examples of these are 'pull a pig' (where a group of guys compete to 'pull the ugliest-looking woman' to win the game) and 'fat girl rodeo' (when a guy pulls a fat girl in a club, whispers this in her ear to let her know, and then holds on to her tight, like a 'rodeo', as she tries to get away). These may sound like urban legends or something I have made up to make my point, but I'm afraid it's very possible to google both of these 'games' and see many examples. And I know plenty of people who have been victims of these 'games'.

When I was twenty years old, I kissed a boy in a nightclub. A few seconds into the kiss, I heard the sound of a group of guys laughing. The guy kissing me started laughing too. I was so embarrassed that I kept kissing him because I thought that it would make it worse if he realised that I knew what was happening.

Only a couple of weeks later, I chatted to a dreadful guy in a bar. I was bored because my friend was dancing and this guy seemed more interesting than staring into a wall. It turned out that the wall would have been a bundle of joy compared to him. I only spoke to him for ten minutes when he suddenly started laughing and said, 'I can't believe you thought I was going to fuck you. Ew, gross,' and then he left. The loud music in the bar made it impossible for him to hear what I shouted at him as he was walking away. I think that might be why people like him enjoy nightclubs. The loud music makes it impossible for them to ever be called 'cunts' to their faces.

I have rejected guys who gasped, 'But you are fat!' as if that was their get-in-for-free card. I have been chatted up at 2 a.m. by men who seemed close to crumbling under the pressure of needing to 'pull', and who had hoped that I would be grateful for their attention.

After a certain point, when men started flirting with me, I stopped trusting them. Even after they eventually wore me down, I would hold my breath and await the inevitable punchline to our night together. There are men I slept with years ago who I still sometimes expect to show up at my door with a sign that says, 'Ha! Joke! You actually think I wanted to fuck you?' and a part of me would be relieved to see them.

I once listened to a podcast in which a comedian joked about fat women in nightclubs. He said, 'Fat women can definitely pull in nightclubs . . . Just after 3 a.m.,' and the rest of the podcast group laughed. Only a year before I heard him say that sentence in my headphones as I was sitting on a bus, he had invited me to his flat at 7 p.m. one night. When he opened the door, he was sober and he had lit candles everywhere. After we had made love, he begged me to spend the night because he wanted to have breakfast with me in the morning.

Shit people say to fat people

A few years ago, a sailor stood in front of me in a comedy club after I had walked off stage. A sailor. In an authentic sailor's outfit. With the hat and everything. I blinked a few times, trying to make sense of the scenario, when my friend, a fellow comedian, swooped in and introduced me to the sailor. It turns out the sailor was an officer in the Royal Navy, who worked in a nuclear submarine. He would be under water, in the nuclear submarine, for three months at a time and then on land for three months till he went back out. And the first thing he would always do, right when they reached land, was to go to this particular comedy club and watch comedy.

Now, I take pride in not finding uniforms sexy, especially when they belong to someone with governmental authority. I absolutely detest war and I think that the fetishisation of the army is disgusting . . . until a sailor in a little hat is standing in front of me with a wink in his eye and a smile on his face. And dimples. I remember dimples. I very well near saluted him. I was not even appalled at how quickly I lost all sense of my principles. I figured that once we were married, we could start working on his values, slowly introduce him to the idea of being anti-military, but you know, we'd keep the uniform.

He asked me my name and said he had enjoyed my set. I immediately interrupted him and said, 'How big is the underwater-boat?' and 'How do you breathe underwater in the big underwater-boat?' and 'Have you ever seen a really big fish?' because I am excellent at flirting.

He tipped his little sailor's hat and said, 'Maybe we should have a drink.'

I snorted loudly, 'MAYBE?' and then, 'I mean, yeah, cool, that'd be . . . cool.'

And he said, 'You know, I heard your jokes about people who like fat people and . . . I just think it's so true. I'm away for three months at a time so my standards are also very low, so sometimes I also just settle for a fat girl.'

It's amazing how quickly you can go from being anti-military to pro-men-in-uniform and all the way back to anti-military again. There was a huge discrepancy between his facial expression and what he had said. He seemed to still be flirting, still be smiling, still be complimenting me. Yet what he had said was fundamentally dehumanising.

'So, what do you want to drink?' he said. There must have

been a long pause, because he seemed confused as to why I was not talking. I figure I must have just been blinking.

'I'm . . . good,' I said and slowly started walking backwards. He looked wounded for a second. Then I couldn't see his face anymore. War sucks.

The big fat friendships

The Big Fat Friend trope is commonly used in modern culture. Like how Fat Monica was Rachel's Big Fat Friend in *Friends*. The woman at the party who is unfuckable, therefore annoying. 'Funny' songs have been written about the Big Fat Friend and performed to sell-out theatres, whole movies have been based on the idea, and it is one of the main 'ways to pick up a woman' in some of the books for potential pick-up artists.* I do not have a count of how many times I have been faced with a completely indifferent man trying to half-heartedly keep me entertained while his friend is chatting up my thin friend. The idea being that I am jealous of the attention that my thin friend is getting and therefore will do anything to ruin her night. So men will have to dismantle me before they can successfully get with the thin friend who is fortunate enough to be worthy of their attention.

---

* What you do is, you just hit on the Big Fat Friend because then the Hot Friend will think you are a great guy who does not care about looks but she will also feel jealousy for the first time in her life and want to convince you to sleep with her instead. If you do not know that a whole world of pick-up artists exist, then I am very sorry to be the one to break this to you.

This is all awfully heteronormative and boring.* However, so is the world we exist in, so I want to address this.

Men's opinions of me are irrelevant. Men's opinions of you are irrelevant too. Yet we are constantly being fed this idea that it matters. Men particularly are told that they should voice their opinions loudly. That we yearn for their approval. And to be fair, a lot of us do – fairly often. Because that is what we have been taught as well. Hello, Patriarchy, my good old friend.

This is how this Big Fat Friend trope can legitimately be harmful. The fact that it is even a thing means that, suddenly, a whole society agrees that you – just by existing in a nightclub or a bar – are annoyingly in the way.

Before continuing with this chapter, I had to ask my friend, 'Do you think everyone gets jealous?' even though I know the answer. She assured me that, Yes, yes everyone has experienced feeling jealous at one point or another. That is also my assumption but jealousy, for me, is such a shameful feeling that I wanted to be sure before I made this next sweeping statement. Because this is something that is so inherently true for me and I wish it wasn't.

Being the Big Fat Friend of your worthy and generally-considered-beautiful friend against your will over and over again is an excellent way of becoming jealous of them. I do not think

---

* You know, how being straight is considered 'the norm'. Straight is the closet we are all born into and, if you are not straight, you have to jump out of it. **Heteronormative** is that idea. That I start talking about dating and, without mentioning it, I refer exclusively to the way straights date. Despite being pansexual I have lived way more and longer as straight, so this is the world I have greater knowledge of. I do not wish to assume how it works outside of this world, although I acknowledge that some of the same issues might be just as relevant.

that this is spoken about much because our thin friends of course do not want us to be the Big Fat Friends. They never asked for us to be put in this situation. Nevertheless, here we are. And you are being forced into a strange competition with your friend where the prize is the worthless attention of a man, a prize which you have been conditioned to believe is not utterly useless.

Friendships between women are empowering. And important. And I treasure every single friend I have. And I appreciate that jealousy is a ridiculously irrational feeling. That being said, let me tell you about my friend Michelle.

Michelle is thin. Michelle lives up to the conventional beauty standards. She is, in fact, quite extraordinarily beautiful. I once put up a photo of her eye (I repeat: of *just* her eye) on Instagram and I got messages from men asking me who my friend was and if she was single. Michelle works out and Michelle eats raw, clean, vegetably food. She is one of *those* people.

Michelle once said to me, 'What do you do when you have *too many* matches on Tinder?'

Michelle has had two – two – men show up outside of her window with guitars trying to woo her. You know, stuff that is only romantic if you are inside of an American teen movie about a guy who is essentially a stalker. One New Year's Eve, she got three phone calls from men declaring their love for her. And we are not talking drunken sloppy phone calls either. These were grown, sober men who had been planning these declarations for weeks. The love for her was overflowing inside of them and they had to, simply had to, tell her now. Only she was busy – just on the phone with that other guy, juggling three pounding hearts and penises in her perfectly small hands.

I had to stop going to my local pizza place after I had gone there with Michelle, because they would not stop asking me about her. Why on earth my friend was single. Where she was. If I could bring her. If I could give her a message? If she wanted free pizza. (That one hurt the most.)

Michelle was at a party once. She realised she had forgotten her lipstick. She hailed a cab. Told the cab to wait for her by her flat. It did. She went up, got her lipstick and got back in the same cab, which then took her back to the party. When she was about to pay, the man behind the wheel said, 'Oh. I'm not a cab,' and she stepped out, without paying and went back to the party. The man drove off, continuing with his life.

Let me rephrase that for you. Michelle stepped onto the pavement and raised her hand and, as if summoned, a man stopped his car – a man, probably on his way somewhere important – a man with shit to do, a life to lead – just to help her out. Drove her all the way home, waited for her in his car – only to drive her back to the party when she returned. She left his car unscathed and with all of her money – and he drove off. I sometimes struggle to get an actual cab.

There came a point where I noticed that whenever I got male attention, I would tell Michelle. I would send her screenshots of flirty messages and talk about it at great length. Regardless of how interested I was in the person I was receiving the texts from. Admitting this makes me feel empty. The way male attention becomes a currency in our friendships. The way I attempted to convince her of my worth, something that she had never questioned.

Michelle and I had to have a talk. We discussed the way we added so much value to whatever men said and did and how it affected our friendship. How interesting and valuable our conversations would be if we actually forgot about men for a second and started talking about work, ideas, art and ourselves. We started sharing dreams and secrets and we embarked on each of our own journeys towards bettering our lives and confidence – both aiming for a life in which our opinions of the men in our lives mattered more than their opinions of us.

It is hard breaking out of this pattern. We are expected to be 'fuckable'. 'Unfuckable' women have no value. 'Unfuckable' doesn't sell cars or gyms. And if you are fat, you are automatically 'unfuckable'.

The unfuckables

There is this notion that fat people are desexual. As I discussed briefly in the previous chapter, fat people are often portrayed as either sexually aggressive or without a sexuality. Fat people rarely get to be sexual or sexy. And so the assumption that we are desperate builds.

Fat people being seen as desexual is more than just a bit offensive. A friend of mine, who is fat, when talking about the time he was raped, is often told that he should just be grateful that someone wanted to fuck him. That sounds desperately similar to a time when I walked home at night and a man spat at me, 'If you weren't so fat, I'd rape you,' which, apart from being awful, is also just not really a way to make me lose weight. Rape is hardly the carrot that's going to make me join the gym.

Fat people are not desexual.* Fat people fuck.

---

* Although, big shout-out to all my asexuals. When discussing sexuality, it's important to just point out that asexual people exist and they are valid. Asexual people are often overlooked, especially when discussing sex. So here's a little footnote to remind you of the existence of asexual people.

I am walking living proof that fat people have sex. I can tell you that it has happened. Quite a few times, even. I can provide you with a list of names and places. Actually, the list of names would probably get me into trouble, but I can get you the list of places:

Various flats in Copenhagen, a hotel in Copenhagen,* a hotel in Leicester, a storage room in a pub in Swansea,† a bush in Copenhagen, another bush in Copenhagen,‡ in a car, two London flats, a flat in Edinburgh, a hotel in Edinburgh, a hotel in Berlin, a hotel in Italy, a hotel in London and an Airbnb in Utrecht. I have had sex with fat guys and thin guys. Guys with rock-hard muscles and tattoos, guys with floppy bellies hanging over their penises, guys in their twenties with impending beer bellies, guys with high standards and high self-esteem and guys with low standards and failing comedy careers. But . . . that's it. I have had sex maybe a hundred times§ since I gracefully lost my virginity in a storage room at the age of sixteen. This is including a three-year-long relationship. But I talk about these hundred times a lot. I am writing this in my book. I speak about my sexuality as openly as I can. And as much as I can. It was not until recently that I realised why.

---

* We couldn't go to my place because I had left an open can of tuna on the radiator. No one believes this and I am okay with that.

† I don't want to talk about it.

‡ Same bush, different guys.

§ When you are reading this, assume the number has at least doubled – after this book comes out, I assume I will be inundated with sexy offers and I'll be knee-deep in lovemaking.

A few years ago, I was at a party. A colleague of mine came over. He was one of those younger white comedians who seem quite nerdy and talk about how they cannot get laid. We talked a bit. He then leaned in (#LeanIn, take notes, ladies) and sighed, 'I just don't know how to talk to women.'

It took me till the next morning before it hit me. But – that was literally what you were doing, white, nerdy comedian-boy. I was there and you were talking.

It was not as much the sentence as much as his voice being unshaken, unbothered by my presence. Because he knew exactly how to talk to women. What he meant was 'women he finds attractive'. Women who are options. Women who are fuckworthy.

As a fat woman, you do not exist.

People will say things like, 'Why is everyone here in a relationship?' and you will want to scream into their face: I am single. I am here. I exist.

But you don't scream. Because they mean well. They never said it to hurt you, they never wanted you to feel bad. They just assumed that you were complicit in the idea that you were not a sexual or romantic option.

They just assumed that you were complicit in the idea that you were not a sexual or romantic option.

I slept with a man in 2010. I slept with the same man again in 2012. Afterwards, as he was getting dressed, he said, 'How many other people have you slept with this week?'

Not in a judgemental way, not in a demeaning way. He was genuinely interested. We were sort-of friends, sort-of colleagues. Both comedians, so there was an implicit acceptance of our brokenness. The question didn't offend me.

'Uhm. I have not had sex with anyone since, well, you. Two years ago.'

He was stunned. His wrinkled forehead and raised eyebrow told me that he did not believe me. 'You don't have to say that, I don't mind.'

It was true. It really was.

It took me a few years to realise that a lot of people in my personal life seemed to think I had a lot of sex, like the vulgar exception to the rule that fat people are not sexual beings. When confronted with this, they barely knew why they assumed so. They put it down to the candid way I talked about sex, my public flirtation with a large number of people and how I often discussed sexual topics on stage.[*]

And one day it all clicked. There is a loudness to my sexuality, because it is so purposefully ignored. If I express it loudly enough, perhaps it will finally be believed to exist. Like everything else about me. My femininity, my emotional complexity, my political viewpoints. It is all loud. In a boring attempt to shout it into existence so it will be heard by the conscience of society. When I look at a person I have had sex with, my eyes

---

[*] And possibly due to the way I refer to myself as the Bang Lord in my book.

are screaming at them, 'You are now evidence that the world is wrong about us.'

We feel, we exist, we fuck.

AN INTERVIEW WITH
Kivan Bay
Southern Oregon, USA

Sofie: Hi Kivan-pronounced-as-Steven. My first question is just to ask you to tell me a bit about yourself.

Kivan: That's a hard first question, describing yourself. I am Kivan Bay. I am, uh, I am a trans guy. I just came out as a trans guy not that long ago, so I guess I'm what they call a 'baby trans guy'. I don't know what I'm doing with my life honestly. (*LAUGHTER*) I am an artist and an activist and a writer and a researcher, a broke academic, trans guy, queer guy, a husband. Cat dad. All that fun stuff. Yeah, that's a good – that's who I am!

Sofie: Congratulations on coming out! Or . . . is that not what you say?

Kivan: I think in my case, congratulations is definitely in order. It is sort of like a birthday for a lot of people – for me, it's just good. I feel less suicidal. I feel less depressed. I am still bipolar as hell but I am doing a lot better emotionally since I came out. Even though I haven't started HRT (Hormone Replacement Treatment) and the hormone therapy yet, I have started binding and doing things like that, so, my dysphoria has been less, people use proper pronouns for me and I feel a lot more . . . grounded in the world. I feel a lot more stable in my identity.

There is a lot to unpack, or well, not unpack but . . . dive into. I want to talk to you about all of that. But first, I just want to ask: when I asked you to describe yourself, you didn't mention fat. How big a part does fatness play in your identity?

Kivan: Oh wow, I did totally forget to mention – I'm fat as hell! I'm 300 pounds! I became what they call 'morbidly obese' in high school on the bullshit BMI scale. I started putting on weight when I was twelve, and I started getting really worried about it and I started dieting very hard. And then, yeah, now I'm at the point where I never forget that I am fat. But I think I often forget to mention because I'm used to being like: Well, look at me, of course I'm fat. Wow, I can't believe I forgot to mention I'm fat. Yeah. I'm totally fat too.

Sofie: Haha, I'm glad we got that settled. Tell me about coming out: how old are you now, how old were you when you came out and did you always know?

Kivan: I always knew that there was something different about me from other girls. I thought I *was* supposed to be a girl. One time I stole my dad's underwear. He got this twelve-pack of underwear and I stole a pair and I wore those every day. I would wash them in secret. One day my mum did my laundry and she found them and I would have been thirteen or fourteen and I had to come up with some kind of bullshit, nonsensical excuse for why I was wearing them, because I didn't actually have any language for what the truth was.

I'm thirty-five, I was born at the very end of 1982. A lot of people knew what trans people were back in the 1980s but *I* didn't know – and that's not really a flaw from my parents, my mum was always involved in theatre, I grew up around a huge queer community, but I did not have the words for it and when I finally did have the words for it, I was frightened. I think it's common for trans men to feel this fear where we are frightened that coming out will be some kind of betrayal of the sisterhood. I didn't want to betray the sisterhood. I didn't want people to think I was just becoming a trans man because I was a failed woman. And that sort of brings us back to fat.

My mum was fat. And she decided that she didn't want to be fat anymore and she's one of the 5 per cent. There is a 95 per cent failure rate for dieting and my mother ran herself ragged and dieted strictly.

So when I couldn't do that, when I was part of the 95 per cent of failed dieters, I figured that made me a failed woman. And when fat activism came along, it really offered me an opportunity to feel like my body wasn't a failure.

And finally when I had grown comfortable with my fat, I had to accept the fact that I still wasn't comfortable with my body. And I still wasn't comfortable with being called a woman and I still wasn't comfortable with *being* a woman. I had to accept that I am a man.

It took a long time. The inkling started probably around the time I went to the Trans Law Center's SPARK Gala and there was this little boy. He was there as a special guest and his dad gave this loving speech about him, saying, 'I am so proud of my son and we were so happy when he came out to us and everyone in his class is so understanding,' and I was just like . . . I literally felt like I was going to die. My heart was racing, my body was shaking, my skin was gooseflesh all over, I thought I was dying. I had never felt pain that intense. It was like I looked down and I was suddenly aware that there was a knife sticking out of me, and I could suddenly feel that knife really, really intensely. Like, it had hurt before but now it was extremely intense.

And I took about three years of thinking and being confused and finally I was like, I'm a trans man. And everything fell into place.

Sofie: Amazing. So how did your relationship with your fatness change after you came out, if it did?

Kivan: Coming out did definitely change my relationship with my fatness. It did make it somewhat contentious and frightening again for a little while, because before I came out, I did this piece called 'The Intersection of Transmisia and Fatmisia'* and it is about how trans people who are fat often get their surgeries or their hormones denied, and this is a global problem.[1] This happens everywhere – I was interviewing people in Africa, Australia, UK, US, Netherlands . . . This is very, very, very common problem for trans people. Their surgeries and hormones are denied because of their weight, and I make the argument that whatever health risks there are because of fatness, they cannot be more of a health risk than the suicide risk that's associated with dysphoric trans people.

---

* Certain disability-justice-activism groups advocate for using '**fat-misia**' (which essentially means fat-hatred) instead of 'fatphobia'. These groups consider the word 'phobia' to be ableist since it is not a mental condition such as agoraphobia (fear of open spaces) or acrophobia (fear of heights). Yet, other groups of disability activists point out that fat-hatred does have basis in fear, essentially.

There's numbers out there that say 40 per cent of trans people attempt suicide.[2]

What it comes down to is that there is a very high suicide rate for trans people, and dysphoria is a trigger for suicidal thoughts. So I feel like denying medical treatment for dysphoria based on weight is more dangerous than the weight could ever possibly be. So I was worried that I was going to get my hormones denied.

But I am fortunate that I have the world's best doctor. He is just great. He is so fat accepting. The office is set up to be super accessible. There are fat people who work there and I just feel very safe in my doctor's office. He totally assured me that things were going to be fine and I felt a lot better.

I'd like to get gender-confirmation surgery. And I'd like to do HRT. I'd like to take testosterone. But I was worried that I wasn't going to be able to do that without first losing weight and I was worried that in order to accomplish that, I was going to have to engage in some disordered eating. And I didn't want to engage in disordered eating. But I also knew that there is a reason that trans people have really high rates of disordered eating according to studies,[3] and it's because we're medically coerced into it in order to receive life-saving care.[4] So that's what I was most scared of.

I mean, we're poor, so we don't often eat as healthy as we should do, but we, you know, we eat pretty healthy. I make us a good chilli. I'm a big boy so I like a big portion. So I was like: I already eat pretty healthy because making lentil stews and chillis and rice and beans is cheaper than other options, so, what am I going to have to do to lose weight? I already watch my sugar intake already because I am pre-diabetic. I am already careful about that. I was worried I was going to have to start monitoring everything I eat and everything about my body and wearing one of those awful FitBits and recording data about my health in order to motivate myself and get into that Foucauldian biopolitics bullshit that makes me so afraid.

Sofie: *I feel like I could talk to you for hours. What I want to know is, is there a difference in how you have been treated as a man and when people thought you were a woman?*

Kivan: I don't get as much yelling out of cars and when men online insult me for being fat now, if they don't realise I am trans, or if they aren't making fun of me for being trans, then they usually call me the f-slur, they call me a faggot, because I'm kind of effeminate for a guy. I like wearing cute striped shirts, cute bowties and cute little-boy outfits, so sometimes people make fun of me for that. I think one of the things that is really interesting is that when people perceive me as woman, my fat is masculinising. When I was in the closet, they would say 'It makes you a man!' or it's ungendering, like, oh your fat makes you not even have a gender. But now that I'm out as a man, I find that people consider my fat incredibly feminising and they consider it a sign of my lack of masculinity. I think that's really weird. When people think I'm a woman, my fat is masculinising, when people think I'm a man, my fat is feminising and makes me a gay boy that they can make fun of. It's something that definitely stands out to me.

Sofie: *Okay, so here is a thought. Do you think that maybe people see fatness as . . . humiliating? Something*

embarrassing? You know, I also get told 'you look like a man' and it doesn't matter if I'm wearing a pink dress or whatever – do you think it is just because fat makes you less of what you are, or what you are supposed to be?

Kivan: I think there is definitely truth there. To be fat is to be 'less', that's very clever wording actually.* Obviously, for women, a certain amount of fat has always been not just acceptable but 'being curvy in the right places' is supposed to be the 'good thing' to be. But too much and you're seen as not exhibiting the kind of control you're supposed to exhibit. People always want other people – but especially women and people they perceive as women – to exhibit this kind of self-discipline that's marked on their bodies, that people can immediately read when they look at them.

I think that, when we see men as failed men, we see them as women. I think that when we see women as failed women, we don't always see them as men. We see them as, 'failed women'. We see them as women who are too masculine but that doesn't make them men, you know what I mean? The failed woman still seems to carry all the other negative traits that people associate with women, all the negative mental and emotional traits that people associate with women; she's still expected to carry those and she's still expected to conform to the thin ideal in ways that, I think, we as fat men don't experience.

Fat men absolutely face that anti-fat bias and it's dangerous and terrible but it would be wrong to say that it's just a simple matter, because, like, fat *is* seen as this *womanly* thing and it's

---

* I could have edited out Kivan saying that my wording was clever, but I didn't. It's in here. You're reading it.

seen as a BAD womanly thing; it's seen as a womanly thing that's *also* bad. So women who exhibit it are failed women who are exhibiting the bad things that women are not supposed to be exhibiting. And men who exhibit it are like women. It becomes another way to hate women.

Sofie: I completely forgot to ask about the queerness aspect – now I believe that when you are fat, you are queer – because you are pushed outside of the norm. But for me, people would still assume that I am straight, my pansexuality is not visible. But you are in a . . . gay relationship. Fuck, listen to me, I sound like a grandmother. YOU ARE IN A GAY RELATIONSHIP. Jesus. But anyways – as you say yourself, in your profile picture on Twitter, you're 'very obviously a gay boy'. So what is the intersection between queerness and fatness? I know that you are a whole person and you can't necessarily separate one thing from the other, but is there anything to say about that?

Kivan: That cracked me up, I was laughing for a good second.*
I identified as bisexual before, but I know what you're talking about.

But I'm suddenly in a same-sex marriage. It was like, more invisible because I was perceived as a woman and I was married to a man and then I came out and suddenly my relationship was much more visibly queer.

---

* If you are reading this sentence, I probably won a discussion with my editor about getting to keep this in. It's my book, I'm keeping the compliments.

There is an experience of 'coming out fat'. I mean, coming out as fat on the internet was a big deal for me, because I'd always presented myself as 'normal', so I had not talked about my body, so people just assumed I was thin because I acted like I was thin. I acted confident. But not confident about being fat.

The history of fat activism has a lot of queerness attached to it. A lot of the members of the Fat Underground were queer women. There's also a gay male community, there's a lot of fat identity at play with Chasers* and Chubs† and the Bear Community.‡ The Girth and Mirth scene.§ All that kind of points to there being a lot of *fat identity* in queerness. But from my personal experience – you don't always feel as visible in queer spaces because queer people will overlook you and you may feel hyper-visible in heterosexual spaces because your fat body is marked as immediately queer.

For a lot of queer women, especially for butch queer women, it can be kind of a bummer to be fat because a lot of straight people will throw around the 'fat butch lesbian' as an insult, and kind of derogate that entire identity, even though fat butch lesbians are *great*. Fat butch lesbians are freaking great! If I was a woman I'd be a fat butch lesbian. But I'm not a woman, so I am not. And then there are gay men, who often fetishise 'bear' – but it's a very specific kind of masculine fatness that is a little

---

* Chubby Chasers: People who are into fat people, in this instance, gay men who are into fat gay men.

† Fat, gay man.

‡ A 'bear' is a hairy, fat, gay man.

§ A subculture based on positive attitudes towards larger bodies and fat fetishism.

bit hard to fit into if you're a short round baby-faced guy without
a beard.

*Sofie: Okay, so. You've previously talked about your life,
which has been all kinds of unfair and horrendous yet . . .
you talk about it with such calm, and with some really
beautiful storytelling. You talk about trauma and make
it sound like poetry. And I hope this is not patronising of
me, but: have you ever had to sit down and, I don't know,
reconcile with your body? Forgive your body? How do
you rebuild the city that is your body after it has been
utterly bombed to pieces by all this shit in your life?*

*(Just to clarify, when I say 'forgive your body', what I
mean is that – at least from my own experience – I know
that we have a tendency to blame ourselves for the things
that happen to us, so I think it would be quite normal for
you to have a difficult relationship with your body. Not
that the blame would be in any way justified.)*

Kivan: I don't want to give the impression that my whole life is
some kind of a terrible tragedy. I have very loving parents, I've
been on some amazing adventures, I've done incredible things,
I have had incredible hardships but I have had really big highs
as well. I don't want to give the impression that my life is just a
horrible terrible malaise of darkness. (*Laughter*)

I don't know if I ever rebuilt my body. And I don't know
if I ever made peace with my body. I think that I am in a
constant state of deconstructing and reconstructing my body
and my identity. And my relationship to my body. Because
I'm learning every day, I'm reading every day, and discovering
new things that teach me new ways of how to . . . like, feel

less like something separate from my body. I feel like a whole and complete unit – not a soul inside a body, but a whole and complete person.

But those moments are fleeting. I also have days where I feel like I'm going to tear my skin off and I have days where I feel like I'm just going to fall over. I have days where the bipolar is really hard. I have days where, just, poverty is hard, or just life.

So I feel like I am in a constant state of not just being shelled but with my own two hands pulling apart and rebuilding myself. And I think that's probably a good state for people to be in, to think of their relationship with their body as a state of permanent revolution. A state of permanent flux and change and challenge and success and failure and all of that, rolled into one, and it's all good and fine to have that because to be static would be more damaging. To be in this sort of constant motion and to have my relationship with my body constantly changing. And usually changing for the positive these days, because I'm feeding myself really positive brain food – like, I am reading a lot of fat studies books, I am enjoying a lot of good food, I am enjoying a lot of good sex with my husband, I am happy. In my body. And I enjoy those moments of happiness. But I also allow myself to believe that it doesn't have to be perfect all the time and it's not going to be perfect all the time, my relationship with my body. There's going to be dysphoric days and I accept that. Not every day is going to be perfect. And not every day of my relationship with my body is going to be perfect and I accept that. That it is kind of a constant work in progress.

Sofie: *Thank you, Kivan.*

6

Why you should chuck your scales in a bin

Oh, how we want to be thin

At age fifteen, I joined a weight-loss group at my local gym. On day one, a nutritionist gave a talk about the basics of 'eating healthy food'. When she mentioned the newest trend, that 'actually, bananas are bad for you', a man in his fifties threw a huge fit and smashed his fist into a wall, screaming at his wife, 'Then why have I eaten only bananas for breakfast for six months, Ellen?'

I think we all have this rightfully furious man in his fifties inside of us. The frustration of doing what you believe to be the right thing, regardless of how dreadful and tasteless it seems in the moment, only to find out that there is now a new trend; a new way in which you are doing it *wrong*, could make anyone want to punch a wall. The frustration of trying to lose weight but nothing happens. The frustration of trying and trying and trying.

I have tried harder to lose weight than I have tried to pass exams, than I have tried to win love from a person I was in love with, than I have tried to patch things up with family members. I have tried so hard to lose weight that I have said no to parties, friends, travelling, concerts, dating – basically, I said no to feeling alive for over a decade of my life, because *nothing* was more important than becoming thin.

So many of us are obsessed with thinness, of reaching that body ideal. We want the flat stomach, visible clavicles, thigh gap, smooth and firm skin everywhere. Absolutely nothing can be floppy, soft, bulging, hanging or bulky, and cellulite is out of the question. It's not just the vision of what's considered beautiful; it is also how happiness looks. It's how love looks, it's how success looks. We are taught to believe that with thinness comes an easy life, a life in which you can pick and choose between lovers, careers and clothes.

My fatness has always been met with either, 'Do you know you are fat?' or, 'What are you doing about it?' as if it is not even an option to just *be fat*. We are desperate to lose weight – and for people around us to lose weight too. It's the reason it's called *diet culture*. It's the all-encompassing obsession with weight loss in an entire society. We live in a culture that praises weight loss and punishes weight gain, regardless of the reasons behind it.

A friend of mine lived with the dangerous eating disorder anorexia for years. When she was at her worst, mentally and physically, she was very thin. Her body was shutting down, due to starvation. She received many compliments about how her body looked amazing and how she looked super healthy – this even came from people who knew the history behind it. When she got better, she started gaining weight again. Her cheeks went from white and almost transparent to rosy red, her hair went from looking dry to looking shiny and strong, and she started smiling again for the first time in years. As soon as people around her noticed the weight gain, they immediately started expressing concern for her weight and her health. They told her, a survivor of anorexia, that she should *watch her weight* because she should *not get fat.* When my friend told me this, she said, 'They'd rather see me dead than fat. It would concern them less.'

She has a point. In an article in the *International Journal of Obesity* in 1991, a study was published. A group of formerly fat people were asked whether they would rather be a 'morbidly obese multi-millionaire' than 'normal weight' and every single person said they would rather be a 'normal weight'. When asked if they would rather be fat again or blind, 89 per cent chose blindness.[1] An overwhelming majority said they would rather be deaf, dyslexic, diabetic, have one leg amputated, heart disease or very painful acne than be fat. In another survey, almost half of those asked indicated that they would happily give up a year of their lives if it meant they were not fat.[2] While we have already established that being fat isn't all super-fun roller-coasters and sunshine,* due to all of the discrimination, I feel like these results are about more than just 'how people will treat you'. They show that fat is *the worst* thing you can be. *The worst.*

So it makes sense, that we are trying to lose weight. Desperately and eagerly.

---

* I mean, even though you're fat, there will still be sunshine, but roller-coasters are out of the picture for many of us.

How we try to lose the weight:
Diets

When I was a young teenager, Sunday evenings were always full of hopeful planning. My mother and I would sit down and embark on a new diet for me. Mostly, we would fantasise about how thin I would be and how much my life would change.

'According to this diet, you are going to lose two pounds a week, so by next summer, you will be thin. Then we can go to the beach and we can get you a new wardrobe.'

We would find a photo of me slightly thinner and tape it to the fridge. We would empty the kitchen – everything that contained sugar, salt, fat or taste would go straight into the bin. This was a fresh beginning. A new start. I was the fattest I would ever be, I was a walking *before* photo. It was thrilling. I can still get excited by the memory. Just the promise of *everything changing* would be so motivating, I could barely sleep. I couldn't wait to wake up and eat a diet yoghurt with apple slices for breakfast. Or wake up and not eat anything till 2 p.m. Or do one hundred push-ups. Or take an ice-cold shower. Or whatever the diet that week suggested.

The first couple of days were exhilarating. The hunger, the intense hunger, the signal that my stomach was empty, was just interpreted as a sign that I was doing something right. The feeling of hunger was the feeling of becoming thin. I would eat carrots, apples, small handfuls of nuts (but not too many) and I would drink ice-cold glasses of water.

I would be invited to dinner parties, restaurants or to have ice cream with friends, and I would be almost furious with them for even asking. Sometimes I would attend and only eat salad;

their pizzas or steaks would look mouth-wateringly delicious to me, and I couldn't possibly imagine a better feeling than eating whatever was on their plates. But they were *thin*, they could eat anything. Mostly I would turn down the invitations and stay home with my carrots and the picture of a thinner me.

Eventually, usually within the week, sometimes within the month, I would crash. I would eat an abundance of food. I would take one bite of a friend's bagel, and it felt as if everything I had been working for was for nothing, everything had been ruined, nothing mattered. I would buy whatever I wanted and stuff my face with it. Pizzas – in plural – coke, sweets, chocolate, crisps, anything that could be classified as a guilty pleasure. Then the wave of guilt overcame me, and the shame often made me crumple into a state of pure depression.

Why am I so weak? I can't do anything. I am so lazy. I will be fat forever. No one will ever love me. Why am I so greedy? I'm unlovable, I'm unworthy, I'm disgusting. I am a pig. Nothing matters, anyway.

The sadness would last a few days as I fell back into my old patterns. I binge-ate what felt like mountains of food. When a Monday was coming up, I couldn't stand making it through yet another week as a fat person, so I would find a new diet. A book at the library, an article in a magazine, a fad, a trend, just anything. Sunday would come and I would sit down with my mother and plan my new life – again.

I began this cycle when I was eight years old and didn't stop till I was in my early twenties. Two things are absolutely certain: I lost *a lot* of weight. I also gained *it all* back, and more.

I read an article in *The New York Times* about the contestants of the American reality TV show *The Biggest Loser* that floored me.

The Biggest Loser, if you do not know it, is a show on NBC where fat contestants have to lose a lot of weight. The one who loses the most becomes 'the biggest loser' and wins the show. They have a nutritionist and a personal trainer on board and the cameras follow them as they suffer through hunger and muscle ache in order to lose weight, for the whole world to see. The winner of season eight, Danny Cahill, had lost 239 pounds – 108 kilos – and stood in a rain of confetti and said, to the world, 'Man, I feel like a million bucks.' Which is fair enough as that is probably close to the amount of money the diet industry made during the season-finale, as hundreds of thousands of fat people watching the show all collectively thought, 'I should probably do something about my weight as well.' Because if Danny Cahill could become thin, we can all become thin.

Well, it turns out, Danny Cahill could not stay thin and neither could the rest of the contestants. Six years after the finale, thirteen out of fourteen of the contestants had gained back the weight – four of them heavier than they started.[3]

What happens when you're on a diet is that your body will fight back hard against weight loss. Danny Cahill's metabolism dropped so much that, even after six years, he had to eat 800 calories a day less than a typical man his size. Anything more turned to fat. The show's doctor, Robert Huizenga, said that he tells contestants that 'they should exercise at least nine hours a week and monitor their diets to keep the weight off'.[4]

Health at Every Size or HAES is a segment of the fat-acceptance movement that argues that traditional interventions focused on weight loss, such as dieting, do not reliably produce positive health outcomes. Linda Bacon, PhD and researcher and the author of the book also called *Health At Every Size*, lists some of the things that dieting will do to you. It:

- **slows the rate at which your body burns calories**
- **increases your body's efficiency at wringing every possible calorie out of the food you do eat, so you digest food faster and get hungrier quicker**
- **causes you to crave high-fat foods**
- **increases your appetite**
- **reduces your energy levels (so even if you could burn more calories through physical activity, you don't want to)**
- **lowers your body temperature so you're using less energy (and are always cold)**
- **reduces your ability to feel 'hungry' and 'full', making it easier to confuse hunger with emotional needs**
- **reduces your total amount of muscle tissue**
- **increases fat-storage enzymes and decreases fat-release enzymes.**

It means that, if you want to keep the weight off, you have to constantly fight your own body's energy-regulation system, and that you will be hungry for the rest of your life. In the 2018 article published on *Huffington Post* by Michael Hobbes[5] called 'Everything You Know About Obesity Is Wrong',* he explains that there

---

* It was quite fantastic seeing this article going viral, seeing as Michael Hobbes is a thin man – quite the opposite of the fat women who made the same points in the 1960s. It seems to take a thin man for anyone to pay attention.

is a 0.8 per cent chance of a woman classified as obese achieving a 'normal' weight,[6] 95–98 per cent of attempts to lose weight fail and two thirds of people gain back more than they lost.

This also means:

Your failed diets were never your fault. It was never going to work. You never failed. You and your body did exactly what you were always destined to do. Lose some weight and gain back even more. Your body and your willpower didn't let you down – the diets don't work. You work just fine.

While this all may seem as if your body hates you, it's actually a really healthy sign. If you are ever on a deserted island and your body senses that you are starving, it will attempt to preserve as much fat as possible, so that you stay alive for longer. Which is great, because then you can listen on a loop to those eight albums that you brought.

It might seem strange that *diet culture* is such a huge thing when it essentially doesn't work.

But the thing is, *it does work* – for the companies selling you these ideals, dreams and weight-loss products. By claiming that *dieting works* and *all you need is willpower*, they automatically put the blame onto you. The cycle of guilt and blame only ends up with you fatter – and poorer – than you were when you started . . . and with an even more urgent need to lose the weight and invest in yet another diet. If you own a company that sells dust- or feet-tasting meal-replacement shakes called things like SuperSlimSuperQuickYumYumTasty, the last thing you want is for your customers to lose weight – permanently. You want them to lose just enough so that, after they crash and gain it all (plus more) back, they will come right back to the thing they *think* worked in the first place.

Weight-loss surgery

I know too many people who have had weight-loss surgery suggested to them by a doctor as casually as a waiter offering you bread in a restaurant. If you have struggled your entire life to lose weight, but the diets just make you fatter, the surgeries sound promising. The idea that you can fall asleep and wake up unable to not lose weight is almost magic. And I want to make it very clear: I have no judgement for the people who decide to get the procedure. It can be a struggle being fat – and we do what we need to do to self-protect. Instead, when I talk about weight-loss surgery, I want it to reflect upon the society that makes fat people feel so hated that this seems like the only way out to a bunch of people. I say this as someone who is terrified of the very concept. Because if I had known that weight-loss surgery was an option when I was a teenager, I would without a doubt have had it. And knowing what we now know about it, I am very glad that I didn't. I have read a few – *a few* – stories of people who have had no complications (yet). I have read hundreds and hundreds of stories of people whose lives have been destroyed. People who go in and out of hospital several times a month, who can't eat, who can't sleep. It's truly haunting.

There are currently three kinds of weight-loss surgery. Gastric bypass, which is making your stomach smaller (by stapling it), so the food will bypass most of your stomach and your bowels, leaving you to absorb fewer calories and be able to eat less food. Sleeve gastrectomy is where they amputate a big part of your stomach, so it becomes tiny and you can eat less. Then there is the gastric balloon, which is just that – a balloon in your stomach that is filled with water or air, giving you less room for food.

One to five per cent of patients die on the operating table during weight-loss surgery. Eighty-four point eight per cent of patients accept 'some risk' of dying to undergo the procedure and then studies suggest that there might be a 20 per cent chance, if you do survive, that you need to go back and have more surgery to get an error fixed.[7]

Now, of course, you would expect some level of risk when someone is about to cut you open. But the difference is that most people don't get surgery unless they *have* to. Normally, you are ill and you get the surgery to get better. In the case of weight-loss surgery, however, you do not actually have to be physically ill to get it. We're not talking about weight-loss surgery that has been recommended by a medical professional because of reasons that are other than cosmetic. We're talking about surgery a healthy fat person can elect to have for the sheer purpose of losing weight. And often, you end up with a lot of uncomfortable – and sometimes lethal – complications down the line.

It is important to stress that we are yet to know the long-term effects of such surgery. They could be much darker than we think. My friend, who is a gynaecologist, told me that if you have any intention of becoming pregnant after you have had the surgery, you are likely to face quite a struggle. Apart from various pains and bowel-movement complications, you might also have difficulties eating the amounts and types of food recommended for a 'healthy pregnancy'.

One complication is simply called 'dumping syndrome', yes, it is exactly what it sounds like. You will be 'rapidly passing food', or, 'you will be shitting yourself to pieces, mate.' And not in a nice 'mm, a lovely healthy poo, I might read a book during this' way. Patients have reported nausea, vomiting, bloating, cramping, dizziness and fatigue in addition to the pooping bit. This is just what is called *early dumping*. *Late dumping* happens one to three hours after a meal, when you will feel low blood sugar, weakness, sweating and dizziness. Like a hangover that you get to have forever and ever.[8]

This happens to about 40 per cent of people who had weight-loss surgery. If you have the shitting-yourself syndrome, you can treat it by avoiding 'forbidden foods', and by cutting food into small pieces, chewing thoroughly, eating slowly and waiting one hour after a meal before drinking beverages.[9] Turns out, you will get to find out if anything tastes as good as skinny feels, because you will be chewing each bite for minutes from now on before you go ahead and shit it all out immediately.

Happy weight loss! That constant toilet underneath you really makes you look thin.

In a study, participants reported a significant increase of substance abuse following weight-loss surgery.[10] Another study showed that self-harm emergencies significantly increased after surgery, leading them to recommend a screening for suicide risk before the surgeries.[11]

I met a woman who had undergone a form of weight-loss surgery, where they had put a sleeve on her stomach, making it smaller. Whenever she ate anything, she would throw up. She said, 'So I lost a lot of weight. Because, you know, I didn't actually eat anything. Right now, I have had them loosen the sleeve, so I can eat. And every time I eat and I don't throw up, I feel guilty. I feel like I am cheating. I can only eat and feel good if I throw up afterwards.'

I am not a doctor and I am definitely not a surgeon. I have very much focused on the negatives in regards to weight-loss surgery because I believe it is being offered too readily, especially when we consider how dangerous it can potentially be. During my research for this bit of the book, I was allowed into a myriad of Facebook groups where people had undergone the surgery, and I listened as members of the group shared the stories of their complications. Again, I understand wanting or needing to be smaller. I understand wanting to risk it, because sometimes the risks of weight-loss surgery may seem smaller than the risk of staying fat. Because I am not a doctor I thought long and hard about whether or not to even keep this section in the book. I came to the conclusion that I wanted you to read the studies I have found about this, so that you *at the very least* know to look into this before you make any decisions.

Diet pills

In 2006, a classmate of mine took me to one side and asked me for a favour. She was larger than me and desperate to shed the weight. She had once given me a 'weight-loss tea' which was pretty much just a shit-yourself-for-two-days tea. Why do they make shit-yourself-for-two-days tea? Who wants that?* My classmate, apparently. She had tried the tea and it did not work. She told me that she had found a diet pill that would help her lose weight. It could only be bought online from somewhere in Europe. She could not have it sent to her house because her mother would be furious with her, so she asked to have it sent to mine. I said no. I think I only said no because I was slightly annoyed with her for a whole other teenage-girl reason, but now, reading this and doing

---

* Sing along, kids: THE DIET INDUSTRY IS WHO.

the maths, the diet pill she had heard about could very well have been Rimonabant.

Rimonabant (also called Zimulti) was an anti-obesity drug that was first approved in 2006 in Europe but was banned worldwide in 2008 due to serious psychiatric side effects. Side effects such as the fact that in clinical tests people were twice as likely to have suicidal thoughts as people who took a placebo, and three patients killed themselves during the clinical trials.[12, 13] A lawsuit was raised against Sanofi-Aventis because they failed to warn against this and instead merely mentioned 'depressed mood disorders, nausea and dizziness'.

Diet pills – as well as weight-loss surgery and most diets – promise the same thing: that thinness will come and it will be quick and easy. The dream of losing weight and finally being thin overrides any carefulness that we might otherwise have when it comes to our bodies. It's like crossing the road without looking because you think that, when you reach the other side, all your problems will be over.

It's really about control

There's an established narrative which says that women have to be thin to be taken seriously, that their worth is based on their fuckability – and so women should be constantly dieting, exercising and chopping up salads *in addition to* putting on make-up, having a straight fringe, wearing painful heels and expensive perfume and focusing real hard on *smiling to everyone* but not too much, not enough to be *asking for it*. They also need to figure out complicated ways of getting home at night in order to not walk through any poorly lit alleyways, and to do reproductive and emotional labour for all the men in their lives. It takes so much hard work, time and effort to be considered an 'acceptable woman' that we hardly have time to just exist. We constantly have to reach an impossible standard in order to just be taken a little bit seriously, and you can't help but wonder if it's all a trick. If we are meant to be too busy applying lipstick to get involved with politics, business decisions and activism. When women are given the impossible task of having to 'get thin and stay thin', and when this is made the very minimum requirement to receive basic respect, we can see that this is less of a focus on beauty and *more* of a way of controlling women.

As Naomi Wolf says in *The Beauty Myth*:

A culture fixated on female thinness is not an obsession about female beauty, but an obsession about female obedience. Dieting is the most potent political sedative in women's history; a quietly mad population is a tractable one.

Mmmmm, control and immortality, yum

Apart from having been brainwashed since birth to believe that thinness is the ultimate ideal, I think we also love the idea that we can control our own mortality. It's astounding how many of the abusive tweets and comments I get on the internet are based on *how I'll die soon*. Almost as if thin people never die. So whilst the obsession with weight loss and dieting stems from a need to *control* women, our personal obsession with it could also be fuelled by our need to just *control something*.

Life is scary when you think of how unpredictable it can be. Fatal diseases and accidents can strike at any time to anyone – or said in another, more upbeat way, *death is coming for us all.* There are people who have eaten kale their entire lives, exercised an hour every day, who have never set foot in a lift but always took the stairs, who turned down all the desserts and who died of cancer at the age of thirty. I know people, like my grandmother, whose diet has consisted of butter and sugar and who was glued to her couch for her entire life, who is turning ninety-five this December. It doesn't make sense, if you are to believe everything you are told about bodies. And I think we all long for things to make *sense*.

I think we all need to hold on to *something*. Something we can believe in, something we can control. Our mortality is the most terrifying thing. Most of us expect and assume that tomorrow will come. We make plans for next autumn. So the idea of being able to prevent your own death is pleasant. The idea that I can eat this carrot and drink this bottle of water and I am adding years to my life – yes, I can understand how that feels good. How it can feel like the one thing you can possibly control in this life. It is definitely true that fat people die at some point. But so do thin people. No one can give you a guarantee.

So maybe what you need to hold on to is *right now*. I know I am being very fridge magnet-y right now, but just like the magnet that says FRIENDS ARE THE FAMILY YOU CHOOSE FOR YOURSELF, it's tacky and nauseating but true. *The present.* You cannot control what happens tomorrow and no amount of yoga or starvation can change that. We need right now to take a deep breath and exist. And do what makes us happy right now. Instead of trying to make things seemingly better for whatever fictional person we imagine we will be in five years, we can focus on who we are now. Even if who you are now is fat, clumsy, lazy, disorganised, always late for appointments, and someone who hasn't visited the gym since you signed up three years ago; even if your hair is greasy because you haven't showered and you haven't seen a banana or even anything in the shape of one for weeks. You could be a hot mess of a person. But you are still utterly deserving of being happy.

And diets never promise that the actual journey towards the weight loss is going to be fun. They promise happiness at the end of it, but we've now established that #dietsdontwork, that *this* happiness doesn't exist. So what you are signing up to, what you are holding on to for hope, is an illusion. So hold on to what you can see and touch and what you know is real – right now. Which is you, your breathing and your fat stomach or thighs.

Food

The body knows what it needs. I propose the idea that we would all have been much better off if we had not all been spoon-fed this idea that there are good foods and bad foods, that we need to look a certain way, and that there is an underlying morality in connection to food.

I also include a lot of general ideas about 'politeness' and 'manners' in this spiel. When we tell children to 'eat up' and 'finish your potatoes so that you'll get an ice cream for dessert' instead of saying, 'What do you feel like eating? Are you full? Are you hungry? What do you like?' we add to the idea that we need to ignore our inner instincts about what we want to eat.

I will be purposely dancing around using the term 'mindful eating' because the term has quickly become associated with another set of rules and morals, impossible to live up to. I read an article in which the list of rules claimed that 'mindful eating' meant that you should *always eat with others at set times each day* – but also that *you should only eat when you are hungry and that you should not be distracted*. I don't know if your family or friend dinners are particularly quiet and serene, but I don't want to have dinners with anyone if I have to focus hard on my burger. A lot of 'mindful eating' articles also tell you to eat nutritional food and to 'consider where food comes from'. So, already, unless you are eating a fair-trade, vegan, organic salad in the midst of five of your quietest friends, you are *doing it wrong*. A 'mindful eating' article said that the practice was both about 'removing all shame and guilt from food' and at the same time 'noticing the effects that food has on your figure'.

(We have to give it to the weight-loss, food and health industries – all the industries behind thick books about How To Do Mindfulness Properly, and TV shows, and articles in women's magazines. It is a matter of pure genius to be able to take a simple concept like 'mindful eating' and make it into yet another thing it is possible for you to be bad at, another thing to spend money aspiring to, another thing to be ashamed of not doing.)*

This is why I don't use the term 'mindful eating'. Instead, I want to call it: *Your Inner Two-Year-Old*. The inherently happy,

---

* It is very similar to what a lot of people are doing with the Scandinavian term 'hygge'. A word that just means 'to chill out'. 'To relax'. 'To hang'. Something that is so fundamentally free. Yet suddenly there are £25 books about 'How to Hygge' and £35 scented candles called 'hygge' and wool 'hygge' blankets for £85. As a Dane, I think this is an outrage. You are already hygging whenever you are just having a nice time. That *is* hygge. Don't give them your money.

clumsy, emotional child that just eats whatever it wants, whenever it wants. It is a matter of being aware of your body. Just being aware.*

Are you hungry? How hungry are you?

What do you feel like eating? The taste, the texture, the smell.

Eat slower, look at the food, taste the food. Feel it fill up your stomach. Bring the focus back to you.

Taste the chocolate, notice when you are full and stop putting food into boxes labelled 'good food' or 'bad food'.

You don't *have to* empty your plate and you don't *have to* just eat the suggested serving.

If you are hungry, eat more.

If you are full, stop eating.

Exercise

If you are physically capable of doing exercise, but you find it psychologically stressful and leading towards damaging thought-

---

* I mean, possibly be more aware than a two-year-old. In that, you should probably stick to eating food instead of rocks you find on the beach. Don't put anything with small parts in your mouth. And don't poo in your mother's mouth, if you can help it.

patterns – but you have a desire to do it, you have to do a full rewiring of your brain.

You have to think of exercise not as something to do with weight loss or morality. But as something completely different. I know people who have got a lot out of running apps that make it sound like you are being chased by zombies.

People walk to work in order *to get to work* – that way the walking seems just purely practical.

Maybe you take up boxing because you want to be able to fight when the revolution comes.

You take up swimming imagining you have been on a sinking ship and you have no other way of surviving than swimming to the nearest piece of land.

You dance just because dancing is fun and the music makes you happy. Or because you are trying to learn a specific dance move, so you can pretend to be in a musical.

There was a flurry of people who suddenly walked to where they were going because of the app *PokemonGo* – where you could catch Pokemons when you physically moved from place to place. It made moving your body fun for people. Instead of a potential chore, something with a dark cloud of shame and guilt hanging over it.

I love moving my body. I love dancing, swimming and I love spinning. But I am weighed down so heavily by everything that exercise has been made out to be. A *health* thing. A *weight-loss* thing. So many times I have planned on exercising in one way or the other but my mind has spiralled and gone straight back into diet-and-lose-weight mode. And this is incredibly unhealthy, in emotional and physical terms. Being a fat person in bad shape who wants to start exercising can be draining. My social anxiety once rose to such a level that I couldn't even imagine being physically active around other people. When I went to buy some exercise equipment online, *all the machines had a weight limit of 110 kilos.*

When you live in a fat body, exercise is always encouraged – in theory. But often the reality is very different when you actually do it. Earlier in this book I mentioned going for a swim and how I had to ignore people staring. In 2017, *Playboy* model Dani Mathers took a selfie in a dressing room at her fitness centre with an elderly, slightly fat woman in the background, showering naked. With the text, *If I can't unsee this, then you can't either.*[14] I remember my initial thought being, 'Oh, I guess I am just never going to the gym again,' because the anxiety of being that woman was too much. We know this thing happens regularly – Dani Mathers just got caught doing it. So, for a fat person, going to a gym, or running in the park, or doing exercise in a place with people, can be anxiety-inducing because you are so on display doing something that is considered uncharacteristic.

So telling fat people to 'just go for a run' is about as helpful as saying 'just eat fewer calories'. What may seem like a 'simple solution' to some people is intensely complicated for others. There are more bridges to cross and not everyone has the ability to get over them.

Imagine if exercise was just something fun to make you feel better, but if you weren't capable of it or if you simply didn't want to do it, that was also just okay. How many negative emotions would we have removed from people's lives?

7

'But what about health?'
But what about you shut up?

One evening I was hanging out with my flatmate in my pyjamas.
I was eating my pasta and doing some work on my laptop while
chatting to him about his latest boyfriend. I was feeling quite
content. Then we got company – my flatmate's friend came over.
I haven't met this guy many times, so we awkwardly said hello to
each other. As he was taking off his coat and scarf, he immediately blurted out, 'So, there is something I've wanted to hear your
opinion on for a while.'

Usually, when presented – by a man – in such a confident and
urgent tone, this only means one thing: *There is something I've
wanted **you** to hear **me** say for a while.*

Then he started talking and didn't stop for half an hour. He
had once been fat and people in his family were still fat, so he
knew *everything* about being fat, he explained. He told me that it
was unhealthy being fat and that, if you are fat, you will die. Soon.
Finally he was quiet, eagerly awaiting my response.

I was still just eating my pasta, living my fat life. I blinked a few times, not quite knowing what to say. It's quite a lot to have thrown at you, on a regular Sunday evening when you're in your pyjamas. That I'm going to die real soon because I'm so fat. I had really been looking forward to this pasta.

He continued, 'So I just think there should be a limit to this *body positivity*.'

Which doesn't sound a lot like a question. It sounds more like a frustration that he had kept inside for a while, that he needed me to agree with. He was eager to make me admit that if we all just love our bodies then everyone will get fat and die. I didn't agree with him, but I wasn't able to tell him that because each time I started a sentence he would interrupt me. I would say, 'Studies show—' and he would shout, 'What studies? I've not read them!' and I would say, 'Well, there is one from 2014—' and he would say, 'I've never heard of these studies!'

This went on for so long that, by the end, I stopped trying to speak at all. I texted a friend under the table to call me and pretend I had to be somewhere, which she did because women are awesome. I excused myself and as I got dressed, he told me that he enjoyed *talking to me* about this and that he couldn't wait to read my book. I'm really glad he said that, because the greatest thing about writing a book is that no one can interrupt you when you are writing it.

✳

There are two types of ways people usually ask me *but what about health?*

The loudest way comes from the trolls on the internet, from the fatphobes, from people like my flatmate's friend who are just looking for an excuse to diminish the idea of fat people gaining liberation. The question *but what about health?* is usually loaded with animosity, and it usually doesn't make much sense within the context of the conversation. A fat activist will ask to be treated with respect and the troll on the internet will say, *but what about health?* as if being unhealthy somehow removes your right to be treated well.

Then there is the quieter type, the type of *but what about health?* that comes from a place of genuine concern, fear and confusion. Often from fat people who have been told that just because they are fat, they are in mortal danger of dying immediately from various diseases, or who have been hit with the less empathetic *but what about health?* whenever they have expressed a desire to feel content in their bodies.

I want to address both and I want to start with the loudest, because it's impossible to not feel affected by their loudness, their anger and their indignation over Fat Liberation and body positivity. So, to the man on my couch, shouting at us all as we are wearing pyjamas and eating pasta, let's just take it one bit at a time.

Q: So, is it unhealthy being fat?
A: Physically? Not necessarily.

The establishment clings to the belief that weight causes disease and death just as people once insisted that the world was flat.[1]

Dr Susan Wooley, Professor Emerita,
University of Cincinnati, 1998

185

In 1993, something very interesting happened. Two scientists called McGinnis and Foege published an article called 'Actual Causes of Death in the United States' that declared 'diet and activity patterns' as one of the main reasons why Americans died, alongside things like firearms, smoking and a lot of other causes.[2] Basically, exercising and eating what is considered a *healthy diet* is healthy. However, their data began to appear in the media and in research articles being attributed not to diet and activity patterns, but to fat. You've seen the headlines before.

THE OBESITY EPIDEMIC

OBESITY KILLS

IF YOU ARE OBESE, YOU WILL ABSOLUTELY DEFINITELY DIE IMMEDIATELY

McGinnis and Foege protested as much as they could. In the *New England Journal of Medicine*, their letter to the editor was published, in which they said:

You and Dr. Angell cited our 1993 paper as claiming 'that every year 300,000 deaths in the United States are caused by obesity'. That is not what we claimed. Instead, the figure you cite applies broadly to the combined effects of various 'dietary factors and activity patterns that are too sedentary', not to the narrower effect of obesity alone. Indeed, given the contribution of multiple diet-related factors to problems such as high blood pressure, heart disease, and cancer, we noted explicitly the difficulty of sorting out the independent contribution of any one factor.

Two things are happening there. McGinnis and Foege are being absolutely badass legends, doing a mic drop in a medical journal. And also, they refer to high blood pressure, heart disease and cancer as *diet-related factors* and not – like most articles do today – *obesity related*. They also point out that it is very difficult to pinpoint just one independent factor.

So, to conclude: scientists did a study about the causes of death and never once mentioned fatness, and suddenly every media outlet blamed fatness anyways. This is one example – albeit a pretty huge one – that shows why we all seem to so stubbornly believe that fatness is the direct cause of all illnesses and death ever. I have seen many instances of this.

Despite *health* being such a super-complex multifaceted concept, covering mental health (which includes anything from stress, depression, anxiety and general feelings of low or high self-worth), metabolic health and lifestyle elements (such as food, alcohol, drugs, tobacco, if you exercise and how, how much you sleep, if you participate in extreme sports, violent sports or if you regularly walk into traffic without looking), it is often assumed that you can tell, just by looking at a person, whether or not they are healthy. *Fat* and *unhealthy* are almost used interchangeably and the connection is very rarely questioned.

Is it unhealthy being fat? is a ridiculously simplistic question, because when is a person ever just one thing? When is health ever just one thing? Which I think is part of the reason why 'fat is unhealthy' is being thrown at people so often: because it *is* simplistic, being fat sounds dangerous, and it takes a lot of explaining to debunk. I tried to get this whole chapter into a tweet but it quite quickly exceeded the 280 character limit.

It's hard to argue against something the whole world seems to think is true. I mean, for example, **let's look at the term**

fat-thin. Remember when that started being a thing? Front covers of magazines warning us: EVEN THOUGH YOU ARE THIN, YOU MIGHT STILL BE FAT!

Fat-thin is actually called 'Metabolically Obese, but Normal Weight' (MONW). It is when thin people are at a higher risk for type 2 diabetes and cardiovascular diseases.[3] Illnesses that we are used to attributing to fat people. There are also fat people who are 'Metabolically Healthy, but Obese' (MHO). Meaning they are fat but otherwise completely healthy. No heart disease, no diabetes, none of that. Actually, some studies show that up to 35 per cent of fat people might actually be metabolically healthy.[4] That's over a third of all fat people.

Metabolically healthy just means no high blood pressure, cholesterol or raised blood sugar. It only covers a small part of health – but it's the one that most people often think about when you discuss fatness and health. High blood pressure, cholesterol or raised blood sugar.

An article written in the *European Journal of Clinical Nutrition* in 2010 by scientists from the Department of Nutrition and Dietetics at the Portuguese Institute of Oncology,* concluded, 'Physical activity increases the likelihood of presenting with MHO, and MHO is associated with a lower prevalence of family history of type 2 diabetes.'[5] Which states that you can be a healthy fat person, if you are physically active. And the article concludes you are more likely to get type 2 diabetes if it runs in your family – not if you are fat.

---

* These long sentences are really good to memorise and then later, you can say them at a party and sound really smart. Please read my next book *How to Sound Like You Went to Cambridge When, Actually, You Dropped Out of Uni Because You Liked Sleeping More than Studying.*

In the research journal *Obesity*, a 2016 paper on a study that looked at data for nearly 20,000 people spanning nineteen years, found that the 'Metabolically Obese, but Normal Weight' were about twice as likely as the 'metabolically healthy fat' to develop diabetes.[6] And in the journal *Progress in Cardiovascular Diseases* in 2014, they stated that fit fat people had the same mortality risk as fit thin people. The authors urged researchers, clinicians and public health officials to 'focus on physical activity and fitness-based interventions rather than weight-loss driven approaches to reduce mortality risk'.[7] And if we turn our heads to the copy of the 2012 January–February edition of *Journal of the American Board of Family Medicine* that we all have on our coffee tables, we can read Matheson, King and Everett's study which shows that healthy lifestyle habits are associated with a significant decrease in mortality (people die less) *regardless* of BMI.[8]

So just to summarise: there are thin people who get type 2 diabetes and cardiovascular disease and there are fat people that don't. Across the board, it looks as if *physical activity* and a *healthy diet* is actually what affects your (metabolic) health. Yet, instead of admitting that it's not *unhealthy just being fat*, but that it's a matter of your lifestyle, we get weird, self-contradictory terms like *fat-thin*. These studies are also referred to as *The Obesity Paradox*.[9] It goes to show just how adamantly we want fatness to be an indicator of ill health. Even in medical science, if someone has a high risk for cardiovascular disease or diabetes, they are sometimes just classified as 'obese', instead of attributing the propensity to the diseases to something other than size. And when an abundance of scientific research shows that, actually, fatness doesn't make you sick, that a bad diet and not moving your body enough can make you sick, then it's a strange *paradox*. Instead of just science. Proving the common discourse wrong.

189

The language around fatness in medical science is a huge part of why we all seem to think that it's just, simply, unhealthy being fat. We have all been spoon-fed this idea since we were born. It makes sense. It scares us. It's scary. It's scary to be told that your body is going to kill you at some point with its fatness. And that fear sends us straight to the gym, straight to Slimming World, straight to our doctors to ask for weight-loss surgery. We're ready to do *anything* to avoid this Death By Fatness, including giving all of our money to corporations. To corporations who happen to sponsor a lot of medical studies.

David Allison and the 400,000 deaths

In 1999, obesity researcher Dr David Allison published a study that claimed that approximately 300,000 people died every year from obesity.[10] In 2004, the *Journal of the American Medical Association*, the same journal that published David Allison, published a new study by the Centers for Disease Control and Prevention which upped that number to 400,000 people. And then it starts to unravel.

In just over a year, Allison's study is picked apart. An American congressman called Henry Waxman requests a Government Accountability Office investigation. The *American Journal of Public Health* and the *Wall Street Journal* criticise the methods used to reach the study's deductions. Researchers Katherine Flegal and David Williamson from the Centers for Disease Control and Prevention start to debunk the study. Finally, in April 2005, alongside researchers from National Institutes of Health, they publish a study in the *Journal of the American Medical Association*, attributing less than 26,000 deaths to 'obesity and [being] overweight'. That's fifteen times lower than the original estimate,[11] and when questioned on it Dr Allison stated, 'These are just back-of-the-envelope, plausible scenarios . . . We never meant for them to be portrayed as precise.'[12]

David Allison has reportedly received funding from basically every big player in the weight-loss industry, including Weight Watchers, SlimFast and a whole lot of diet pill companies. An article in *Scientific American* from 2006 reports that he 'discloses payments from 148 such companies' – all companies that profit from people being terrified of dying from fatness.[13, 14]

It's worth thinking about. That there are people and companies financially benefiting from the idea that there is an 'obesity epidemic' which is going to kill us all.

And that the truth is, actually, it's *not that bad*. The truth is it's not as simple as equating 'fat' with 'unhealthy'. That you can't just look at another human being and determine if they are sick or not.

I am not saying that it is without risk being fat. I am saying that perhaps the risk isn't what we think it is. We are used to believing that fatness is unhealthy because of the actual cells of fat that exist on our body – instead of looking at the effects of the outside world on our bodies.

Q: So, is it unhealthy being fat?
A: Oh, you mean because people treat fat people like shit? Then yes, definitely.

Fat people going to the doctor

I had a bit of a scare recently when I went to the doctor's. I was there to ask for a prescription for a contraceptive pill as I had recently – and quite mistakenly, as it would later turn out – entered into a committed relationship with a sperm-producing man. It was the first time I had seen this particular doctor. Before I even had a chance to tell her why I was there, she asked me my weight, so she could check my BMI.

'BMI? Wasn't that debunked decades ago?'* I asked, more perplexed than upset. She didn't react, she just sighed and awaited my response. The very mention of weight and BMI came as a shock. I had not prepared myself to discuss my fatness.

I said, 'Well. I don't know what I weigh. I have not weighed myself for six years. I have an eating disorder – and it's under control now, but I don't want to trigger it, which talking about weight will do.'

She got up and walked over to the scales. 'You will have to be weighed.'

---

* BMI is the simple calculation of your 'body mass index'. Your BMI is your weight in kilograms divided by your height in metres squared. I am surprised that people still use BMI seeing as it really should not be used in any medical sense. It is a 200-year-old mathematical formula which is ultimately flawed. It was created by a mathematician. And it makes no sense – it does not, at all, touch upon waist size, which has quite a bit to do with your level of fatness. Moreover, it ignores the fact that bone density differs from person to person – and that muscles can add to your weight too. So incredibly fit people and athletes can be classified as 'morbidly obese'.

I said, 'Why? It will without a doubt say that I am "morbidly obese". It won't say I am skinny. We can both see that I am fat.'

She remained silent next to the scales as if she was a parent waiting for her difficult child to stop acting up. I got up and walked over, not quite believing what was happening. I stepped up on the scales and as I was about to ask her to at least not tell me the result, she did. *Oh.* I stepped back down and we walked back to her desk. She typed the numbers into the calculator and said, 'Ah. You are morbidly obese. You'll need to lose weight.'

At this point, I had tears in my eyes. Not because of the wild revelation that I am fat. Nor was it because I believed that I needed to lose weight. I know that if I even begin to consider attempting to lose weight, my mind will spiral within minutes and less than a week will pass before I have two fingers down my throat after having sucked on a frozen grape for an hour. And I know that diets don't work. I had tears in my eyes because I never asked for her opinion about my weight. I did not come to her with any symptoms or illnesses. I was, for the first time in my life, psychologically healthy. I was beginning to see my way out of a stressful life in which I never knew if I could pay my rent or not. I no longer surrounded myself with people who were toxic and who made me feel bad about myself. I slept well each night, I didn't have any obsessive thoughts about food. I had begun to love myself and my body. I had started performing, which filled me with joy. I even moved my body way more than I ever had before – not to lose weight, just because I was busy with life. And now I also had this boyfriend who was kind and respectful. I had finally reached a point in my life where weight didn't hold me back. It didn't make me miserable. I was happy. I *felt* healthy. But now, due to her comments, I was spiralling.

I shouldn't have been surprised that she disregarded my protests. I had read and heard about medical bias – the statistics had been bouncing around my brain for hours before my appointment. In a study from 2012 made by the North American Association for the Study of Obesity, two out of three doctors say overweight patients 'lack self-control', and 39 per cent said obese people are just lazy. Forty-nine per cent of nurses say they're uncomfortable working with fat patients, and 31 per cent of nurses indicated openly that they would rather not have to care for fat patients. Twenty-four per cent of nurses said working with fat patients repulsed them.[15]

There is even the mindblowing survey that had a control group of a couple of hundred people, and was carried out over a time period of fifteen years, which showed that the fatter a patient is, the more likely a surgeon is to leave sponges or even surgical instruments behind, which necessitates further surgery for 69 per cent of such cases.[16]

I had heard all the horror stories about fat people going to the doctor with a broken finger only to be sent home with a Slimming World introduction pamphlet. In online circles, where fat people feel safe amongst fellow fatties, stories like this are being shared all the time.

Not to say that medical professionals are necessarily more biased or fat-hating than other professions – although it would make sense as a lot of science regarding fatness is inherently fat-phobic, since there is a lot of money for research if you are intent on proving that fat is dangerous, all sponsored by, guess what, the weight-loss industry. So if you are a doctor, you are pretty much surrounded by studies that say that if thin people have diabetes, it's because they're *actually fat*. But also, fat bias is inherent in all cultures, so it affects everyone. I am sure that the same numbers go for bus drivers, waiters, teachers and lawyers. Of course doctors will be biased towards fat people – a bitter assumption to make, but there is no reason why our cultural bias would have passed doctors by. I am not saying that all medical professionals are evil or out to kill all fat people. In fact, I have had two very positive experiences with doctors – where my weight was rightly never brought up because it was not relevant to the reasons I was there. But I still arrived anxious – because it is part of being a fat person in a doctor's office. *Oh no. What are they going to say now?*

It's one thing hearing about the statistics and the stories, but it's another thing altogether having them happen to you.

'I can't attempt to lose weight,' I just stuttered through the tears. She immediately started talking – turns out, all I needed to do was exercise a bit and then eat fewer calories than I burn. I wanted to start explaining to her that all she had to do to be a doctor was to wear a white gown and say *scalpel* a few times, in the hope that she would see how surreal it was for her to tell me – a fat person – about losing weight, as if that option had never occurred to me before. As if I am not very much the number one expert in the field of My Own Attempted Weight Loss.

'No, I can't – if I start counting calories or exercising to lose weight, my, uh, eating disorder will come back and . . . I will be very sick,' I mumbled.

She then suggested that I could just wake up thirty minutes earlier than usual and go for a walk. I whispered the words 'eating disorder' again but she didn't react.

She brought out the blood-pressure machine. She wrapped the bond around my arm and tightened it. As the monitor started working, she looked concerned, like the scrunchie in her hair was too tight. She released the band and wrapped it around my arm again. Then looked at the monitor again. She left the room for a decent amount of time. Then returned. As usual, when a doctor looks scared, I start to accept death. *Oh, I have cholera. It's definitely cholera. Or rabies. Or I have no blood. I have been drained of blood. I want white roses at my funeral.*

The doctor came back, sighed and sat down.

'Your blood pressure is—' she began and I finished her sentence in my mind. *Non-existent because there is no more blood.*

'Normal.'

Once you get a diagnosis, your world stops for a second before you realise you now have to live the rest of your life in a different way. When I was diagnosed with 'normal blood pressure', I knew that, from then on, I would have to start taking precautions, such as, for example, keep doing whatever I was doing, because apparently, it had all been fine.

My doctor put away the monitor, which she had thought was broken. She then refused to give me the contraceptive pill.

'It is dangerous, if you have high blood pressure.'

'But. You just said I had normal blood pressure.'

'Still.'

I left without my prescription.

On my way home, I bought a bag of apples. I don't particularly like the taste of apples; they are too sour, too hard to bite into; nothing about them is appealing to me. Apples are what I buy when I am headed face first into disordered eating patterns. I turn to food I dislike, because food immediately becomes about punishment – instead of about joy and nutrition. I sat at home, staring at the apples, feeling like running. Running so fast and so far that every muscle in my body felt like it was on fire, till I couldn't breathe and till I would collapse. Because movement no longer felt playful, it was a necessity to *get thin. Get thin quick.*

My relapse lasted a few days, when I finally managed to work through it in therapy. Ironically, I decided that to look after my mental health I might need to stay away from my doctor, because she seemed to make it all a lot worse. Finding a new doctor seemed like a big task. It was hard to imagine that the next one would be more understanding or less fatphobic.

In 2015, sixty-year-old Kevin Daly from Hoboken, New Jersey went to the doctor, complaining that his stomach felt too big. The doctor told him to lose weight. After having lost 35lb, Kevin Daly's stomach still had not shrunk one bit. After he had demanded a scan, it came to everyone's attention that he had a 30lb tumour in his stomach. That is, in medical terms, a fucking huge tumour.[17] In 2017, 57-year-old Roger Logan had a 130lb tumour removed after having been told by doctors for years that he was 'just' fat and should lose some weight.[18] Trevor Smithson, fifty-three, from Yateley, Hampshire, was told to lose weight by experts at the Royal Berkshire Hospital in Reading and they failed to notice the 55lb tumour in his stomach despite carrying out three operations on him.[19] I have yet to meet a fat person who is surprised by this – and I am yet to meet a fat person who is not afraid of going to the doctor for this same reason. Studies show that fat women are less likely to seek medical help than non-fat women.[20] They are worried that the 'diagnosis' will just be 'fat' and the cure just 'to lose weight', regardless of why you are there.

Ellen Maud Bennett did not know she had a tumour until three days before she died in 2018. Her obituary in the *Victoria Times Colonist* went viral as she had decided to make a very special point:

A final message Ellen wanted to share was about the fat shaming she endured from the medical profession. Over the past few years of feeling unwell she sought out medical intervention and no one offered any support or suggestions beyond weight loss. Ellen's dying wish was that women of size make her death matter by advocating strongly for their health and not accepting that fat is the only relevant health issue.[21]

We want to trust doctors and we want to feel safe in the knowledge that we can always get the medical help we deserve and need. Fortunately, we can discuss our experiences online and, at the very least, get support from our community. Because it's important that we know that we are not alone in being discriminated against in the doctor's office. And that we are not wrong when our gut feeling tells us that *something isn't right*.

Linda, who is behind the blog *Fluffy Kitten Party*, often discusses her experiences as a fat person with an illness. In one post,[22] she describes how she went to the doctor because she kept waking up with really painful acid reflux. When the doctor was to take her blood pressure, he simply refused to touch her. Instead, he put in a number he made up into the system which then ended up informing them that her blood pressure was way too high. She later demanded that someone did take her blood pressure – and when they did, it turned out to be just fine. The medical professional simply did not want to touch her.

A survey in 1998 by researchers Fontaine, Faith, Allison and Cheskin at Johns Hopkins University School of Medicine looked at 6,000 women, and when age, race, income, education, smoking and health insurance status were adjusted for, it showed that fat women (defined by having a BMI over 35) were more likely than non-fat women (defined as having a BMI of 25) to delay clinical breast exams, gynaecological exams, and pap smears, which the researchers said could exacerbate or even account for some of the health risks associated with fatness. In the foreword of *The Fat Studies Reader* (which is amazing and absolutely necessary if you want to get into fat activism) written by Marilyn Wann (who is amazing), she notes that mammograms, which do not require physician/patient contact, were unaffected by BMI. She writes this 'may indicate obstetric/gynaecology physicians' hesitation to touch fat patients'.

✳

The Fat Liberation Movement isn't centred around health at all. It's all about ending discrimination and achieving equal rights. I know many fat activists, such as the fatlicious Cat Pausé, who have simply started to refuse to answer questions about health. Because it's *not the point* of the movement. It derails from the *actual* and *urgent* need for equal rights. We should not have to be deemed 'healthy' to be treated with respect.

It's overwhelmingly dangerous for your mental health to be reduced to your weight, which is subsequently treated like an illness that needs to be cured, when whatever you actually went to the doctor's to address has been overlooked.

Fat people are discriminated against in pretty much every thinkable situation. All public spaces are potential threats, all popular culture either confirms our worst thoughts about ourselves or erases us completely. Other people will most likely either hate us or ignore us, doctors will refuse to look past our stomachs in order to cure us, dating is a whirlpool of rejections and humiliation and we will get paid less,[23] hired less[24] and can be legally fired for being fat.[25] There just does not seem to be room or want for us in the world.

To say that being fat is stressful is an understatement. In 2010, Professor Michael Inzlicht from University of Toronto wanted to find out the long-lasting effects of having experienced prejudice. Inzlicht and his team found out that even in the time after having been stereotyped, people were less able to control their aggression, or make rational decisions, and they would overeat.[26]

In writing this book, whenever I have described a fatphobic incident, I have physically felt the effects in my body. I have had to take a step back, consult with my therapist and work through the frustration, the sadness and the, in lack of a less overused word, trauma. I could feel it, in my stomach. Even remembering some of these events made my heart beat faster and made me want to go back to bed.

In a study published in the *American Journal of Public Health*, they asked Latin Americans to deliver a speech to a racist person. The people's reactions were tested before and after and there was overwhelming evidence that even just the anticipation of prejudice leads to both psychological and cardiovascular stress responses.[27] Other studies have shown that discrimination can lead to depression,[28, 29] common colds,[30] hypertension,[31] coronary artery calcification,[32] breast cancer[33] and death.[34]

These all sound painfully similar to the diseases usually attributed to fatness. We need to consider if the supposed correlation between fatness and cardiovascular diseases, diabetes, cancer and death is actually to do with the cells of fat (for which there is not a lot of direct science) or could just as well be due to lack of access to proper health care or the discrimination fat people face on a daily basis.

Does it work to make people feel ashamed of their weight? Does that make them actually lose weight?

Peter Muennig, assistant professor at the Mailman School of Public Health at Columbia, published an article in 2008 in *BioMed Central*, a peer-reviewed portfolio of scientific-research journals. His article contemplated the idea that any correlation between fatness and health might not be to do with weight.

In his conclusion he states, 'Obese persons experience a high degree of stress, and this stress plausibly explains a portion of the BMI-health association. Thus, the obesity epidemic may, in part, be driven by social constructs surrounding body image norms.'

To come to this conclusion, he examined the relationship between what people think about their bodies and their health. Peter Muennig makes it clear in an article, published in the *American Journal of Public Health*,[35] that he has used 2003 Behavioral Risk Factor Surveillance System* data to figure out the impact of the way you see yourself on your general health. This study showed that the more people wished to lose weight, the more unhealthy days they had a month. For example, people who wished to lose 1 per cent (basically, people who don't want to lose any weight) had on average 0.1 physically unhealthy days per month, whereas people who wished to lose half of their body

---

* The Behavioral Risk Factor Surveillance System is a system of health-related telephone surveys that collect state data about US residents regarding their health-related risk behaviours, chronic health conditions, and use of preventive services.

weight suffered approximately six physically unhealthy days per month.[36] Bear in mind that this is all about what they wanted to lose and regardless of *actual* weight.

A clinical study in the *Journal of Obesity*, published in 2013, showed that people who were dissatisfied with their weight had poorer health than their similar weight counterparts. Fifty-five point three per cent of dissatisfied women experienced yo-yo-dieting compared to 25 per cent of satisfied women. Dissatisfied people had the highest rates of hypertension, diabetes, and hypercholesterolemia.[37] And a study published in the *Health Psychology Journal* in 2014 showed that chronic weight dissatisfaction, regardless of BMI, increased the risk for type 2 diabetes.[38]

Basically, the shame (and discrimination) makes us physically and psychologically worse. This isn't hard to imagine. Stress and low self-esteem can make you not want to take care of yourself, because what is even the point? Why get that mole checked out, why drink water, why even try to go out and hang out with friends, when the message you receive on an hourly basis from the whole world is: You shouldn't exist. You have no worth. When your inner voice is just one, long, loud scream, there is no room to feel.

Feel what you really want, feel how you really feel, feel what you really need. The healthiest thing you can do is reach a point where you are happy with your weight and your body. And the healthiest thing we can do to fat people is stop shaming them. Trying to shame people into being healthy is like trying to get someone to smell less of piss by pissing on them.

A study from 2004 about shame[39] found that feelings of 'low social standing' increased people's cortisol levels and their sensations of low self-worth. A 2002 research report funded by the US Government came to the same conclusion.[40] Cortisol is fairly important – it's a stress hormone that manages how you use your fat, it regulates blood pressure, increases blood sugar and controls your sleep cycle. If you have high levels of cortisol, you are stressed. Your body gets the signal that it's in danger. And stress can lead to heart disease, anxiety, depression, diabetes and weight gain.

So to summarise again, just so that we're all on the same page: wanting to lose weight seems to be a higher predictor of ill health than BMI or, just in general, how fat you are. Whereas it is clear that experiencing shame and discrimination can lead to diseases that are usually associated with fatness.

Seeing fatness as a disease to be cured dehumanises the many, many fat people in the world. We become those headless fatties on the news with the word EPIDEMIC underneath. When fatness becomes synonymous with illness, it erases all potential for other dimensions of fatness to thrive.

Simplifying *health* and *fatness* is impossible. Both are complex, ever-changing and multifaceted: they don't exist on their own or outside of an elaborate context. All of this complexity is lost as soon as we accept as a fact that *fat is inherently unhealthy, thin is inherently healthy*. When actually, this couldn't be further from the truth.

What do we really want? Do we actually want for fat people to be *healthy* or do we want them to be ashamed?

✳

Just a reminder to maybe give your stomach a cuddle. We have talked a lot about disease and discrimination. Let's just, for a moment, remind ourselves that we're okay and we will be okay. That our worth is not based on our health.

But is it really about health?

The question 'But what about health?' usually comes with negativity attached. From people who are angry at fat people on the news, from trolls on the internet, from people sitting on my couch. There is rarely much 'caring' in their intention when they ask the question. Usually, when they tell you to lose weight, they just want fatness to disappear. Fatness is scary, wrong, excessive and contagious. 'Lose weight' is presented as a rule, almost desperately, because, if only you were thin, it would be easier to relax around you. When you are told to 'lose weight', it is almost said with a hint of 'how dare you?' How dare you be fat, when we have accepted that it is wrong? How dare you be fat, when I am not allowing myself to be fat? Or, how dare you be fat when I am fat too and I hate it?

The lack of genuine concern here is obvious: people don't interrogate thin people about their health in the same way. People don't ask 'but what about your health?' under the photos of people going bungee jumping. There is not a moral outrage when a thin person posts a photo of them eating a burger or drinking a beer. There is actually a whole trend on YouTube of small, beautiful, cis women eating large amounts of food. It's celebrated. When fat people eat food, it's demonised. 'You shouldn't be eating – think of your health.' These people are not concerned about our wellbeing. They don't want us to be happy. They want us to not exist.

Also, have you seen men's football? It is very entertaining. But it is also a bunch of tall, muscular men running with full speed and throttle into each other, causing other tall, muscly men to roll around on the grass, screaming in pain. We are talking ankles being twisted, shoulders dislocated, teeth being knocked out by an elbow, hamstrings snapping. However, I am yet to see anyone be furious about the health risk that these men put themselves through. I can't wait till a fat footballer arrives, so that a whole lot of people on the internet can tell him to get healthy and lose the weight so he can properly get kicked in the face by another grown man in the name of sports and entertainment.

People who care listen. And if they will only listen, they will understand that shaming and discriminating against fat people is as damaging as they claim being fat is. If people actually listened, they would notice that Fat Liberation is about fat people's right to live without being discriminated against. In the Fat Liberation Manifesto, published in 1973, which I've placed in the back of this book, two of the seven points are: 'WE believe that fat people are fully entitled to human respect and recognition', and 'WE demand equal rights for fat people in all aspects of life . . . We demand equal access to goods and services in the public domain, and an end to discrimination against us in the areas of employment, education, public facilities and health services.' These are our basic rights. Even if we were all unhealthy, that would be beside the point.

(The other way we know that they definitely don't *care* about us is that the first Fat Liberation Movement took place in the 1960s. That's decades ago. I'm not making any new points that other people haven't already made. If these people *truly* cared, they would have separated fatness and health back when the first studies proved them wrong. But it is more lucrative to categorise an entire population group as 'forever and fatally diseased' than it is to dismantle the patriarchal and capitalist system that actually kills them. We call it *concern trolling*. When someone disguises their contempt with the illusion of wanting to help.)

We need to stop glorifying health. It is a privilege to be healthy. Not everyone has the time and the money that it takes to 'get into shape' and 'start eating healthy'. Nor does everyone have a brain that's willing to give them the emotional energy that is required to start cooking your own vegetable-y meals, or to even leave their house. There are people with eating disorders for whom any kind of food restriction can be triggering. And there are enough instances of people taking photos of fat people in gyms in order to mock them online to demonstrate why there are fat people who would never come within an inch of a gym. Not to mention that there are bodies that are just chronically ill. Bodies that are just sick.

When we glorify health, we demonise and marginalise disease and disability. We *cannot* allow for the healthy to be seen as superior to those who are not healthy. We are all worthy of respect, regardless of what we eat or how much we exercise or whether or not we bother to make a smoothie in the morning.

By the way, get the fuck out of my health

Not only is it wildly complicated and individual, but my health is also *no one's business but mine*. Seriously. Chances are that there will be people in your life who have asked you to *take better care of yourself*. And maybe your family members or friends mean well. But no one is entitled to judge you on how you live your life, and no one can tell you what to do. You have full autonomy over your body. **You do not owe it to anyone to be healthy.**

Choosing to eat ice cream over a carrot affects no one but yourself. We are so tempted to apologise for ourselves all the time. I have certainly done so myself, and perhaps I have even done it subconsciously in this book. *I don't exercise because it triggers an unhealthy psychological circle of shame to do with my body, I don't eat well because it triggers my eating disorder, I got fat because I was depressed and a victim of bullying.* And while all of that stems from the truth, **I shouldn't have to make these excuses**. It's no one's business but mine why I eat what I eat or why I don't do the yoga that I don't do. Health is, *first and foremost*, personal. You don't owe it to your partner, your family, your doctor or to strangers to live a healthy life. If you choose to be healthy – and if you have the resources and abilities to do so – that is one hundred per cent your own decision.

So, imagine . . .

Imagine if we weren't shamed into losing weight. Imagine if weight loss was just simply never mentioned. If instead, nutritional and healthy food was made more accessible and affordable.[41] If gyms no longer had fat-shaming messages on the walls and there were no calorie-counters on the machines. If you were encouraged to exercise because moving your body can be fun. Imagine if the messages you got about your body were all positive. If there was no shame attached to fatness. Imagine if there were no discernible economic inequality in the UK[42] and therapy was free and accessible to everyone. Imagine if there were no 'good foods' and 'bad foods'. Imagine if it was illegal to financially benefit from people feeling miserable about themselves. It makes me feel wholesome and happy just imagining this and yet I understand why they hired John Lennon instead of me to write that song.

AN INTERVIEW WITH
Matilda Ibini
London

Sofie: Hello Matilda, thank you so much for wanting to do this. So, would you like to introduce yourself?

Matilda: My name's Matilda Ibini and I am a 27-year-old British-Nigerian playwright and screenwriter from London. I'm disabled and use a wheelchair, and I ascribe to the social model of disability* and I am totally obsessed with Afrofuturism,† so I would definitely consider myself an Afrofuturist. I live with a condition called Limb Girdle Muscular Dystrophy which is a muscle-weakening and -wasting condition.

---

* The **social model of disability** says that disability is caused by the way society is organised, rather than by a person's impairment or difference. It looks at ways of removing barriers that restrict life choices for disabled people.

† I had to look up what Matilda meant by **Afrofuturism** and I found this description by Jamie Broadnax in an article from February 2018 in the *Huffington Post*, 'Afrofuturism is the reimagining of a future filled with arts, science and technology seen through a black lens. [. . .] What makes Afrofuturism significantly different from standard science fiction is that it's steeped in ancient African traditions and black identity. A narrative that simply features a black character in a futuristic world is not enough. To be Afrofuturism, it must be rooted in and unapologetically celebrate the uniqueness and innovation of black culture.'

Sofie: *So how does your day to day look? What are your biggest challenges and how does it hold you back in life in society?*

Matilda: The best advice that I ever got from a doctor was, 'Just live the life you want, and make sure you get the support you need put in place to be able to do so.' What has been really helpful is identifying quite young what I wanted to do with my life: to write, and then pursuing that relentlessly. Which has then meant I'm self-employed and I'm my own boss because, unfortunately, in the capitalist society we are literally judged and valued on our ability to work.

I'm able to set days flexibly around my condition. Working from home means I have most of my amenities and adaptations in my flat: my adapted bathroom, specialist bed, my wheelchair – I have everything I need in my flat to be able to get work done. It is very flexible and that kind of work structure just doesn't exist in the capitalist world. People just don't yet have an understanding of what it means to live with a disability or live with an impairment. So day to day my work involves answering emails, pursuing opportunities, writing funding applications, meeting people or facilitating workshops. I'm only really able to do that with a team of awesome carers. (And I know some people aren't comfortable with the term carers, some people use the term 'personal assistants', some people use the term 'support workers' but I'm used to 'carers'.)

My team of carers carry out all my personal care, which is anything that involves my body physically, for example dressing, showering, brushing my hair, making meals – as well as the upkeep of my flat and making sure I can get from A to B when I'm out working, which as you can imagine in a wheelchair in London is very difficult. Whether it's public transport or people's attitudes or taxis.

I think that the thing that I've learnt most about living with this condition is that *everything* is a fight. There's the fight for the right care package so I can live independently in my flat; the fight to have a social life, and how that is just as important as my work life; the right to work as and when I am able to; the fight to do the things that I want to do in life. Then there's the daily fight just to get on the bus. London buses can only take one wheelchair at a time and if there are two prams in the space, you can't get on. There truly should never be a fight about who has what priority. Buses should be able to take both wheelchairs and prams, like the buses in Barcelona or Brussels, where they have multiple wheelchair and pram spaces.

Sofie: Why do you think this is?

Matilda: I personally think that the government wants to keep division because that's how they control us. If we're divided and too busy hating one another they can pass through any disgusting abhorrent laws that infringe on our rights and we won't have time to look or do anything about it because we are too busy, tired, and fighting one another, and not being paid enough. But that's just, like, my conspiracy theory.

Sofie: Can you comment on the intersection between the things you mentioned – Nigerian, wheelchair user, woman – because there's quite a few intersections of oppression and discrimination happening. How do those things kind of play with each other?

Matilda: Yeah, it is interesting. Unfortunately, that's just
by default of being born in the UK that there are more nondisabled people than there are disabled people. When I
attended writing workshops I was frequently the only black
person or the only Nigerian-British person, and definitely
usually the only wheelchair user in the room.

I used to joke that other wheelchair users weren't allowed to
leave their homes because only one of us was allowed to be out
per night, or that there's only one wheelchair user within every
five-mile radius and our radiuses never intersected. We all buy
into the idea that success looks like a white, heterosexual, cis-
gender, able-bodied man. And if you're not that, you will never
be successful. And we're all sort of indoctrinated into the idea
that beauty is a certain dress size, white, Eurocentric features
and when you are the complete opposite of what the beauty
standards are, you are the opposite of what success looks like.
You're the opposite of who or what fairy tales are written about.
It can warp your view of yourself.

I'm going to get really personal here – for a while I did think
I was like this disgusting unlovable monster, because that is
what society reflected back to me. That most representations
of disabled people I saw were of villains who were bitter
and vengeful that they were disabled, but also angry that
they hated the way that they were made. So of course I was
going to internalise that. I had such low self-esteem and
self-worth because the world reflected back to me that I was
not acceptable. It took a really long time to unlearn that and
actually find beauty within myself, within my skill-set, to
understand that I had value, that I had something to contribute.

It's seven years on from when I first met my counsellor, who was amazing, and I am definitely a different person with more positive views about myself and my circumstances and also the way the world operates. I don't want the next generation of black people or the next generation of disabled people or the next generation of British-Nigerian people or the next generation of women to grow up in a world where they hate themselves simply for existing. So I'd like to think my activism is through my work, and my work is about dismantling those oppressive systems or helping people to understand that being able to identify those oppressive systems is the first step in dismantling them. So yeah, having so many intersections has meant that I've always been an outsider from society. It's very messy. It's very beautiful. I couldn't imagine existing any other way. Though it hasn't been without its challenges.

I've had to find not just my community of artists or collaborators but also just my community of people who I can turn to, these people who know and understand and who have an intersection that chimes with mine, and we can vent and come together and know that we're not alone, and that one day those systems of oppression will be dismantled once and for all. And I'd like to think we've all played some part in dismantling them. That's what's scaring a certain group of people (the elite especially), and it's why they are doubling down. They should be scared. People are becoming more aware of those systems and how they harm so many more people than they benefit. And is that a world you want to live in? So no wonder they're doubling down their efforts to tear the country apart, because those systems are starting to malfunction and people are starting to wake up, as it were. Well, at least that's what I like to think, because I have to have hope.

Sofie: *What has your relationship with your body been like?*

Matilda: Growing up I had incredibly low self-esteem, especially around my body image, because I have two sisters who aren't disabled. And when I was younger I would look at their bodies because I could see that my body didn't look like theirs. And not only does my impairment affect my mobility, but as a consequence it affects the appearance of my body. It was something I had a lot of insecurities and hang-ups about, and it's something I think I'm still coming to terms with. So my relationship with my body wasn't very positive because my deteriorating condition meant my mobility gradually declined to very little mobility. I still have some mobility but that's made my relationship with my body incredibly complicated.

However, what I think I have learnt to understand, was that there is only so much you can do about the body that you're given. The times where I felt incredible about myself is when I had good consistent care, which lifted my mood, which meant I dressed better, I ate better foods and felt better about myself. My mobility was still the same. My condition was still there but I felt better about myself because there were people on hand to support me when I needed support.

When my body image has been at its worst is when there was little to no support. It was when I was struggling and when I was very conscious that people could see that I was struggling. So when I used to walk with a crutch, I would walk very slowly. I was putting on weight because I was moving less and less so my body was changing in terms of size and shape.

But again through ongoing therapy and even sometimes just through chats with friends I've realised that all of our bodies are so different. My sisters' bodies are not the same, so why would my body be the same? But then also I've learned to understand beauty is so subjective and that the people that have set the ideals for beauty have closed themselves off to so many other beautiful things in the world and beautiful shapes and sizes and abilities. And it's not to say I'm at the point where I'm totally 100 per cent fine with my body but I like to think I'm getting closer with each year, that I'm just becoming a little bit more comfortable in just how my body looks and feels.

Actually, one of my counsellors once asked, 'Do you really want to be friends with people who are judging you on your body or how it functions?' I realised those are people I don't want to be associating with or having in my life, like, why would I go out of my way to impress people who are already so shallow? But then also I've learned that it's not always bad that my body can't do a certain thing, and this has forced me to think far more creatively and far more outside of the box to explore what this body is capable of doing. So for example, I've been swimming recently but I don't actually go swimming. Physically, I can't swim, but I do have fun thrashing about in water for an hour each week and that's my way of swimming. So it's sort of like having to learn to love the model that your body comes in and that it won't be like other models that you see.

That didn't happen overnight. That was years. Years and years and years and years. At the beginning hating my body, hating the way it looked and hating its limitations. I think with a disability it can always feel like your condition undermines who you are. Recently, I have felt that my condition elevates who I am. It elevates what my body can do, or at least what people think my body can do. They see the wheelchair and think, 'Oh

she's capable of nothing' but then when people get to know you
and realise actually, 'Oh, wow, you're fun to hang out with,' or,
'You're living your best life,' and that's all I ever want to do is
#livemybestlife. And if that means with carers, then so be it.
And if that means having to force myself to learn to like what
I see in the mirror – because for a long time I couldn't look at
myself in the mirror. I just didn't want to see what was staring
back. But actually what was staring back is a pretty decent
human being, with a killer smile.

Basically, being disabled has added pressure, because your
body won't look like the ideals of what we believe women's
bodies should look like. So first you don't look like what you
think you're meant to look like and then because there is no
representation of you anywhere, and I mean literally anywhere,
the only representation you find of disabled people now is
online, if you find sort of Instagram models, vloggers, etc. So
lots of representation is now online that still hasn't quite yet
transferred to the mainstream.

What I did when I was really really young was just to cover
up – you wear winter coats, and turtlenecks in the summer. I
didn't wear bright colours. I wore black all the time. You just
cover up every aspect of your body because you think, 'I can't
let people see this,' because it's not, you know, 'the norm', and
only slowly have I started wearing colours again and not feeling
afraid or embarrassed by the way that my body looks, and, if you
want to be mates, great, but if you don't, just keep out my way
and keep your comments to yourself.

**Sofie: *In terms of the size of your body, which words do
you prefer to use? And how do you feel about it?***

215

Matilda: I find it quite hard to use those same words that have been weaponised and used negatively towards me. I'm not yet at a stage where I could reclaim them. I think I would describe myself as like basically a black curvaceous woman who is a wheelchair user – because I don't think we get to see wheelchair user and curvaceous used in the same sentence often.

I'm getting more comfortable with my curves and having hips like my mom and having big boobs. It's something I'm learning to embrace. It's all a journey, I'm not even sure there's really an end point. It's kind of weird, the idea that equality for disabled women isn't being leered at or like, 'Oh you can look at . . . ' or deciding whether or not we're fuckable, but to me, it is seeing us as human, as potential partners, as someone you could fall in love with, as someone you can be attracted to.

And, at the minute, representation of disabled women (and disabled people overall) is that we're not interested in sex, we're not interested in relationships, we're incapable of having the emotional maturity or even emotional understanding to be able to be engaged in relationships, which is obviously bullshit.

There are very few occasions where I can tolerate being spoken to like a five-year-old. And there are other days where I will just stare someone down until they get the hint that I don't like how they're addressing me. Like talking to me slowly, talking to me loudly, asking me personal questions that are literally none of their business in a public space.

Society has tried to construct one disabled narrative, for all disabled people. But it's a myth. We constantly run into these awkward, weird situations where nondisabled people are like, 'Hold on, I've been told disabled people are like this, and in fact they're not like this at all: they are intelligent and they can communicate and are aware of situations,' and this chimes

with being black as well. There are so many connotations about
being black in general, in terms of micro-aggressions and anger,
and all these sort of colonial associations and colonial myths
that were created about black people.

People have to do the work and by doing the work that
means not trying to categorise everyone as the same, not treating
disabled people as if we all experience disability in the same
way. It means treating disabled people as individuals. Being
person focused – so speaking to the person directly, talking
to them, not touching their wheelchair or mobility aid. It's so
weird when people do that. Because one hilarious thing about
my wheelchair is that it's electric. So it has automatic brakes
meaning if I'm not moving you cannot push my chair but so
many people have come up behind me even when I've been
out with carers and tried to push the chair, whether it's to help
me get up a ramp, up a kerb or whatever, up into a taxi and it's
like, no, no, don't touch the wheelchair. Treat the wheelchair
like my legs. You don't go around touching people's legs without
their permission so don't touch my wheelchair without my
permission. Don't assume because I can't walk that therefore
my brain doesn't work, so I'm not a functioning human being.
People make such wide leaps in their brains. Start small, by just
asking the person their name and if they would like your help.

You are not a doctor so you don't need to inquire about my
medical condition and diagnosis, because you have nothing
to offer in that realm as well. I find that quite strange because
I spend a lot of time in the back of taxis (because public
transport in London is so shit for disabled people, and actually
public transport in the UK is so shit). I use taxis so frequently
that taxi drivers on numerous occasions have tried to become
consultants, and are telling me to eat certain foods or try

exercising more or doing this or taking a special vitamin. And it's just like, Oh my god, why do I need to?! Nope, you're not a doctor, so you don't need to know my medical history. It's so weird. I give them false information as in like I won't tell them the name of my condition because it's not necessary.

Sofie: This is all incredible. In terms of unlearning all of this internalised ableism and toxic stuff . . . I know it was a long process – you said seven years – but would you happen to have some advice? Tips?

Matilda: Two thoughts popped into my mind. The first one is to stop comparing yourself. The idea that I could only be happy if I didn't have this impairment. I am not my impairment. I think that's the biggest takeaway. I am not the symptoms of my impairment. I am not weak, I am not degenerative, I'm not a muscle-wasting condition, I'm Matilda who is this very kooky, lovable, patient person, and that has nothing to do with my condition – or rather, yes, I've been influenced by my experiences, but I'm not my condition.

It is a day-by-day process of actively being kinder to myself in a world that reflects such negativity about people like me. There's one exercise, where my therapist is like, 'The things that you say in your head, would you say them to another person that you cared about?' and of course I wouldn't. And then she asked, 'Why do you say them to yourself?' and I was like, 'oh', and that was sort of step one of many, many other steps. Of trying to stop berating myself and beating myself up and holding myself up to these standards that are really not realistic.

Once you interrogate them, once I had the time, space and support to interrogate these thoughts and where they came from, realising how absurd they were, how unrealistic, and how ridiculous. Those thoughts lost their power. If I can adapt parts of my life to be able to accommodate living with this condition I too can adapt parts of my thinking to counteract the negative experiences that come with living with this condition. Realising those negative thoughts and feelings don't necessarily come from me – these are things I learned as a child. Because when you're a kid, all you were doing was trying to reflect your environment. You were trying to fit in. And I think there's an aspect of forgiveness in a way.

As a disabled person, all my life, because of lack of representation, I've had to be able to see myself in so many people's lives and stories where I have nothing in common with them. I've never experienced what they've experienced and yet I've been able to find common ground or a connection. And so when you're out in the world and you see a disabled person, whether or not it's visible (because some people have invisible disabilities), you need to be able to see yourself in them. A whole generation were able to relate to the fictional characters in *Harry Potter* – people were able to see themselves in people and stories far removed from their own realities and existences. So why is it so hard to see another disabled person and think, 'Oh, they are like me,' or, 'I am like them'?

That they too have history, family, friends, relationships, ambitions, dreams, nightmares, flaws, scars, wounds, whatever. Even though you've never had a disability or you may not know anyone with a disability, to be able to find a connection with another person irrespective of their background, irrespective of their aesthetic, is to be able to see the humanity in another human being. With enough varied and authentic representation, you'll be able to see a disabled black woman and think, *she is like me*.

PART TWO

How to lose weight and get thin

Just kidding.

It's about how we fight for fat bodies –

for our own fat bodies

and for other people's fat bodies.

8

How to be a good friend to fat people

When I was seven years old, I was sitting by the side of the road in the tiny village of Søndersø next to my friend. We were both chubby children and it must have already got to us that this was a wrong thing to be. Every day, a fat woman rode her bicycle past us. Every day, we shouted at her. I do not remember what we shouted. I am quite sure it was not a positive 'Nice bike!' or 'Love your hair' because we were children with intense internalised fatphobia, so it was probably something a lot less pleasant. I am as ashamed as I can allow myself to be about this. I was a tiny, self-loathing child lashing out. Hoping to elevate my own self-confidence by tearing down someone else's. It must have seemed to work – because we kept doing it. Until one day. I remember the lady stopping her bicycle and I remember immediately cowering with fear. She stepped off her bike and turned around. She was crying, which hit me in the gut. When you are a child, adults are not allowed to cry. Especially if you were the reason for it.

The woman approached us and calmly asked us to stop. I do not remember her exact words because the whole world froze. But I know we never did it again, and we probably developed quite a healthy dose of empathy by realising that fat people are actual human beings with feelings.

It has taken me many years to learn to be nice to fat people, because all fat people have felt like an extension of myself – and I hated myself. I hated my fat and what it made me: unworthy, unlovable, unattractive. I am oblivious to what came first: my love for fat people or my love for my own fat. Nevertheless, I am here now. In love with my own fat and in love with others' fat. Learning to embrace fatness elevated me as a person, opened my horizons, filled me with compassion and emotional energy. I no longer felt the need to hold on to negativity, which all seemed to link to childhood trauma and deep, internalised shame. I can recommend becoming a friend of fat people.

And if even just a tiny part of you is thinking, 'Well, surely, it should not be hard to be nice to fat people,' strap in, because I have got news for you. Only days after one of my first Facebook statuses about fatness went viral, I went to a party. I felt slightly relieved – I had just started talking about the difficulties of existing in a fat body and I was surprised by how positive most of my friends' reactions were.

So when a colleague of mine came up to me at the party, I was naively expecting nothing but another positive response. He seemed distressed, pearls of sweat bouncing off his forehead. He said, 'Sofie, I just want to thank you so much for your article. It really resonated,' and I smiled because it is still my favourite thing when another fat person tells me that something I have said has been in any way helpful to them. I was happy for him – that he had perhaps started on his own crusade towards self-love and maybe my article had been the first step. He then said, 'Because I know exactly what you are talking about, you know, people hating fat people. Like, I would never fuck a fat woman. Ever. I just . . . could not,' and he made *the face*. The face of someone about to throw up. The sick face. The ew-face. To my face. To my shocked, fat face.

The shock had barely subsided when another colleague of mine waddled up to me. She was the level of drunk where tears came easily to her eyes, and she wanted to share her grievances with anyone who would listen. She came close and I could smell some fierce alcohol on her breath and she said, 'I read your article. It really hit me in the gut. I have been in love with this woman for years – Sofie, she is the one. We get along so well and she is just incredible. But she is fat, so I could just never be seen with her,' and I blinked a couple of times, trying to let it sink in. The odd discrepancy between the seemingly loving tone of voice and her grim and brutal fatphobia towards someone she supposedly loves – and me.

I had to re-read the article I had written several times, dissecting it to find the possible sentences that could be misconstrued to mean that we should feel sorry for people who hate fat people. Of course, if I was to take my own head out of my ass for a bit, I can fully see that there are not many people who are not somehow victims of fatphobia. That, in a way, if you love and are seen publicly with a fat person, you become a target as well. And if not a target yourself, you do suddenly become the witness of seeing someone you love being a target. I get that. I am merely suggesting that you do not flaunt your fat-hating opinions in the face of fat people. Perhaps you can create your own little club where you fat-hate together – maybe you can call it, oh I don't know, Reddit?*

Reaching out to non-fats or smaller-fats,† asking for help and understanding, is not something I am comfortable doing. When the majority of your life consists of you feeling like you are *too much, too big, not welcome and in the way*, the last thing that feels appropriate is asking other people to give up more of their time and space for you.

Asking people to empathise is one thing – I am sure if most people tried to, they can imagine what it must feel like to not be able to fit in a plane seat or find clothes in straight-sized stores. As someone who, at the age of ten, attempted to ride in a little mechanical car meant for toddlers at the local mall,‡ I understand that it does not matter how small you are, the experience of not fitting physically into something is a universal feeling that everyone can relate to. Empathy should not be the hardest thing for people. But identifying which situations call for your empathy is different and a lot harder. On a daily basis, we are reminded of ways in which we could be a better ally to people. Little things we can do to make everything easier for other people. So many

---

* **Reddit** is a forum on the internet. It has some truly hell-holeish subgroups – it is the best place for trolls to blossom and share hateful memes and discuss how to attempt to break down women online. Fun times.

† My new word for 'people who are less fat than me'.

‡ I had one leg all the way in and half an arm and then I got stuck. That is when my mother leaned in and put money in it and the loudest music you have ever heard blasted through the speakers and the whole mall became intensely aware of this fat ten-year-old stuck in a mechanical car for toddlers, being shaken back and forward to the rhythm of a kids' song. Just in case you ever wondered why I became a comedian.

people have different lives to you and why would you not look into that and figure out how you can make everyone feel better?

Which is all very nice, gentle and suggestive. Other people, more angry people, whose editors have not asked them to have a 'nicer and more inclusive tone', might suggest that these are things you fucking should be doing because no one is free until we are all free.

Understand your thin privilege

I know that fatphobia affects everyone. I know we are all made to feel *too big*. Capitalism thrives when we hate ourselves and look to buy whatever we can get to make us feel good again, so of course, it's not just fat people who feel bad about themselves. So it might feel provocative when I say that you have thin privilege if you are not fat. The word 'privilege' always feels icky at first because your initial reaction is always, 'I don't feel particularly privileged!' which makes sense. You don't feel the ways in which you are *not* discriminated against. For example, if you can fit into any seat – be it airplane seats, cafe chairs, cinema seats, the chair at the hairdresser's – and if it's never on your mind if a chair can support you and won't crumble underneath you – then you are a lot more privileged than those for whom it is a massive part of their day-to-day life. If you can buy clothes in any physical clothes store, you're a lot more privileged than those who are bigger than you, who have to either buy clothes online or have it tailored.

The fatter you are, the harder it gets. Your life could still be hard right now, even though you are thin, but all 'thin privilege' means is that it would get a lot harder, if you were fat. Privilege is a fun thing to become aware of – because you will start to realise how much space to take up. You have probably, without realising, talked over a fat person at some point. You have probably made a comment or a decision that negatively affected a fat person because your privilege made you blind to the fat person's reality and how different it was to yours.

If this resonates with you, your instinct might be to message your fat friends (I hope you have fat friends) and apologise to them or ask them questions about their day-to-day life. And while there might be some value to that – maybe your friend is relieved to finally be acknowledged – be aware that you wanting some kind of forgiveness, emotional labour or education from your fat friend is another way of draining their energy.

When I was in the process of understanding my white privilege, I made these mistakes in the most problematic and cringeworthy of ways. I would message my black friends and ask them, 'Is this racist?' and 'Why is this racist?' and 'What can I do to help?', and it took too long for me to realise that it's not the job of the oppressed to explain to the oppressor how to stop oppressing.

There are plenty of resources out there for people to find and read. The questions, 'Is this wrong?' and 'How do I help?' have been answered a million times before and the experiences of marginalised people have been documented just as much.

But the first thing you need to do is acknowledge and understand your privilege. Particularly if you are *a bit fat* – which can be hard to quantify, of course – and you can still fit in a plane seat but you can't buy clothes in any physical shops. You still have more privilege than those who can't do either. I am currently in between *fat* and *super-fat*, and I constantly make sure that I also include people fatter than me in my activism and that I amplify their voices and experiences more than those who are the same size as me or smaller. This is all difficult and it can feel like a lot of work, but to be honest, it's simply the right thing to do.

I listen to the American body-positive podcast *She's All Fat* a lot. In episode two of season three their focus was on people who are super-fat, and they interviewed a woman called Alex, who is super-fat and incredibly articulate and her words really resonated with me. Upon discussing what it's *like* being super-fat, she said,

'It's very challenging, I think, to try and exist in a world that isn't meant to accommodate you ever. You go to a restaurant, sometimes there's a wider chair, if you're a mid-fat, you're comfortable. Sometimes you get lucky and you go to one of those movie theatres that has those reclining armchairs, and they're wide, and they're nice. That experience never happens to me. Nothing is built for me. There is panic every time I go somewhere new. That level of panic is extremely psychologically draining.'

And then, when April and Sophie, the two brilliant hosts, asked Alex about how other people can be a good ally to super-fats, Alex explained perfectly:

'The best gift I think anyone can give if you have a fat friend is just listen to what their needs are, and don't make them feel like a freak for having needs that are different than yours. At the same time I would say, the worst thing? It's really hard listening to people who fit into the normal standard of what it means to be socially acceptable body-wise, it's very challenging to listen to them complain about their bodies. They totally have the right to do it. I know they are hit with as much messaging as I am about why their body is flawed because it has a quarter inch of fat on the back of their arm. You know what I mean? I fully respect their need to talk about that, their need to process that, and their need to be frustrated with that. I am not the person to talk about it with. Because you may think that I have more understanding, or more

compassion, or I get it. *I do get it, and you actually don't get it.*
And that's where I think the disconnect can be really challenging
is that I want you to receive that support, but you're not going to
get it from me because it's too painful. I think people in the fat-
positivity community want to sort of undercut, I think, a lot of the
time how much pain there is, because we're trying to legitimise
ourselves as a movement, right? So you want to be saying all the
time, "Things are great, we're doing great, everything is okay. We
have a right to be here. We're happy the way we are." And we are.
That's not up for debate. But that doesn't mean that there doesn't
exist lingering pain, and resentment, and frustration at a lifetime
of rejection. One doesn't negate the other. You can have both.
Both feelings are allowed to coexist, as my therapist tells me all
the time. So while I care that you've put on fifteen pounds and it's
hard for you, I care, I don't want you to be unhappy, don't talk to
me about it. It's too hard. It's just too hard.'

Understanding

Recently, I was on a plane. I had managed to convince the woman
at the check-in counter to hold a free seat next to me, so I would not
be uncomfortable. I said to her, 'It is not just about my comfort, it
is also because people sitting next to me will be quite annoyed',*
which made her, I swear to God, burst into tears. 'Oh honey,' she
said and blocked the seat next to me. It is difficult to explain the
relief and joy you feel when you have a spare seat — and you do

---

* I am in no way asking for a spare seat next to me for other people's comfort. It's one hundred per cent for my own. It's a sentence I use to create as
much empathy for my situation as possible, so the odds are in my favour.

not have to be in intense physical pain for ten hours. In the row behind me on this particular flight, there was an equally fat man. He was placed in the aisle seat with a much smaller woman sitting by the window. He was making jokes from the second he sat down. 'Let us hope no one claims this seat, because then I have to sit in the middle,' he nervously chuckled. I remembered a line from activist and illustrator Stacy Bias' 'Flying While Fat' guide in which a woman revealed that she always made polite small talk to the people sitting next to her in order to force them to see her as a human being and not a nuisance. It was impossible to know if the man did this for this reason or if it was just an instinct. Again, he repeated, 'I hope no one sits there, because then I'll have to sit next to you and I'm uh, large.'

I felt his pain deeply as I knew the terror and frustration of being in that situation. He was apologising for himself with desperation. But then the woman said, cheerfully, 'That is okay! It will just be like a soft pillow!' and he laughed with such relief. I just took a deep breath on his behalf, very aware of the fact that I was not just listening in on a conversation that had nothing to do with me, but I was also projecting years and years of my own fear and oppression onto this guy with whom I suddenly felt immense kinship. I also felt incredibly grateful for the woman's reaction. She could have sighed, scoffed and rolled her eyes, and that would not have given her more space on the airplane, and it would have made the man feel awful about himself.

Being accommodating towards fat people does not take a lot of extra work. It can be a matter of practicality – checking the restaurant you are about to go to to make sure they have chairs without armrests. It can be making sure that your birthday party is being held in a venue that has a lift, as stairs can be a struggle for some fat people. Even nondisabled fat people do carry a lot of weight, so walking up stairs can be a hard task and it can demand that we take a lot of breaks.*

I recently went to see a comedy show in Melbourne in a venue I had never been to before. I went with two non-fat friends. We were a bit late so the front-of-house manager had to lead us to the room. We went to the back of the enormous building and started going down a flight of stairs. Then another flight of stairs. Then another. Each time we reached a new floor, there was another flight of stairs going down. I had cruel flashbacks to my trip to the catacombs in Paris, and the very narrow, steep and long staircase that nearly killed me. At one point my knees were so acidy from carrying my weight upstairs, they were turning numb and I had to stop. The staircase was so narrow that I was blocking the way for the twenty impatient tourists behind me. The embarrassment of not being able to make the trip up made me force myself through the pain and upwards, upwards, upwards, till I saw the sun. I couldn't walk for a couple of hours.† I saw all of this before my eyes as myself and my two friends descended down into the actual centre of the Earth on a seemingly never-ending flight of stairs. After seven minutes of walking down stairs, we arrived at the show. Throughout the show, I was nervous about the trip up.

---

* #NotAllFatPeople – some fat people are also capable of running up stairs with no issues whatsoever. I am #NotOneOfThoseFatPeople.

† I am primarily unable to walk up loads of stairs because I am in 'bad shape' or whatever you call it when you don't do all the exercise. The fact that I am fat does make this aforementioned exercise a bit harder, as I am carrying more weight, but I don't want you to assume that being fat equals an incapability of walking up stairs. By the way, there is nothing wrong with being unable to walk up stairs. Get your morality out of my stair-climbing, please.

I started coming up with possible reasons for hanging out in the room till everyone had gone, so I could walk up last and not be in the way or be seen struggling by too many people. But I somehow could not find the words to say to my friends. I was too ashamed to say what I wanted to out loud, regardless of how much I knew the shame was unwarranted.

The show ended and I catacombed my way up the stairs. I ended up behind two old people who also had to take their time. I hid behind them for the whole ascent and I was so grateful for them. At the top of the stairs, I became very aware of how good I am at not sounding like I am out of breath – a technique I have developed through many years of trying to hide it, because being out of breath was somehow associated with my fatness in my head.

(It's a strange one – I know loads of thin people who are in as bad a shape as I am. When I hear them try to catch their breath after walking up stairs, I never connect it to body size. I don't think it's shameful at all. But even when I regularly did hard-core cardio and was naturally out of breath after a work-out, I would *still* somehow connect the shame to my body size. As if I would be less out of breath if I was thin. When actually, you can be fit and fat and you can be unfit and thin. As we saw in Chapter 7.)

I once challenged my very thin friend to carry a heavy back-pack on his stomach for a whole day, after he had pointed out that he walked a minimum of 16,000 steps a day. I received a number of voice messages that day in which he was out of breath and considering taking a cab everywhere. And my friend said to me, after she had given birth, that she had never understood why I was not up for 'going for a brisk walk' until she became pregnant. She said, 'Everything is just heavier,' and I nearly cried.

A few years before she said that, I had a one-night stand with a musician.* On the way back to his place, he casually mentioned that he lived on the fourth floor. The anxiety slowly started building within me.

I had been in a similar situation once – ahead of a Sexy Time, I had been texted a man's address. Even though this guy lived on the fifth floor, I was calm – because I was alone, so I could take my time reaching his floor. But when I arrived, he had to let me in through the door phone. So he would know how long it took me. So I leapt up the stairs, ignoring the pain in my knees. When he opened the door, I eagerly said, 'Oh I have to pee so much!' and ran past him and into the bathroom where I took deep breaths until my heart stopped pounding and I wiped the sweat off from everywhere.

With the musician on the fourth floor, I was planning to do the same. Except, I would not need to. Halfway up, he stopped. He took my hand and kissed me for a bit. It struck me. *He knew. He understood.* We stood still for a bit and kept kissing. And then took the remaining length up.

Because, sometimes, what you need is someone to be understanding. If instead of being fat, we were people carrying a big, heavy suitcase, people would kindly ask us if we were okay getting it up the many flights of stairs. People would understand if we stopped halfway up. Our friends would not have any qualms about asking a restaurant if there was a place we could store this luggage while we ate. It would not be a loaded, emotional thing. It would be purely practical.

---

* No, it is not relevant that he is a musician, but why sleep with a musician if you are not going to mention it in your book?

There was no way for my friends to know how to deal with the situation with the venue that existed in the core of planet Earth. I was not even really sure what I wanted them to do. In retrospect, I think that them being understanding would have made it better. Perhaps, as we descended, someone could have asked the venue manager how far down this show was. And then suggested that we did not go – asked me my opinion. I would have demanded that we still saw the show, but I would have felt relieved and not alone with my fat angst. Sometimes it is so simple. Sometimes it is just someone saying 'Oh, that's okay, it is like a soft pillow' or 'Is this situation okay for you?' or 'What do you need?' or 'Hi, I am a bass player in a successful band, would you like to have sex with me?'

'You can just borrow one of my shirts!'

I was sixteen and fat. I was five or six sizes larger than all of my friends. I had ventured outside and agreed to come to a pyjama party at the popular girl's house. In a cruel twist of fate, they decided that the pyjama party would turn into a house party which would then continue to a nightclub. I was there, in my Westlife pyjamas.* All the girls stripped out of their pyjamas and started going through the popular girl's wardrobe. I sat back knowing that there was no way I could fit into any of her clothes. When they saw me sit there, they started suggesting outfits that

---

* 'They SOLD Westlife pyjamas?!' you may think. And no. No, they did not. I had them especially made. Shut up.

I could borrow. Denim shorts that would barely get around my ankles. A top I could use as a small hat. I kept saying 'no' and tried to casually suggest that I could just 'you know, go home or whatever'. But they protested *too hard*. 'Come on, just try it on, you can definitely fit into this – it's really big on me.' Well, guess what, Karen, even if it's humongous on you, it still can barely make it over my face. I would eventually stretch out a T-shirt and feel every stomach roll fight to get out of it till I made up an excuse to go home anyways. I knew they would secretly be relieved. It's tiring having to convince a fat person that they are not fat.

There is a scene in the US version of *The Office* in which a large man has started working at Dunder-Mifflin. The awkward boss Michael wants him to get up on a table and sit on a chair as part of an initiation process. The man gently says no and mumbles that he'd rather not, to which Michael exclaims, 'It's all right, don't be shy,' and he and his assistant (to the regional manager) Dwight try to forcefully push him up on the table. Watching that as a fat person is intensely relatable.

I will sometimes look at a chair and say out loud, 'I don't think that this can support me,' and nine out of ten times, people around me will say, 'Oh, you'll be fine,' and often they will add, 'I can sit on it!' even though they are smaller than half my size. When actually, some of those chairs have not been able to support me. People just desperately wish not to realise that. *You'll be fine* turns into *We'll all be fine. It will all be fine. No one will fall on their face because that would be uncomfortable to watch.*

People refusing to acknowledge your own perception of the world and attempting to force you into spaces you don't want to be in or that you are unable to be in. The man in *The Office* quit his job immediately. The chair broke and I landed on my face. And

I went home from the pyjama party and slept with the perfect man – a cardboard cut-out of Mark from Westlife.

Fat people experience this kind of gaslighting on a daily basis our entire lives.* When you are told, often enough, that your perception of reality is false, you will start to doubt your instincts and to some extent, who you are. If you tell a fat person often enough that they *can* fit into a shirt or a seat or that *that person didn't shout at you* or *look at you with disgust* or that *you're not fat, you're beautiful*, you can end up with a warped sense of self. We are already taught to distance ourselves from our bodies as much as possible, we cannot afford to distance ourselves further from our perception of our lives.

This whole 'Oh you are not fat' is unhelpful and destructive. Erasing someone's experience is not a way of making *us* feel better; it's a way to make *you* feel better. You can tip-toe around fatness all you want, like it's a dirty, smelly poop in the middle of the dance floor that you don't want to pick up. But the fact is, if it hurts so much to talk about and look at, the best thing to do is to try to remove the source. The person at this party pooping on the floor. Or, to narrow down this metaphor, figure out how you can be a better ally and help erase fatphobia *instead of* the fat experience.

---

* **Gaslighting** is when a person questions another person's reality in order to have more power over them. In Patrick Hamilton's 1938 play *Gaslight*, a man is quite obviously cheating on his wife and she knows this, but to get away with it he tries to make her think she is insane. The husband starts to make the gas light dimmer, and his wife points it out, but he pretends that it's not dimming. In relationships, you will often see a woman calmly pointing out that her partner is acting weird (because they *are* acting weird) and he will then raise his voice and call her paranoid and crazy.

Watch your fucking language

It seems as if there are two main ways to interact with fat people. People either acknowledge your fatness negatively – or it doesn't get mentioned at all. You are either unhealthy, unattractive, 'something to be settled for', unintelligent – or your body does not exist.

There is a certain way in which people say, 'You have such a pretty face,' or, 'She has a great personality,' which creates a sphere of 'Do not talk about the body.' Even though everyone knows that 'pretty face' and 'great personality' are probably code for 'fat body'. It is like they are trying to erase the fat body. As if my fatness is a T-Rex that can only sense movement.* As long as we stay quiet and still, it won't attack us with its floppy belly.†

It's the same reason many people use words like 'curvy', 'voluptuous', 'bigger', 'thunder thighs', 'voluminous', 'larger', 'full-figured', 'thick', 'plus-size', 'big-boned', 'chunky' to describe FAT. It's the same reason why there is sometimes a slight hesitation between, 'She's a, uh . . .' and '. . . a big girl'. Because something uncomfortable is about to be said, something we would all rather wasn't true. So we wrap it in cutesy and glamorous words.

When we talk about fat people, we very rarely say the word 'fat'. And when we do, it is loaded with all of the fears and hate.

---

* I know that it has been debunked that the T-Rex could only sense movement, but I am specifically talking about the fictitious *Jurassic Park* T-Rex. Not the weird one that had feathers and was a vegetarian. I'm talking the original OG T-Rex, the Hollywood star.

† Just try and imagine a fat T-Rex. Do it. Imagine it right now. Isn't it cute?

The popular phrase, 'Does my bum look big in this?' which is usually said to a partner by a woman who is trying on an outfit, is a classic example. It is so often used in popular culture as a great set-up to a joke. The obvious answer is 'no'. If you even hesitate before you say no, you might insinuate that yes, she does look fat in it and then all hell breaks loose.

Columbia professor Derald Sue coined the term 'micro-aggression' (originally used to describe the kind of casually racist insults that people of colour have to endure on a daily basis), which covers this sort of interaction quite well. Like saying, 'No, but where are you really from?' to someone after they have explicitly told you the answer. Or, as one of my friends told me she gets all the time, 'You don't act like a black person', which is another way of saying, 'I usually associate black people with something negative, but you are actually quite nice, so you must be more like a white person.' Saying, 'You have such a pretty face,' is often a microaggression if said to a fat person. So is, 'Oh my god, you look amazing, have you lost weight?' and, 'Is *that* your boyfriend? Oh.'

Part of being a better ally is recognising how the stigmatisation of being fat hurts everyone – and that it gets worse, the bigger you are. When you talk about wanting to lose weight next to a person fatter than you, you are, whether or not this is your intention, making a dismissive statement about their body. Understand that your negative feeling towards fatness – your own or others' – has a directly negative effect on people around you. It is worth weighing up your words and maintaining a general awareness of what you say, when you say it, and around whom it is being said.

I have sat next to self-proclaimed allies who suddenly made a fatphobic comment about another person. Now, we can all do that by accident. Fatphobia is horrendously ingrained within us. A very prominent fat activist told me that when her girlfriend recently said that she had gained weight, her instant response was, 'No, you look hot!' and she told me this in a fit of laughter because the irony of her seven-year stint within fat activism combined with those words coming out of her mouth was simply too much. And we have all been there and we will all continue to go there. The reaction, however, is very important. I have sat next to people who made a fatphobic comment and then did nothing. No apology, no 'oops!', no correction. Just gross, unedited, genuine fatphobia that hung in the air and stank.

When you speak about food, remove all the fat-oppressive language and stop mentioning dieting. If you tell me you are on a diet, you are telling me that you are trying to look less like me. Stop it. Try – really try – to eradicate language that has its core in fatphobia. And specifically definitely do not comment on a fat person's body or food intake. No 'Are you going to eat that?' and no advice like, 'If you just cut down on calories and do some exercise . . .'

Get out of people's bodies. Let people live in peace.

Amplify

We have a tendency to mainly post content on our social media that relates to us, personally. You can use your platform to amplify the voices of the oppressed. *Orange Is the New Black* actor Matt McGorry posted a photo on Instagram of him holding the book *Health At Every Size* by Linda Bacon with the caption, 'I wish that all people, and especially health-care providers, fitness industry professionals, and nutritionists would read this book.'

Matt McGorry is not only thin – he is a Hollywood actor with no obvious horse in the race. I can only talk for myself and not on behalf of the entire Fat Liberation Movement, but when a non-fat person shows public support for us, it feels like when someone helps you carry your suitcase up a load of stairs.

Be intersectional

It is truly confusing when people who identify as feminists make derogatory comments about fat people. Say, with former President Trump,* somehow him being fat was the go-to put-down when criticising him. The man is an actual fascist. Yet, his fatness is what makes him evil. Will Donald Trump go to bed crying over the fat-shaming comments? Probably not. The man does not have a soul. But will all of your chubby and fat friends hear you call him fat and then feel bad about their bodies? Damn right they will.

Feminism includes fat people. Feminism includes people of colour, people with disabilities, trans people, queer people, non-heterosexual people, people without beauty privilege and non-binary people. You can't cherry pick which causes you are going to support. I get it. You're doing your very best and then someone calls you out for having used an ableist term. You want to punch a wall and exclaim, 'Oh fuck this, it's too difficult,' but maybe the best way forward is to say, 'You're right, I'll do better,' and just try doing exactly that. Try to do better.

---

* As I am writing this, he is very much still the president, but I am writing this book in the hopes of a better future. Also, my editor wouldn't let me write 'now deceased'.

We have a tendency to always approach the world from our very own and very limited point of view. Being truly intersectional means to constantly take into account the groups of people who are marginalised in different ways to ourselves. And use our privilege to help them.

So when you amplify the voices of fat people, check if you are only retweeting fat white people's voices. Make sure you include everyone, especially people whose voices are particularly silenced.

Speak up

It is hard to call out your friends when they are being problematic. Changing the social structure was never meant to be easy. It is, however, necessary. It is especially important to do so when you are part of the group that is not being oppressed.

So your friend Steve makes a comment at a house party. He shouts, 'I fucked this girl but she was so fat, I couldn't even throw her out of the window the next morning – I tried, though!'* and what do you do?

People are sort of chuckling to themselves. A few people stay quiet because they know it is a bit too far. Some people are laughing hard because there are no fat people present, so it seems to be a victimless crime.

You raise your voice and say, 'I am not okay with that kind of talk. It is toxic and hateful and I am not here for it.'

You can also start a lecture on fatphobia in our modern

---

* An actual thing I heard someone say.

society or bring out the charts proving that capitalism is the one true enemy. Feel free to use the sad statistics from this book.

What you do *not* do is text your fat friend about what the guy just said with a sad emoji afterwards, because we do not need your witness statement, we need you to educate that guy. We know that these things happen, we do not need thin people giving us first-hand accounts of horrible people being horrible. It does not help that there is a middle-man between a hurtful sentence and you. You still hear the hurtful sentence.

Take action

If you really want to make a difference, there are some pretty radical things you can do. You can, for example, boycott places that are not accommodating towards fat people. Venues without wheelchair access or lifts. You can stop buying clothes from shops that do not cater to plus-size people. You can stop going to restaurants which only have chairs with armrests. Stop going to comedy clubs that book comedians who consistently make fatphobic jokes.

Or take it one step further: Call and email the places and ask them to change their ways. Make them aware that they are excluding a group of people and that you will not accept it. Put pressure on them.

I met a colleague a few days after I had been under a massive attack from trolls online. He gave me a big hug and said, 'Just so you know, I spent a whole night reporting the trolls that sent you abuse,' and it was so simple and so nice. He said he simply had to do something. Later that same week, I met a guy who told me to send him all the abusive tweets that Twitter refused to take down, because he would figure out who to speak to at Twitter and make sure they corrected their mistake. I doubt that it ever worked, but the desire to help felt incredible.

Know your place

Acknowledge your thin privilege and understand that you should support fat people but stay in the background. You have no actual place in the Fat Liberation movement; it is not for you. By all means, amplify fat activists' work and donate to the Kickstarter campaigns, but do not start a podcast called 'My Fat Podcast' where you, a non-fat person, talk about fatness. Do not speak over fat people and do not attempt to lead the movement.*

And why should you care about fat people?

It is no secret that it is difficult to be a friend of fat people. You have to make changes in the way you use your language, you have

---

* Listen, I know all of this sounds like I'm being really angry and harsh. And if you are a thin person reading this, you might want to put your hand on my shoulder and say, 'Look, I would *never* do any of these horrible things,' and yes, I know. The anger stems from the fact that so. many. people. do. these. things. I am not talking from the point of view of someone who is scared of this happening, I talk from the point of view of someone who has seen this sort of stuff happen *over and over again*. Also, now your hand is already on my shoulder, would you give me a backrub? I've been dealing with a lot of fatphobes today and could use some relaxing.

to do a little bit of daily research, perhaps you even feel inclined to doing some activism. It would, without a doubt, be easier to just continue living your life, letting fat people fat on their own.

But you are currently living in a world that allows for certain groups of people to be oppressed, bullied and discriminated against. As long as that is a possibility, you are not safe from this. Especially when it comes to fatness, you are possibly just a pregnancy, half a decade or suddenly acquiring a taste for ice cream from becoming fat yourself. The hatred of fat people is not limited to fat people – it is directed at fat in itself. So even if you have one per cent body fat, that one per cent is something you are meant to hate, even if it does not mean you need two seats on a plane. If everyone decided to take one stab each at the monster that is fatphobia, it would not have to be just up to the fat people to battle it.

'Until we are all free, we are none of us free.'
Sofie Hagen (quoting Emma Lazarus)

9

How to love your body

I wish I could tell you that this is going to be easy. It is probably not. If you are like most people, you have, in your life, tried to lose weight. Quite possibly, unsuccessfully, seeing as that is the very nature of dieting. We now know how near-impossible it can be to lose weight – and shedding the weight of society's expectations and body-image standards is difficult too. The difference is the following: You could lose the weight and still end up miserable. You would just be miserable and thin. Or you can lose the weight of societal pressure and that might just be the only chance you have of truly finding joy within yourself. Of being truly happy.

I am sorry that this is a chapter. And that it is the longest one in the book. You were not born hating your body; this would not have happened without the interference by an entire industry that thrives off people's insecurities about their bodies. In theory, this chapter should not be directed at you and it should not be called 'How to love your body'. It should be directed at them and it should be called 'How to Stop Making Other People Hate

Their Bodies', because this is a huge and comprehensive problem that affects everyone and the responsibility and blame lies with *them* and not you. The focus should never be on you and all the things you could or should do to become happier. The focus should rest on those who made you feel this way in the first place. So let us all collectively send a proper stink-eye to those who created this internalised hatred as we delve into your safari towards self-love.*

✳

When I started this peregrination towards self-love, no one warned me how difficult it was going to be. How literally everything was going to change. You essentially need a complete rewiring. This is going to be hard. This is the Mount Everest of challenges you might face. In a lot of ways, ironically, this chapter starts the exact same way a lot of diet books start.† With asking you to please see this through, to be strong. The difference between learning to adore your fat and trying to lose it is this: learning to love yourself – or unlearning to hate yourself – will essentially make you feel good. It will feel good in your core. You will gain autonomy, confidence and your own humanity. You will look at yourself and

---

* I refuse to use the word journey anymore, so I have found a thesaurus and looked up synonyms for 'journey'.

† Diet books and 'lifestyle change' books. Fun fact: lifestyle change is just another word for dieting. People often think they are being super clever when they exclaim, 'Actually, you are right, dieting DOES NOT work, what you need to do is actually to make a LIFESTYLE CHANGE.' Just shut up, Sebastian.

see someone who is attractive and worthy of love.* So – same results as what all the diet books promise you, except you can eat whatever you want. And not in the diet-book way, where 'everything you want' has a fun caveat when you actually open the book. Turns out, you can eat everything you want as (sing-song tone) long as it's kale. It is never kale. No one ever wants kale. I mean 'you can eat whatever you want'. You can eat pizza for breakfast, sweets after 6 p.m., drink wine with friends and you never, ever have to count a calorie or weigh yourself again.

All of that ends now. You are now free. Imagine looking at a menu, deciding what looks the most delicious and ordering it – without feeling guilt or shame. Without apologising with your words or your eyes to the waiter and the people around the table. Imagine having dessert, not a single part of you thinking about calories or weight. You will come home, happy and content after a huge, delicious meal – you will look at your stomach in the mirror and you will smile. You will think 'I am one hot piece of ass!'† and you will mean it. You are free. You no longer have to be thin. You no longer have to apologise for who you are and how you look. You are fat and happy.

If that is a place you want to go, I need you to know that it won't be easy, but it will be worth it. Keep that in mind.

---

* Another fun fact: You don't have to live up to society's or really anyone's idea of attractive. You can be ugly. You're allowed to not care. One of the main problems with the term 'body positivity' is that the word 'positive' is in there. You can also just be 'body neutral'. Where looks and appearance simply don't matter.

† I am not sure what the hottest piece of an ass is. Is it the bumhole? I have a mole on my bum – allegedly – maybe that is the hottest piece of my ass.

Unlearn everything

This guide starts with me telling you that you need to doubt every-thing that you think is true. It will be like when you start a diet by taking all the good-tasting food in your house and throwing it in the dumpster and pour soap all over it, so you cannot later go back and eat cake out of the bin.* Except, instead of food in a bin with soap all over it, it is society's fucked-up beauty standards in a bin with soap all over it.

Once you know about fatphobia, you start to notice it in even the smallest fragments of your social life. From your friends saying, 'You look amazing, have you lost weight?' which suggests that thin simply looks better than fat, or from all of the headlines on the covers of magazines urging people to try their new diets. It might be the lack of fat characters in movies and TV, or the way 'fat' is constantly used as a derogatory term.

Fat being a negative thing seems to be largely considered a truth. I am here to tell you that it is not. One of the most difficult things to do is to question what other people deem just common knowledge. I am pretty sure that the first time someone pointed out that the Earth, perhaps, was round instead of flat, everyone around the table looked at each other, rolled their eyes and said, 'Steve is drunk again.'†

---

* This might sound like an exaggeration but no, this is actually quite common advice. It even happened in a popular *Sex and the City* scene. Isn't diet culture fun?

† Steve being a very common name in ancient times.

If you start believing that fat is not a bad thing, your life will get simultaneously better and worse. Let us start with how it will get worse.

I keep imagining the weekly brunch I participated in with some women from my work, a good seven years ago now. We liked to *Sex and the City* it up* on a Saturday late morning, drinking cocktails and gossiping. It was the highlight of my week. It felt good. It felt like I was living up to the expectations of how I should act as a woman. Women Do Brunch. Women Gossip. I felt like I was a *real woman*. They were also the only friends I had. Among the commonly discussed topics at the Saturday brunch were boys, fashion and weight loss. We discussed how we were all too fat, too big, too much. Which diets we were trying out, which diets we were failing this week and which diets we would try the next. Plans for the future were discussed – the future, in which we were all thinner. I did not discover Fat Liberation till years later, when the friendships had all faded.† I often think about how I would have felt, if I had discovered it during that time. Realising that our discussions about weight were toxic and damaging would have meant that I would have had to take a step back and not engage with them. I would have had to confront

---

* I don't mean that 'we loved to sit around being homo- and transphobic while cheating on only the best guy ever, Aidan'. I mean, we were four ladies in a cafe and is there any better example of that than to reference a nineties hit show? I think not.

† It started fading because during one brunch, I laughed loudly and one of my friends told me that I laughed weird. After that, I stopped laughing with sound for a whole year. When I realised what she had made me feel – shame over laughing – I started to end it with the whole group. It felt toxic. Who shames someone for laughing?

my friends. I would have had to explain to them why I would no longer participate in weight-loss chat and that I would rather not have to listen to it. I'm pretty sure this would have ruined brunch. It took me years to acquire the vocabulary to have these discussions so I am pretty sure I would never even have been able to explain to my friends why I suddenly needed to distance myself from the Saturday brunches. And I think of this so often. How you might be in the same situation.

If this is the first you ever read about fatness in this way, chances are, you are surrounded by fatphobia in your workplace and your family and social life. Because, let's face it, we all are. In order to properly embrace Fat Liberation, suddenly your whole world view will need to change. Every little conversation can become a possible battlefield. If you want to completely rid your life of toxic fatphobia, you may need to have some difficult conversations with colleagues, friends and family.

I acknowledge that this is terrifying. There are friends I no longer see, family members I no longer speak to, movies I cannot watch, music I cannot listen to, because of fatphobia and my awareness of it.

Excluding fat-hate from your life is not a necessity. You can carry on the way you are now and still work on your feelings towards yourself. I am just telling you that it is difficult. And there is a chance that you might not *want* to carry on the way you live now. Cutting the fatphobia out of your life is one of the most helpful and healthy things you can do. It is toxic – and it is scary and difficult. Loving yourself wholly is difficult and scary. But once you get to the other side, the grass is actually greener. Not only is the grass greener, but it is positively trampled flat by a horde of fat people dancing happily on top of it. Naked, flaunting our big, floppy bellies about the place.

I want you to feel warned. If you embark on this pilgrimage*
towards self-love, you have to be prepared for things to change.
There is something very sweet and comforting about societal conventions.

An acquaintance of mine raised a question at a dinner party
a while ago. She has a son who was being bullied for being fat.
She posed the question, 'What do we do? Do we tell him that
he is fine the way he is or do we help him lose weight?' Initially
this sounds as though it shouldn't even be a question. To me, the
answer should be so simple. When I unleashed all my suppressed
fat anger onto the table and started defending this poor boy –
napkins, butter rolls and cutlery flying freely across the table – I
realised that the answer was not simple. Teaching the child that
he is okay is the noble and right thing to do. But it will not align
with the world view he is being subjected to every single day
of his life. Children are logical creatures. How will you respond
when he says, 'But if I am all right, why do they make fun of
me?' and there is no way out of it unless you manage to somehow
explain that the whole world is bullshit. Of course, it is important
to teach your child that they have worth and that they are perfect
just the way they are, but is it possible to explain capitalism,
feminism and fatphobia to a child? Is it even possible to explain
that things are fundamentally unfair?

I understand the people who would decide to just help the
child lose weight. I understand that, even though I know first hand
how damaging that is. The alternative is imagining a child rock-
ing up to school, trying to become friends with a bunch of kids
who are just trying to live up to society's expectations of them.

---

* I still refuse to use the word 'journey'.

I have been there and I know that it is lonely. So what do you want your child to be? Full of self-love but lonely or self-hating but conforming?

This is why these conversations need to be had from the earliest age possible. I have heard horror stories about Other Parents and how it's almost impossible to speak to them about their children. I know that I, childfree, can't easily tell you to have a little fat-positive chat with all the parents in your children's school or nursery because I don't know any parents who wouldn't throw something at me if I suggested that. Make sure body-shaming is forbidden in the playgrounds and classrooms. Ask the teachers to not use anti-fat language or teaching materials. Suggest to parents and teachers that the children are taught about fatphobia, homophobia, racism, sexism, Islamophobia, transphobia, queerphobia and ableism and that there is an on-going conversation about how to make sure that the classroom is not a toxic space. Now, I know from first-hand experiences that teachers and parents (like all people ever) will not necessarily be super open to change themselves* – and all we can ever do is try – but what I am saying is: It seems like the temporary solution to the problem. Until, of course, the actual solution: a complete dismantling of the structurally oppressive system.

---

* The school system is flawed in so many ways. Institutions that have to constantly battle financial cuts will often not have the resources to attend to the special needs of one specific child – or one specific group of children. It often ends up being thirty highly individual kids in one classroom all expected to learn the same material in the same way. Me suggesting that you, the reader, singlehandedly attempt to change the way your children are being taught is, if anything, quite optimistic. I realise this.

As an adult, it is easier not being lonely. The internet is a wonderful place where you can essentially find anyone you want to mingle with. Facebook groups full of glorious fat people arranging fat-positive nightclubs, fat clothes swaps, fat art shows, fat conferences. There are podcasts with and about fat people in them, fat summer camps, fat fashion shows. Fat blogs and vlogs and Instagram accounts. You do not have to be alone with your fatness.

And that is the positive side of this – learning to love yourself and accept your fatness might create some imbalance in your life and it will take some adjustment. But there is this glorious world full of fat people ready to welcome you into our world, where you are considered beautiful and worthy and deserving of the same rights. Where there is no wrong way to be. It is a wonderful little corner of the world and it does not seem as if a lot of people understand us or accept us. So you no longer have to be sad or lonely.

The road to here is long and difficult but I hope you are willing to go down it and begin your excursion towards self-love.

Here is the thing. There is a good chance that it is too late for you to go back. You now know and understand what the alternative to accepting this new world view is. You can continue to believe that fat equals bad, unhealthy or unattractive, and you can continue to attempt to lose weight, knowing that the chances are that you will never be thinner than you are now. Being thin makes life easier, as you are no longer part of *that* oppressed group of people. But you are not *guaranteed* happiness, regardless of how privileged you are. Happiness is easier to achieve when you are not battling structural oppression on a daily basis, but when it comes down to it, the subjective hatred you feel about your body is just that – subjective. Meaning it is something you can change – without having to change your body.

You can just change your mind.

If you continue to believe that fat is inherently a bad thing, you will spend the rest of your life fearing it. Each meal can become a threat. A life full of limitations, restrictions and negativity. All in order to become or stay thin. Most people live like this – because we have been taught that thin means happy. Look at those beautiful and thin women in the diet ads, laughing at salads. Who would not want to be so happy that they find themselves erupting into laughter over lettuce?

So here is the trick. You can actually be just as happy as legume lady without having to limit your intake to stuff that is green and tasteless. You do not have to be thin to be happy.

You do not have to be thin to be happy.

You do not have to be thin to feel good about yourself.

You do not have to be thin to be loved and wanted.

You do not have to be thin to think you are sexy and beautiful.

You do not have to be thin to do yoga or to go swimming, to wear a bathing suit or a crop top, you do not have to be thin to follow your dreams.*

You do not have to be thin.

---

* Yeah, huge caveat right here: there are a lot of systems in place that are directly going to try and stop you from achieving your dream. If your dream is to play opposite Chris Pratt as the female lead in a Hollywood film, I'm pretty sure they would not allow that (I've asked). But if your dream is not dependent on other people's permission or commission – if all you've ever wanted was to take up dancing or sew your own clothes or write a book (hello) – don't wait till you're thin. Do it now. I once found a diary I wrote when I was sixteen where I had written down, 'Things I Will Do When I'm Thin'. One of them was: 'kiss a lesbian'. Now I know that you can do that while fat. Thank God.

Challenging 'the truth'

The gist of it: The very first step is learning, accepting and believing that being fat is not a bad thing. It seems like such a simple thing to state towards the end of the book, because by now I hope I have sufficiently made that point, but it *is* absolutely crucial. Society has successfully placed a voice within all of us that constantly tells us that fat is worth fearing. I can go into a random cafe and say to a group of people, 'I feel fat,' and they will say, 'Don't say that, you're not fat,' regardless of the fact that I am actually fat and that the word fat is technically just a descriptive word and not something I can feel. I cannot feel brunette. It is widely accepted that 'fat' equals 'bad'.

And it is wrong. You need to believe that it is wrong. If we take it one step at a time.

✳

The notion that fat is not beautiful: There are two sides to beauty. There is beauty in the socially acceptable sense. *The beauty ideal*. What has been deemed beautiful. It is this idea of beauty that is terribly damaging because it leads to people who do not fit into this category being discriminated against and oppressed. This definition of 'beauty' is very carefully constructed and forced upon us from a very early age. In this understanding, *fat is not beautiful* because fat is not acceptable. This idea that beauty is objective is the reason why I, throughout this book, have used Chris Pratt as an example of a *Classic Hot Guy* that we can just all agree is sexy. He is completely interchangeable with other white, cis Hollywood hunks like Brad Pitt, Ryan

Gosling or Channing Tatum. (In reality, if I really had to fantasise about marrying a cis man I found attractive, like John Goodman or Danny DeVito, the jokes would not work. You would be slightly confused and not certain if the people I mentioned *were* somehow the joke.)

The other side is the individual's perception of beauty. The subjective interpretation. Naturally, a lot of us are prone to preferring society's idea of beauty because we are so easily manipulated. But to a certain point. From then on, what happens inside of our brains is the very definition of subjective. There are loads of people who find fat people beautiful. I believed that beauty was *one particular thing* for most of my life. Until I rewired my brain. And what I saw in the mirror seemed to change, even though it remained the same. I suddenly found and saw the beauty in the body that I had hated. When you think of it, it is ridiculous to assume that we all find the same thing hot. It's important to attempt to dismantle the beauty ideals that we are all forced to survive under, but it's also important to dismantle those beliefs within yourself.

$$*$$

The notion that fat means lazy, greedy, unintelligent, evil, non-sexual, etc.: You can continue this list yourself – all the personality traits that you subconsciously combine with fatness. The fact that none of these are true should be so obvious that I feel bad even spending precious space in this book saying it. You know it is not true. I know it is not true. Even the most fat-loathing person in the world would do a double-take if you asked him to bet all his life savings on this being true. Despite this, we often swing these words around alongside 'fat', like it is a fact.

'Oh, he is so fat and lazy,' and it just *sounds* true. If I said, 'You thin lazy bastard,' it would seem weird. We should have reached a point by now where we know that how a person looks does not mean they are a certain type of person with specific traits.

✳

The notion that fat is unhealthy: See Chapter 7. If you still disagree, meet me at the car park closest to your house at 4 p.m. on Friday and I will fight you.

✳

Perhaps it is easier to look at it like this: being fat describes that your body is rounder and softer than people who are less round and less soft. That is it. Fat describes a body shape or the amount of fat you have on your body. It is a neutral thing. If you must add any emotional connotations or moral connotations to it, add positive ones. Most importantly: get rid of all the negative ones.

Owning the word 'fat' was the most important step of my pilgrimage towards self-love. 'Fat' was a weapon that had been used against me my entire life. Taking the word, using it about myself, stripping it of its negative connotations was like grabbing the gun out of someone's hands and pointing it right back at them.

And essentially, it was fairly easy.

'Fat' is not a negative word. I repeat: 'fat' is not a negative word. 'Fat' has been made to mean something negative through society's fatphobia. 'Fat' has been made to mean greedy, lazy, selfish, unintelligent, annoying, evil, unattractive, in the way and excessive. But actually going back to basics, to the actual origin and meaning of the word: it is not a negative thing. It is a descriptive word describing the size of your body.

The upset or hurt that you have been taught to connect with the word 'fat' has nothing to do with the actual word or – and this is very important – with any facts. Being fat is not intrinsically a negative thing, in the same way as being a redhead or tall or wearing a purple T-shirt says nothing about what your core values are or how objectively good-looking you are.

I understand that the word 'fat' can hurt. For many of us, it has been thrown at us from moving vehicles, from family members who were meant to love us, from people on the internet whose sole intention is to hurt us. If, every time I left the house, someone tossed a cinnamon bun in my face with fury, I might actively start to dislike cinnamon buns after a while as well. But if I somehow managed to figure out a way of catching the cinnamon buns so I could eat them later, all the tossing of them would stop hurting. Quite the contrary: it would mean that I would get to eat a lot of cinnamon buns.

So, if you can start accepting and using the word 'fat' as a neutral – and eventually a positive – thing, it will stop hurting. As with most things, it will take quite a lot of time. The more you use it, the more you say it, the better the cinnamon will melt on your tongue.

In the beginning, I used to add sentences to the phrase in my head. I would say 'I am fat' out loud and then add whatever I needed, but I would not always say it out loud.

I am fat – and so what?
I am fat – and that is a not a bad thing.
**I am fat – I also have brown hair and I am
    kind.**

I am fat – why would that make you feel uncomfortable?
I am fat – and I am allowed to be fat.

Because it will make people feel uncomfortable at first. Get ready to be met with a stream of, 'Oh my god, you are not fat, how dare you say that about yourself?'and similar comments, but hang in there. You can choose to either ignore them or confront them. 'Why do you say it as if it is a bad thing? I am fat. It is not a secret. This is how I look. Why would I not want to be fat? Do you think it is a bad thing to be fat?'*

The first step is removing the negative connotations – the next step is to replace them with positive ones.

I am fat – and I love it.
I am fat – and squishy, soft, round and beautiful.
I am fat – and I love my fat stomach.
I am fat – and glorious.
I am fat – and that is wonderful.

I can only recommend this solution if you love making people cringe and blush and change the topic quickly. Which is one of my favourite pastimes.

---

* The word 'why?' is so important when you are starting to face people with a newfound positive attitude towards fatness. 'Why are you asking me that? Why are you assuming? Why are you reacting like that?' – it is equally powerful to use against yourself as well. 'Why does this photo showing my chins make me sad? Am I currently believing that I should be ashamed of my chins? Why am I reacting like this?'

This goes for all the words that we perceive as something negative. Fleshy, big, fat, cellulite, heavy, large, chubby and floppy arms. It is not necessary for any of these words to be anything but neutrally descriptive. I look at my body and I state: my stomach is big and rotund, my thighs are fleshy, my upper arms are floppy and my butt is full of cellulite and I say all of this and feel happy. I say these words with the same tone that I would use if I told you I had won a million pounds. I am proud and happy and exclusively with positive connotations. It has taken me so long to get here, but it is definitely a possibility.

Just keep saying it. The words, the word 'fat' and your daily affirmations:

Daily affirmations

I am the first person to refuse, stubbornly, to stand in front of a mirror and speak to myself out loud. I will happily talk to myself when I am walking down the street, faking a phone call in order to make sure no one speaks to me.* But there is something ever so awkward about standing in front of your own reflection saying 'I am beautiful.' I believe that we are taught that we should never be too self-involved, too confident, too full of ourselves. We should keep our heads down and stay humble.

---

* Also, every once in a while, so that I can live out that fantasy where I met Fat Chris Pratt at a house party, and he is now obsessed with me, which means that I one day on a busy street in London shouted into a phone, 'We can have this conversation again once you finish shooting that dinosaur movie, Pratt,' because I call him Pratt – it's like, our thing, you know?

Fat people are more than anyone barred from feeling beautiful and from taking up space. And when you plonk your feet down in front of a full-size mirror, you are meant to focus on all of your flaws* and on how you want them fixed. You are definitely not meant to praise yourself for being wonderful. So when the majority of the self-help books that I read over time asked me to do so, I refused to do it. It felt silly.

Until I did it, of course. Do not get me wrong, the first time you look at yourself and say 'I am beautiful', it will not seem natural. Not the fifth time either. I hate to tell you that it works. I wish it did not work. I wish it was a wishy-washy American daytime chat show temporary solution. It is that too – but it is also a way of actively fighting the voices in your head that tell you that you are not good enough.

We receive negative messages about bodies on a – dare I say – hourly basis. From the adverts on television, public transport, social media, all telling women to buy a certain product to become 'better', to have smoother skin, shinier hair, a smaller waistline, redder lips and you have to be able to laugh at salads and yoghurts.† To the messages you get from friends and family, telling you that 'you've lost weight – you look great' or 'are you

---

* I need you to listen very carefully: You do not have any flaws. You do not. There is no such thing. You are perfect. I do not care how large your nose is or how much cellulite you have, you are perfect. When I say 'flaws', I mean it in the way that magazines mean it – and when they say 'flaws', they mean 'things we can pretend to fix if you give us your money'. Don't listen to them.

† Adverts directed at men seem to be telling men to use a body-wash-shampoo-conditioner-toothpaste-shaving-foam-all-in-one because EXPLOSIONS AND WAR.

sure you want to eat that?' – all with the same fundamental view-point that fat is bad and that you are not good enough.

So who is going to tell you differently than yourself? Who else than you will provide you with positive messages, with counter-arguments and with what is essentially love?

Your brain cannot necessarily differentiate between the sources of the messages. It takes an unbelievable amount of self-awareness and energy to separate each individual comment from each other and make individual judgement calls. So instead, bombard your brain with messages of the opposite values.

Do this.

Write down your insecurities. What are your most prominent thoughts about yourself and your body? Be honest with yourself. No one has to know this or see the list. Just be completely honest. Write it down. Dig out all the self-hatred and put it down on paper.

Then change the statements to a positive. Even if you struggle to believe it yet. If it says 'my thighs are gross' on the paper, you write down 'my thighs are wonderful' on a new piece of paper. 'I am unattractive' becomes 'I am beautiful' and 'my boobs are too saggy' becomes 'my boobs are saggy and that's perfect'. #Saggy-BoobsMatter.*

Congratulations. You now own a list of statements to tell your-self as much as you can. Figure out when you want to say them. Is it every time you take a dump? Each morning, during your morning coffee? Is it right before sleep? When you are on the bus to work? Will you draw a heart on your hand to remind yourself?

---

* #SaggyBoobsMatter is a hashtag coined by the Slumflower, Chidera Eggerue. She is a kick-ass powerhouse of a woman fighting the fight for no-bra-saggy-boobs to be free, free from judgement.

Keep saying it. Even when it feels like you are lying to yourself, when it feels like acting, when you feel silly and over-dramatic.

Because once upon a time, you were a tiny baby and you were not aware that anything about yourself could be wrong. Then a bunch of adults, who should have known better, made sure that a cascade of negative messages were drilled into your tiny child's brain. That is the child to which you are speaking. That is how far back you have to go in order to change things. Even if you now, as an adult, feel like you have learned that logically, there is nothing wrong with you, there is still a child-version of you somewhere who was taught the opposite.

Keep repeating your affirmations to yourself. Say them out loud. Listen to them. Believe them. And eventually, feel them.

Exposure

There is a good chance that you have rarely seen fat bodies. You will certainly have difficulties finding us on television, in magazines or in mainstream pornography. We are rarely written about and described in novels. Even in negative portrayals, it is rare to actually see a full-bodied fat person, apart from, of course, when we are mentioned in the news and we are only headless bodies with EPIDEMIC written underneath. Or we are a meme that someone posts on a friend's Facebook wall with the caption: 'Your girlfriend, lol', because people are just so funny, so, so funny.

So considering how often you even see fat people, imagine how little you see naked fat bodies. There is a good chance you have only ever seen yourself, maybe one or two fatties on some beach, a parent or if you have been so lucky to have sex with one.* Compared to the vast amount of naked thinnies out there, it is very unbalanced.

This makes fat bodies – and particularly naked fat bodies – seem strange. Like an oddity, something secret and possibly unacceptable and wrong. Whereas the thin body or the muscly body is normalised and idealised. Even if the thin or muscly body is not your sexual preference, it probably does not disgust you. It's just neutral. It's just a body. The fat body, however, might disgust you. I had to look at many fat, naked bodies before I stopped cringing and wanting to look away. Even though I knew that this body was as worthy of love as all other bodies and even though I felt it in my heart that this body was a beautiful body, my instincts all told me that this was a bad body.† A wrong body. This is a normal reaction to have. I have spoken to a myriad of self-loving, fat-glorifying, super-cool fat activists who found fat bodies repulsive, some did so for years into their fat activism. This feeling does not make you a bad fat person – you are simply indoctrinated to hate fat bodies alongside the rest of society. The hatred and invisibility of fatness is taught to us before we even start having a language. And so subtly, that we do not even realise that it is happening. Part of this is simply because we do not see it often enough for it to be normal.

But hey, should we not change that?

Look at fat people's naked bodies. The ones that have consented, of course, I do not suggest you go out and buy yourself some binoculars and start roaming bushes. I actually actively

---

* A fatty, not a parent.

† I keep reading this as 'bad boy' and I love the idea of calling my body a 'bad boy'. I think it might be a bad boy.

forbid you to do that. But look at them. Go on the internet and look up the Adipositivity Project.* Two wonderful photographers called Substantia Jones and Shoog McDaniel take nude photos of glorious fat people and put them up on the internet. There are fat nude calendars and prints that you can buy. I suggest you make it your wallpaper on your computer and your phone, that you get the calendar and put it up on your wall, that you make the website your homepage, so it pops up whenever you open your computer. Make sure that wherever you look, there is a naked fat person. Until it becomes normal. Until it stops feeling dangerous or wrong. Try looking at fat bodies – not as a warning or 'thinspiration'. Just as a fat, glorious body that exists and is allowed to exist.

Allow me to talk about porn for a second. People with fat bodies are hardly ever seen as sexual. If they are, it is often grotesque or hilarious. It will be a fat woman trying to sexually assault an innocent man because her sexuality is so laughable and aggressive. Or her dildo will require car batteries. I once exclaimed, on a podcast, that I watched porn and that this was a feminist sin. I declared that I would stop watching porn and become a good feminist instead. A few months later, a couple of women came up to me after a show I had done. They had the attitude that I adore the most in people approaching me after gigs. The attitude of, 'Right, we really want to like you, but you massively fucked up, so allow us to educate you for a second.' Being called out on your problematic behaviour is painful to the extent that I almost enjoy it as a physical, masochistic pleasure. This group of women told me that feminist porn exists. They gave me the names of websites

---

* Or go to shoogmcdaniel.com

that I should check out. I said 'I will give it a look' in the only way you can ever tell a group of people that, yes, you will soon be masturbating to something they have given you, and inevitably your mind will occasionally wander and you will see their faces. Hopefully, by providing you with this feminist porn information, you will now be imagining my face the next time you masturbate to it. Hi.*

Watching feminist porn was very different to watching mainstream porn. First of all – you have to pay to watch it. Which is the ethical thing to do, when you think about it. My first instinct was a feeling of entitlement – why should I pay, when I can get it for free elsewhere? And then you realise: it costs money to produce. When shooting a porn film, you need porn actors, camera people, light, a pizza for the pizza delivery person to arrive with, a couch, hopefully a bunch of wet wipes, you know, all the porn things. Of course you should have to pay for it. If you don't, you are essentially stealing from porn actors. And we† support people working in porn and sex workers.

---

* Please imagine me nodding approvingly. Maybe I do a thumbs up. A sexy wink. Yes, a sexy wink. They exist and I know how to do one. I am doing one right now because it is hard to write about sexy winks without attempting to do one. If you are on public transportation as you are reading this, watch out, because you are probably attempting to do a sexy wink and you are attracting hordes of people who now want to be your sex-partner. Quick! Make a disapproving face to make them go away. Good. Well done. Now, back to the book.

† Feminists. Feminists support sex workers. Because we, of course, don't think it's right to tell women (in particular) what to do with their bodies and their lives. And criminalisation of sex work has proven to be very dangerous to the sex workers. The International Union of Sex Workers (IUSW.org) can give you more facts and tell you how to help.

Second of all, feminist porn included people of all shapes and sizes, colours, genders and sexualities. It was a complete and utter mind-fuck.* There was not a single moment where I even considered questioning if any of the people involved had consented to it. It was clear and obvious that everyone enjoyed being part of it. That everyone was turned on by this – and by each other. I saw fat people being allowed to be sexy and wanted and fucked by people wanting to fuck them. Lesbian porn that felt so different from all the lesbian porn I had ever seen before. I could not figure out why it was so different – why it was better – until I realised that we were seeing it through the eyes of someone actually lesbian. Not a straight cis man. It felt like the difference between kissing girls at private parties when I was a teenager, with one eye open to see how the boys were reacting,† and when I finally kissed a girl because I fancied her, because I wanted to kiss her because I wanted to feel her lips. And there is a massive, massive difference. One is for the pleasure of men and one is for the pleasure of us. After I watched feminist porn, watching the mainstream, free porn felt wrong. It felt like watching Barbie dolls rub up against each other. It killed my boner. And I started looking at bodies differently – and my own sexuality differently.

Cut it out

You have done it before, during the myriad of awful diets you have taken upon yourself to finish. You have removed 'toxic stuff'

---

* It was also a body-fuck because, well, porn.

† Well. They were reacting very well.

from your life before. Only, they told you that the toxins were sugar, carbs, pasta, soda water and cake. Yet, for days, sometimes weeks, maybe even years at a time, you managed to live without it in your life because you believed, hand on heart, that this was good for you. That this would lead to happiness.

Has it ever worked? Have you ever thrown a chocolate cake into the bin and poured dishwashing soap all over it, to make sure you could not dig it back up later, when the cravings kick in – and then felt an overwhelming sense of calm and happiness?

I think it is time to eliminate other toxins from your life. I urge you to remove everything from your life that makes you feel bad about yourself. When you look through your social-media feeds, be aware of how you feel. In a world of filters, selfie sticks and teenagers with social-media experts on their payroll, there are a lot of posts that are incredibly staged and with the potential to make you feel bad. If a photo makes you feel bad, you spend money on feeling better. That is the simple reason why this happens. That is the reason why adverts will have thin women laughing at salads, and hair adverts where the hair is thicker, shinier and less static than yours will ever be. 'Likes' on social media have become almost a currency – where, if you have enough likes, brands will get in touch and give you free things. So when you see someone drinking an expensive cappuccino in a fancy cafe in a sort of blueish faded filter with a model friend of theirs, while you are sweating at your desk with a stained tea mug in your hand and pimples all over your face, you are meant to feel bad. You are looking at someone whose job it is to make you feel worse about your life. And I do not blame these social-media personalities – if anything, I am impressed that there are now teenage girls who are millionaires because they found a way to start a business without having to get a white, rich man in a suit to hire them. But back to you.

When you are going through this odyssey towards self-love, you do not need anything to startle you and get you off your course. Unfollow, unfriend, hide, block, mute. Do this to every single social-media account you follow that makes you feel bad. Whether it's your friend from school or whichever famous vlogger. This does not make you petty or jealous. It just makes you a person who is susceptible. And, we all are.

Once you have blocked, removed, unfriended and deleted all the accounts that make you feel bad about yourself, add new narratives. Find all the fatties on the internet that you feel inspired by. There are fat people in sports, fashion (fatshion), popular culture, science, art, porn, comedy, dancing, yoga – whatever you are into, there will be fat people there that you can follow. There are accounts specifically for photos of fat people eating, fat people flipping you off, fat people doing everyday things, fat people travelling. Fill your life with fat people.

Do it now, I'll wait.

Have you done it yet? I'm serious. Do it now.

If you wait, you'll forget. Don't you dare not do this. It's detrimental.

Do you think I don't know you're cheating?

Have you done it? Good. I'm proud. You've done a good thing for yourself. Unless you cheated and didn't do it of course, in which case, we'll never be friends.*

You are going to feel much better, I promise. I recently went to see a musical – something I love to do, seeing as I love the dancing, the music, the emotions. Musical theatre is everything that I, as an introvert, am not. Loud and expressive. This musical took place in a warm place, so all the women in the cast wore tiny shorts and crop tops. And they were, of course, all thin. While I was blown away by the music and the show in itself, I left the theatre feeling quite bad. I realised that I had not looked at flat stomachs for quite some time. When I go through my social-media feeds, there are fat people upon fat people. Of all colours and shapes. I no longer watch adverts on television. I stopped watching free mainstream porn. I stopped watching TV shows that did not feature a diverse cast. Sure, this did limit my television range quite a lot. But at the same time, now when I do, for some reason, watch a regular look-there-are-only-thin-white-cis-people-in-this-world TV show, I can now feel the difference. It feels strange and odd. And I see it very clearly.

Stop fleeing

Our bodies have become deniable to the extent where it is almost a sport. Ask most people and they will know exactly what to wear in order to make you look thin (black) or fat (vertical stripes) or which angles make you look thin (up) or fat (down). When I

---

* However, you can go back a few pages and start over and actually do it and then you can read this page again without feeling guilty. #lifehack

was a child, I would watch the sitcom *The Golden Girls* on TV. I remember ever so vividly a scene where Rue McClanahan playing Blanche Devereaux explained how, when she has sex, she never goes on top, because she would look fat. She hands her co-star a mirror who tests the theory by holding the mirror first above her head and then from underneath, and her co-star realises that Blanche is right. I remember it so vividly because I took note. *Right, seven years from now, when I will eventually have sex on a Portuguese guy's couch during the afternoon, before his mother comes home from work, on top of a carefully laid towel, whilst* Shrek 2 *is on the DVD player, remember to never go on top. You will look fat.* That was my first lesson about sex. Make sure you do not look fat.

We do everything we can to not look fat. This gets increasingly difficult, the fatter you actually are. If you are a fully formed adult fat person, there are not many angles or clothing that will hide the fact. And to be honest, it is the most stressful thing in the world. We have all had people fly across a table, nearly giving us a heart attack, because we took a cute picture of them, and they are about to slit our throats if we put it online for anyone to see. My heart drops almost every time I show someone a photo of themselves and I see in their eyes that they hoped it would look different. That they would look thinner.

I did a gig in Belfast a few years ago. It was a fairly stressful gig already – I was trying out new material in front of an incredibly lovely crowd, so I felt responsible for their night. I wanted them to enjoy it – but the jokes were not fully formed yet. So I was very much in my own head as I was talking down the microphone. The comedy festival had a photographer who was taking photos. At one point, he kneeled at the side of the stage, and took a photo. Instinctively, that tiny part of my brain that still remembered watching *Golden Girls* twenty years before made me say to him, 'Don't take the photo from that angle!' and there was laughter from the audience – laughter of recognition. I immediately stopped dead in my tracks. Oh . . . no. The photographer was halfway up on a table to take the photo from above, when I started ordering him, 'No! No, get back down. Take it from below!' and he reluctantly did so. I did the rest of my show very aware that there was a man on the floor with a camera and he seemed too scared to get up in case I would shout at him again. And I knew the photos would end up making me look fatter. And I knew that that was a good thing. Because here is what I have learned.

The escape from your body has to stop now.

My fatlicious friend Cat Pausé once shared with me that she looks at herself naked in the mirror every day. When I started talking to people about this, I was expecting them to react as if that was a normal thing to do. Instead many of them shuddered and told me that they did not even have mirrors in their houses. So, that ends now. Go get yourself a full-size mirror and put that in front of your naked body and look at it. Until you are comfortable with what you see. There will be no sucking in of stomachs or angling the mirror so it is hanging over your head, no soft lighting. Just you. FAT. NAKED. You can, while you're at it, try to note all the negative voices in your head, and tell them to stop talking, or try to replace them with positive thoughts. Look at your naked, fat body in the mirror, and tell yourself that you are beautiful. You are worthy. You are fatlicious like Cat Pausé.

Touch yourself. Right, calm down, this book is not about to take a shocking – but sexy – turn.* Touch your stomach, your

---

* Although, touch yourself in a sexy way if you want to. It's a good way

thighs, your floppy arms. Caress all the areas that body-shaming TV shows would call 'problem areas'. You have spent your entire life trying to ignore, avoid, deny or remove these areas – how often have you shown them affection?

Cuddle your stomach. Breathe in so it grows big. Gently touch your thighs. Say, 'I am sorry I was so mean about you. You are soft and wonderful and sexy.'

I would suggest you do it at home, in bed or in front of the mirror, but part of me wants to suggest that you can do it any-where. Just because it is now my new favourite dream to sit on the bus and see a fat person feel themselves up as they whisper, 'I am sorry, stomach, you are squishy and lovely.'

Break the rules

I find breaking the rules incredibly therapeutic. You already know all the rules, even if you have never actually seen them written down: Thou shalt not wear crop tops, thou shalt not eat fast food in public, thou shalt not look like you do not have shame over your own fat body. So we wear black, oversized clothes and only order salads in restaurants. It is an unspoken way of saying: Do not worry. I know I am fat. I am ashamed. Carry on with your day.

My older brother lived in Dubai for most of his adult life. When I visited him in Dubai a few years ago, he was vegan. Not

---

to release stress, to get in touch with your body and to recall any time in *Great British Bake Off* where Paul Hollywood is very, very disappointed in someone's cake. Mmm. Hey! We are sex positive. We don't judge each other's fantasies here.

only was he vegan, but he was into 'healthy living' and he did CrossFit and ran up the eighty-six storeys in his building. Once, he and his girlfriend went out and I was alone in his flat. After a desperate search in all of the cupboards, feeling like I was eight years old again scurrying around desperate for sugar, I found half an 86 per cent dark-chocolate bar. It tasted of death. I shoved some organic almonds into my mouth and left the house to eat something that did not remind me of the ground I will eventually be buried in.

I found a greasy, American-themed diner. I ordered a burger, some fries and a coke. I was not very comfortable – Dubai is already an incredibly hot place and I was sweaty and very aware of my size. Being a fat person in a restaurant is daunting in a lot of ways – but I was too focused on the taste of dead rat in my mouth and the fact that I was incredibly hungry to even consider that I looked like a cliché. A fat person eating a burger and fries. I noticed a group of women in a booth close to mine. I only noticed them because they noticed me first. I started sympathising with zoo animals. I bet that giraffe just wants to be left alone too, but, the people going to the zoo want to stare at the giraffe because they rarely see giraffes and, ideally, they want the giraffe to do something fun. I ate my burger as the women were giggling and whispering amongst themselves. This is the mode I usually go into when I am fat-shamed.

I cower. I lower my head, carry on with my day, ignore the threat. I wish this was a choice; it isn't. I know people whose instinct it is to attack. Who will shout effortlessly at strangers and tell them to fuck off. After which they say something like, 'I am sorry. Sometimes I just lose my temper, how embarrassing,' and I want to kiss them on their necks and say, 'That was not embarrassing: you are a hero and I want to be you.' Me, I behave like a giraffe trying to be an ostrich;* I bury my head in the sand and then I later think of the perfect comeback. This time was not different. I ate my burger, pretending that the stares, the laughter and the whispering were not there. But I felt it all burning on my skin. I am not sure what then happened. I did not lose my temper – that sounds like a sudden thing. It was more like I picked apart my anger, bit by bit and threw it away very gently and carefully. I allowed my temper to evaporate to the point where I felt nothing but coldness inside.

When the women had started giggling, I had squashed down all that felt like me, so that I almost did not exist. Slowly, I inflated the parts of myself that I had instinctively pushed down until I became myself again. I was full after the burger and fries. But the women were still laughing. I called the waitress over and said – as loudly as I could – 'Can I have another one of these? Thank you,' and then we all waited. The laughter had turned into confused giggling. Like the giraffe was doing a handstand† and no one could believe that this would happen on the day they had gone to the zoo. Like watching a viral video happen in real time.

The burger arrived and even though I was full to the brim of delicious burger, I turned to the women and started eating the second one. I looked them straight in their dead, evil eyes.

---

* When I googled 'animal that hides its head in the sand' in order to find out how to spell 'ostrich', I learned that, actually, ostriches do not actually do that. According to San Diego Zoo – http://animals.sandiegozoo.org/ animals/ostrich – when ostriches are threatened, they attack with a kick powerful enough to kill a lion. One animal that does hide when it feels threatened is a turtle. It simply pretends it is a rock. I can relate to that.

† Hoofstand?

The laughter died down instantly. They quickly turned away and started pretending to have normal conversation. But I kept staring at them and I knew that they could feel it. I unapologetically ate that burger, staring at the women with so much rage, I could barely taste the ketchup which was now on my cheek – unapologetically. Because no. Because no: that is not how this world will work anymore. You do not get to do this to people. I chucked down the burger, staring at them as they quite quickly got the bill and left. I had switched it around, the narrative. I had been the object of their fun little lunch – suddenly, I was the subject and they became the object of mine.

It feels powerful to break the rules. When one lays down a rule, such as 'thou shalt not wear crop tops' there is a subtext that says 'or else'. I want you to challenge that 'or else'. Or else what? Does someone die? Do you see me as less of a person? Will I get arrested? Because guess what, I am already seen as 'less'. I am already unwelcome. I am already being discriminated against. So tell me again why I cannot wear a crop top while I am being discriminated against.

By following the rules, we are attempting to cover up the fact that we are unfuckable. We are trying to become more fuckable by wearing slimming clothes and drinking veggie smoothies in public. But consider this: do you want to be fucked by people who won't fuck fat folks? Do you really want to be fucked by people who can't handle you wearing a crop top?

It is a blessing more than a curse to be seen as unfuckable in the eyes of bigots.

Here is the thing. If you wear a crop top in public, a few things might happen. You might get stares. You might get looks. You might get comments and abuse. These things also might happen if you do not wear a crop top. You are a fat person being fat in public. There is always a risk. Yes, if you appear as if you are unapologetically yourself and you are part of a marginalised group, there is the actual risk that you are *more* vulnerable to abuse and discrimination.

But if you wear a crop top, chances are you will feel empowered. Of course, there are people who do not like to wear crop tops – in which case, by all means, do not wear a crop top. But if we look at the crop top as a symbol of 'what you are not allowed to do when you are fat – but that you want to do' – it can be anything from doing yoga to dancing at a party to wearing vertical stripes and eating burgers in public – then I am willing to guarantee that it will feel freeing. Because, essentially, you are taking up the space you have been trying to avoid for so long. Like having been in a prison your whole life only to find out that the bars are an illusion and you can break free easily. The guards are mannequins, your orange prison uniform is actually a crop top and leggings you wear as trousers – it is your life, you can do what you want and you are free.

The first time I took a photo of my stomach was in New York, in a cheap hotel room.* Even though it was just a normal mirror-selfie of my stomach, like so many fitness gurus on Instagram have done since the dawn of time,† to me, it was huge. Both the stomach and the act of photographing it. My stomach felt and looked excessive and the photo made my heart jump into my throat, because – there it was. With all of its stretch marks and

---

* It is not important where it was – it looked like any other hotel room. It is merely important to mention because I remember it vividly (and it sounds cool, let's be honest).

† You know, from whenever Instagram and selfie-cameras came to the world.

just its pure volume. I looked at the photo once a day for a few weeks. One night, I held my breath and posted it online. I was not sure what to actually expect. The 'what if' took up so much space in my mind, I did not have space to fulfil the sentence. Turns out, not much happened. A lot of people liked the photo and wrote appreciative comments. A lot of people called me fat – Really? Wow. This photo of my fat stomach sure could have fooled me – and told me to kill myself. You know. The usual. But no one actually died from it. I stood tall, even after (what felt like) the whole world had seen my stomach. Since then, I have posted several photos of my stomach. At one point, I painted eyes over and a mouth under my navel and it was the most adorable thing I have ever seen. I shared that with the world too. I wore bikinis to the beach and I started feeling comfortable changing my clothes in front of my friends. I did the opposite of the rule – to hide your stomach, at all costs. I showed it. Big, fat and bare. If you can, draw a face on your stomach and show the world. I recommend it.

This is all part of the same strain of the 1-2-3 step advice: acknowledge, accept and appreciate your fatness. It will be difficult, and your mind will try to fight it with every trick in the book, because it goes against everything you have ever been taught.

And: it feels good. To hug your stomach and to start believing that it is a sexy, beautiful stomach – it feels good. And if you have gone through life being told you are worthless and undeserving of good things, sometimes good feelings can feel uncomfortable. We need to get over this because this is essential work – you are going to be you forever.

There is no escaping your body. You can ignore its signals to the extent where it is almost invisible to you, but it is there.

It is time to face yourself – terrifying as it may sound. It is time to acknowledge that you are fat. That your body looks the way it does.

Your body is a mishmash of blood, veins, skin, fat, organs, nails, hair and brains. It is an incredible machine as well. Your body is busy trying to keep you alive: a process that looks different depending on how your body works. It is healing wounds and growing hair in places you have been conditioned to think of as inconvenient. Leave it be. Thinking of it as a machine or a car might make you appreciate it more.

By fleeing from the fact that you have a fat body, you become invisible to yourself. You owe yourself more than this. You deserve to be a full, whole, visible, fat human being.

✳

Because this is your body. There is no getting away from that. And when summoning my sixteen-year-old self, I also know what you might possibly think at this point: I will get along with my body – once I am thin. So let's address your inner thinnie.

Your inner thinnie

In 2017, I was a thin model on the front cover of a magazine. Full disclosure, it was a fake magazine and the photo of me as thin was Photoshopped. It was part of a day of filming for a documentary about fatness in Denmark. We thought it would look 'dynamic and fun' if I did a photo shoot in order to put a fat woman on the front cover of a magazine to see how it looked. While the designer was toying with the editing afterwards, I looked over his shoulder to see what he wanted to change.* Reluctantly, I allowed him to make the photo look more 'magazine-y' since the whole point was that it had to look like a regular women's magazine – with the exception of the model being fat. Then he turned to me and said, 'Do you want me to make you skinny, just for fun?'

Ever since I started becoming aware of my fat body being unacceptable in the eyes of society, I have imagined and longed for my thin body. It's hard to find a weight-loss book without such messages as 'imagine yourself thin' or 'you have a thin you inside of yourself wanting to get out'. It is fairly common for people to put a photo of themselves at their fattest on the refrigerator to remind them of why they deprive themselves of food – because they can 'never again' look like that. The concept of the 'thin you' is strong. It is the good future, the future in which you are happy and content and everything is perfect. The 'thin you' has everything you want so badly. When I imagined the 'thin me', not only was she happier, but she walked differently, acted differently, lived differently; actually, I think that 'thin me' was just Zooey Deschanel, but ideally, less annoying than the characters she always plays.

I did more things for 'thin me' in the future than I ever did for 'fat me' in the present. I bought better clothes to hang in the closet as a motivation for losing weight. One day, I thought, 'thin me' will walk down the pavement in those tight, skinny jeans with her tight, skinny butt and she will be smiling, finally, for the first time ever. Every time I outgrew clothes, I would keep them,

---

* Not in a playful and curious way, more in a 'I am about to rip your motherfucking throat out if you as much as crop this photo, because I am perfect in every single way and if you even consider removing even a single one of the hairs on my legs, I will maul you' kind of way.

just for whenever 'thin me' came back. I would turn down parties and events because it did not feel like something 'present fat me' should attend, what with being a big, fat ogre and all. Instead I would postpone and plan to go to the parties and the events when I would eventually become 'thin me'.

If there was someone I fancied, I would not make a move – that was for 'thin me' to do. This lovely person whom I wanted to kiss on the mouth with my mouth did not deserve to have big, gobbly me drool all over them. No, they would appreciate it if I just waited till 'thin me' arrived. Then I would not even have to make an effort, I would get to pick and choose between everyone I wanted. In my tight, skinny jeans and with my tight, skinny butt.

I would tell everyone about 'thin me'; that she was on her way and that I was doing what needed to be done, in order to summon her. There would be such pride in my voice when I would announce that I was on a diet or that I had cut out sugar. Within fat activism, this is called a 'good fatty'. Society can just about accept you if you are fat but you have acknowledged that this is bad and you are trying to lose weight. They are all waiting for you to get to 'thin you'. It is the same reason that you can barely mention your size without people erupting into a cascade of, 'Oh no, you are not fat,' or, 'Do not say that about yourself,' because they see fatness as so awful that they think that acknowledging your fatness would be insulting towards you. If you say, 'I am fat but I am trying to lose weight,' you put everyone at ease. Don't worry: I will soon look acceptable. I will soon fit in, I will soon conform. The 'good fatty' is essentially a 'soon-to-be-thin person'. A fat person exercising, a fat person eating salads, a fat person being apologetic. It is the most acceptable way to be fat.

The best explanation for this, in my opinion, is to be found in

Jes Baker's description of 'body currency'. The concept of body currency was originally coined by her, in her wonderful book, *Things No One Will Tell Fat Girls*, which you have to read.

Body currency goes a little something like this: Through mainstream media and advertising, we are all being sold this idea, that if only we work hard enough and spend enough money, we will achieve happiness. If only we go to the gym, shave our woman legs, put make-up on our faces, get muscly man arms, get a tan, a nose job, a tight butt, I mean: fill in the gaps yourself. Every single one of these cost you so much time and so much money, so you can put an actual price on your 'looks'. The reward for this expense is supposed to be happiness, freedom. So when people see someone fat – or someone not conventionally attractive, someone not following the rules – someone fat with hairy legs, wearing no make-up in a crop top, someone living an unapologetic and happy life – people lose their shit. Because you have not *earned* the right to be happy. You have not worked as hard as everyone else. Imagine spending hours and hundreds of pounds on attempting to achieve happiness, and then some prick just gets it all without doing any of the work, without paying any of the price.

We put in so much effort and money into becoming thin, into striving for thinness, and so when someone does not equate thinness with greatness they are basically telling other people that their currency is valueless. The savings they have been accumulating their entire life now cannot buy them anything. You know that boat which you bought with your entire life savings? We just got it for free, just by deciding that we wanted it. The fury this can provoke in people is astounding. When you denounce thinness as an ideal, and all those years you spent starving yourself, all the hours you spent crying in a gym, all the meals you turned down with friends – you see it was all for nothing. Accepting that you may never be thinner than you are now can easily feel impossible.

My 'thin me' never came, and as I embarked on my jaunt towards Fat Liberation and self-love, I forgot about her. And I thought I had let go of the idea of her completely.

Until I looked the visual artist from the magazine in the eyes and said, 'Yes, please. Make me skinny,' and he started working on the image of me. It only took him a couple of seconds to make me thin. And then time stood still forever.

I gawked at 'thin me' for the first time. This woman I had spent most of my life thinking I was going to be. It felt weird watching her. She was so real. And I knew I had to eradicate her.

As long as 'thin you' is a possibility, a goal, something that could be reality one day, it is difficult to accept and embrace your fatness.

Killing your inner thinnie does not have to mean that you are not allowed to ever lose weight. It means that you choose yourself and who you are now. Look at your body right now. Imagine that this is it. This is you for the rest of your life. That there will never be a thinner version. Even if you have decided to embark on a diet, if you have just started a new sport, if you feel absolutely confident that you will definitely be thin one day: imagine that you will not. Insert your fat self into those future situations in which you imagine yourself being thin. Your wedding day, the beach in the summer, the date with that cute person. Throw out the jeans that are too small, and stop using photos of yourself as motivation to starve yourself.

Live your life as if you will have this body forever – because then you start living *for you* and not for an imaginary version of you in the future.

293

Unlearning food guilt

Stop apologising for what you eat, for what you want to eat or what you are about to eat.

Food guilt is so ingrained in our culture, that it is part of our language. 'Cheat days' are days where you allow yourself to eat the 'wrong' foods – a cheeky comment about that one day where you can eat the things you actually want. But by calling it a 'cheat day', you have already drenched that day in guilt and shame. Eating certain foods is deemed weak, shameful and wrong.

I am not a therapist, so in order to fully escape your own personal food prison, I suggest you speak to someone who is. Being able to afford a therapist is an incredible privilege – if it is possible, I highly recommend it. No book written by a comedian can be a substitute for proper therapy. But what I *can* do, is tell you what helped me.

The very first step is getting rid of all emotional baggage put upon food. There is no such thing as 'good food' and 'bad food'. 'Good calories' or 'bad calories'. 'Guilty pleasures' or 'cheeky' anything. Notice how often you do it – excuse what you have eaten or what you are about to eat. Notice how often you see someone nervously rub their hands together and say, 'I didn't eat lunch, so I think I will have a pizza,' or, 'I'll go to yoga tomorrow, so I'll have dessert.' This needs to stop right now. It is all connected – the food shame is only there because we feel like we know that an abundance of food leads to fatness. And fatness is what we fear; fatness is what we try to avoid at all costs. But remember it is not bad being fat. So we have to end the food guilt immediately or it only adds fuel to the fatphobic fire.

Join the community

Join the community. I cannot emphasise enough how important it was to me and every other fat person I have spoken to to find that there is a community of fat-positive people out there. If you go online, these are relatively easy to find. There are big communities like 'Flying While Fat' or 'Fat Girls Travelling' (both groups on Facebook which you can join) and fat-positive products and events such as Club Indulge – a fat-positive club night in London, or *She's All Fat* – a fat-positive podcast mentioned earlier. If you are a user of Tumblr, it is worth searching for certain keywords there. It is hard to promote specific hashtags, because by the time you are reading these words, chances are they will have been taken over by white cis women who are a size 12. Follow some of the people I have introduced you to throughout this book. Substantia Jones, and the Instagram account, @Shooglet, are excellent places to start. Listening to community-based podcasts like *She's All Fat, Friend of Marilyn* and *Bad Fat Broads!* can make you feel less alone.

You might even be lucky to live near a place that has actual fat events. Like FatSwap in London and across the UK – an event where fat people go and swap clothes they no longer want – or Fat Camps in the States – not weight-loss camps, mind you, just fat-loving camps. Camping with your fat friends. In 2018 I went to the 'Fatties: Politics of Volume' fat-activism conference in Amsterdam, where I first read out a few paragraphs from this book to some of the coolest fat people I have ever met. You are lucky if you live near any of these events or if you have the means to travel there. If you cannot travel, perhaps you could start something in your local community. I have heard of people starting a fat-creativity night. Once a week, a group of fat people meet up and knit, draw and paint.

Failure, flaws, mistakes, and not feeling good enough

You are so used to self-hating and focusing on mistakes and failing, so I need you to know this: when it comes to 'how to be fat', you can do no wrong. You have only ever tried your best.

Our end goal is a world where fat people can live without being discriminated against, without being abused. You do not have to like the way your body looks to be able to achieve this. You can fight alongside fat people and be self-loathing at the same time. It is not a requirement that you love yourself for you to be welcome into the battle for Fat Liberation.

It is so easy to replace rules that say you have to lose weight with rules that say you have to love yourself. These are guidelines that you can follow if you want to. You do not have to love yourself or your body. I promise you that life is a lot nicer if you can, but I understand that this is hard and that I could be talking from a very privileged position compared to yours. I do not know you or your struggle or your past. It is not for everyone to love their bodies.

And you can be on your very own march towards self-love and still every once in a while start to hate yourself again. I am a good seven years in and there are still days when I dislike myself. Sometimes all it takes is a mirror you did not plan to see, or a comment you did not expect to receive. It can be a rejection from a love interest or having gained weight and feeling like you have to start all over again. Learning to adore yourself is an ongoing battle, and as long as there is fatphobia in our world and culture, it will not be easy.

All you can do – and all I can ask you to do – is to try and show yourself affection. Most of us have been deprived of that to some degree, and often this is where our feeling of emptiness comes from. I do not want movements such as the body-positivity movement or the Fat Liberation movement to be yet another thing you do not feel like you can live up to. To be part of this you do not need to be fashionable, to have followers on Instagram, to debate on the internet, to wear crop tops or even to fucking like your body.

There is no such thing as failure. You have already been failed by the people you expected to be able to trust. You have already felt guilty enough. You have already blamed yourself enough. Part of the hike towards self-love is reuniting with your body and the instincts you had when you were born. Accepting that you act a certain way, eat a certain way, look a certain way. And that it is all okay. You are okay. And you have always been okay. You only ever tried your best.

10

Afterthought

On a summer evening, only a few months before this very moment, in which I am writing this final section of the book, I was walking home from the bus stop. My head was heavy from everything I was carrying: the heartbreaking statistics about the effects of fat bias, the personal childhood stories about the fat little child I was and how awful things were then, the fictitious pressure I felt from the fat-activism community about the book (I want to impress the people I admire) and the thoughts about structure and what I wanted to put in my conclusion. Two young men were walking towards me. I could see my front door but I clutched my keys in my hand. Just in case. When I passed them, one of them said, 'Fat cunt!' and the other one said, 'I wouldn't even fucking touch it.'

That has happened before, loads. My usual reaction is to ignore it. Ignore it and process it later. I'd love to say that my reaction is to take a brick from my bag, like a character in the book *Dietland*, and scare the shit out of the pricks. But bricks are heavy and I'm not looking to fight (let's be honest: be beaten up by) anyone. So I usually lower my head and continue to walk, pretending it didn't happen. Later, I will write an angry tweet or shout to my therapist. At this moment in time, though, something clicked. Or snapped. Or fractured. Or popped. And I started laughing. I tried to stop, but it was too late; the men had heard it. It was a deep, bellowing stomach-laugh.

In many ways, scarier than a brick.

These two men verbally abused me because they felt insecure about themselves and probably their own masculinity. They have been brought up to believe that fat people are to be mocked, that women are to be submissive, and that *real men* are entitled to basically every single thing they want. We have all been brought up to believe this. And when we rise above it, we win. And that was funny to me. It was funny that they were so transparent and that they assumed I couldn't see right through them. I felt in my gut that the opposite of cowering – of immense shame, of hiding and self-hating – is laughing, loudly.

And there we were:

Me: a fat person. A fat person who has spent upwards of eight years unlearning fat-hate and learning self-love.

Them: just two random men. Two random men who have been bombarded with fatphobic adverts, TV shows, movies, stand-up comedy routines, news reports and history lessons. And whose default setting is to believe all of it.

It's safe to say that most people *have not* spent years unlearning fat-hate. Most people are probably unaware that it's even an option. For every person who reads a fat-positive book and starts to slowly open themselves up to the possibility of spending a lifetime of attempting to believe they are worth something, there are millions of children who are taught that their bodies are definitely wrong and that they should feel shame about this.

It doesn't add up, this business plan of telling all fat people that they are okay the way they are. If we keep focusing on the individual's quest towards unlearning fat-hate, the problem will never end. However, if we start focusing on the systems that *teach* us to hate in the first place, we stand an actual chance.

I once received an email from two twelve-year-old girls. They asked me if I would answer a few questions for their school assignment – where they had chosen to write about body image.

Whenever I have time, I will always say yes to these. I answer them with more care than I have ever answered a journalist. When I answer journalists, they will most likely water down my replies before it goes into their newspapers, and the children are unlikely to read my words there. So when I get direct emails from the kids themselves is when I unleash. (Although, I'll be honest with you, sometimes these children take the piss. They'll ask, 'What is body positivity?' as if they didn't have Google and as if they haven't been able to google questions like this since they were infants.) These twelve-year-old girls didn't do that. Their first question was:

When you are twelve years old, you hate your body. How do you feel about yours?

When you are twelve years old, you hate your body.

There is no academic study, no fat-activism think piece, no statistics, no hypothetical discussion, no artwork that can prepare you for two twelve-year-old girls telling you, with almost a virtual shrug, that they hate their bodies. It is something that should affect all of us on such a personal level. It should hurt your actual heart physically. That this is the world in which we live.

We *can* no longer focus on the individual, on you and me. We have to start working towards an end goal: for fat people every-where to be free from discrimination, objectification, oppression and abuse. We have to get there and we have to get there soon, before I get another email from twelve-year-old girls that will send my stomach into a tumble dryer state.

Fat people deserve to be treated better.

Even those who stubbornly insist that fatphobia only stems from the desire to help people to be healthy and feel good about themselves, must admit that this has not helped so far – in fact, it has only made it worse. If they are truly in the business of making life better for fat people then surely they will have to be open to the idea that maybe treating fat people well would be something worth trying.

And we can no longer allow them to keep the focus on us. I am now the author of the book in which a chapter called 'How to love your body' exists, so I am obviously guilty of keeping the focus on the individual, instead of the system, myself: I am invested in you and all fat people feeling great about ourselves. This in itself is somewhat of a flaw. We need a complete financial, governmental, socioeconomic and political change. Because what we are doing now, this neoliberal wet dream, of blaming and focusing on the individual's responsibility, is not working and it is not fixing anything.

The fact that we have been made to believe that it is up to us to change our own opinion of ourselves just proves how powerful and dangerous structural and systemic fatphobia is. It has been rigged against us from the beginning. They made us into consumers the second we were born, little fat babies with not an ounce of negative body-awareness. They started working on us the moment we started watching Disney films. By the time we had an allowance, we began filling their pockets. They taught us that we were wrong only to be able to sell us products that would eventually fail to make us feel better, so that we would buy more products. When we get in a plane seat, we blame ourselves for being too fat, never the plane for being too small. We start diets in order to lose the weight and every time we fail, we blame *ourselves*. Never them, for they are the saviours, there to sell us the stuff that can help us. Meanwhile, they teach us to be thinner, smaller, quieter, scared, timid, careful and obedient, as they tell us to smile and not make a fuss, not to complain and to only focus on how we could do everything better ourselves. While using their products. I buy make-up to make myself feel better. I have a whole chapter in this book about clothes – consumerism is the norm now; their system works. We are funding our own oppression.

And this is not one company, one guy in a suit, who is breaking the law in order to do this. It's the financial model on which we have based our entire political system. Making people feel inadequate in order to sell products is not only legal, it's *financially viable*. And it's not only legal and financially viable, it's the business model upon which our society is built.

Capitalism is a system based on the accumulation of profit. It puts the individual's right to earn money above ethics and morals. If everyone loved themselves, if no one thought materialistic goods could make them truly happy, if poverty didn't exist, a whole lot of companies would declare themselves bankrupt. The system values profit more than the safety of children.

So it is all well and good if we manage to change the way we think about ourselves and our bodies, but it benefits just ourselves and it will most likely include a life-long struggle. It's important that we do not stop there. Some would say that it is vital that we do not even start there. The change we actually need is *not* within the individual. *You are not the problem.*

We need a complete financial, governmental, socioeconomic and political change

It doesn't happen overnight and it doesn't happen without all of us standing together, collectively. I know there is a chance that you have read this book because you wanted to learn how to be fat and happy and that the idea of fighting against the capitalist and oppressive system never even crossed your mind. Before I met Andrea at university, it never crossed mine either.

But it is all interconnected and tangled up – your initial sadness over your fat ankles to the company making diet pills lobbying to legalise drugs which have been proven to be fatal.

I have jokingly mentioned the *revolution* and the *dismantling of the system* throughout this entire book and I have hinted that I would eventually try to draft you to be part of some kind of anti-capitalist army.

That's both *just a joke* and also the truest thing I have ever said.

I don't have all the answers; I don't have a list of Ten Things you Can Single-Handedly Do to Eradicate Fatphobia. Sprinkled throughout this book, there are suggestions. Ideas. But even though I don't know exactly what you can do, I know you need to do something. Not just to be a person who will help in changing the world, but because it is very probable that you have spent your whole life consuming messages telling you to be passive, to be small, to be invisible, to be quiet. *Doing something,* saying 'Screw you!' to the patriarchy, is powerful. Because you are finally taking control of your own life. You are finally gaining ownership of your own body.

And fat people deserve autonomy. You existing in your body is not an invitation for anyone to comment on your body, to ask you questions about your body, police what do you or don't do with it, or label your body with anything unwanted by you. You are a full, whole person deserving of respect and the same rights as everyone else. This is important.

And then I can only hope you will engage with the fight. I hope you realise how incredibly valuable your input would be. How much we need as many people as possible to actively fight anti-fat bias. What would be particularly great would be if our thin allies would take the wheel for a bit. Fat people spend every day fighting the notion that we are worthless. How lovely it would be if non-fats would step up and help us eradicate fatphobia.

This exists on the personal level – we have to eliminate fatphobia from our own actions in our day-to-day life. We have to be a good ally to (other) fat people (see chapter 'How to be a good friend to fat people'). We, at the very least, have to make sure we do not actively contribute to fat-hatred existing in society. We have to talk to teachers at our children's school about what they are doing to make sure there is no body-shaming in class, it means telling our bro-friend to stop mocking fat people, it means asking our local venue if they cater to all accessibility needs. It means looking inwards and working on changing our own bias against marginalised groups.

This exists on a slightly larger level – we need to make an effort to stop companies doing damaging work. This means calling out campaigns that are not inclusive and intersectional, signing petitions that ban truly horribly fat-shaming TV shows, and stop fat-shaming adverts from being made. It means making sure that you include all marginalised groups in your activism because none of this will work if we only fight for a few selected groups. I encourage the smaller acts of activism. In my podcast, *Made of Human*, I used to have a segment called Acts of Disobedience. A listener emailed me to say they had made small stickers with fat-positive statements on them to stick all over fatphobic adverts on the train. It is a perfect example of using whatever strength you possess to fight for something better. Like Substantia Jones or Shoog McDaniel who take beautiful photos of naked fat people for the world to see, like Kivan Bay who educates anyone who follows him on Twitter about fat studies for free, like Cat Pausé travelling Europe to teach about fatphobia, or like Cameron Esposito, a perfect example of an ally who is not fat, making sure to include queer, fat voices in her podcast *Queery*. Not to mention all the activists whose actions are borderline (if not completely) illegal and who therefore cannot be mentioned by name or actions.

But the fight exists on a global and all-encompassing level. By now, it's safe to say that I have pointed the finger at capitalism as the main enemy. This *means* something. Fatphobia, homophobia, racism, sexism, transphobia, Islamophobia, ableism and queerphobia thrive under a capitalist and right-wing government. If we want the complete financial, governmental, socioeconomic and political change (and oh, we do), your fight has to stretch itself into your political involvement. Figure out which politicians are actually fighting for marginalised groups and vote for them. And do vote. When possible, join anti-fascist protests. Protest for all the marginalised groups. Pay your taxes.* Donate to or volunteer for charities that help the groups affected by fascism, such as Stonewall UK, a lesbian, gay, bisexual and transgender rights

---

* I'm looking at you, huge corporations.

charity, or Help Refugees, which provides humanitarian aid to, and advocacy for, refugees around the world. Use your voice, your resources and your democratic right to fight.

And demand the right to take up the space you deserve.

I know it's hard. There is a loneliness to being fat. It's ostracism. We go to cinemas, on planes, in public bathrooms, to restaurants – hoping we will be able to fit into the seats. Hoping that their chairs can hold our weight. Hoping that we can wipe our own butts after we have done a very human and natural poo. And each time, we know that there is a risk that we are not able to. We go to the doctor's, hoping to be seen as a whole person who is judged on what is inside (literally) rather than what you can see with your naked eye. We go to swimming pools, hoping we can enjoy the feeling of the water surrounding us without being stared down or ridiculed. We go to gyms and hope that no one will take our photo and post it to the world with a snarky comment. We seek a meaningful relationship or a night of sex and we have to hope that the other person isn't playing a prank on us. Each let down, each disappointment and each rejection can feel like a punch in the gut.

It is a very specific feeling. The one you get when all your friends sit down to eat – and you are left standing because you recognise the chairs. And the last time you sat in one, it broke. I have tried finding out what the feeling is called.

You feel unwelcome, embarrassed and excluded at the same time. But I believe there must be something deeper behind it. If the whole world is a DO NOT ENTER sign that no one else sees – surely, that must do something to you. That must stick to your core.

As fat people, we build an entire world around us where we can sort of breathe for a bit. Where things can be made slightly bearable. A lifetime of not fitting into seats and thinking about how we cannot fit into seats. We are used to problems, we are prepared for them and some of us are even okay with that. For an outsider, the world looks different. For a thin person, an airplane is full of seats – not torturous chairs that you might not even be allowed to sit in.

How do you explain to someone that you are not welcome in the majority of places – but that there are no signs and it's an unspoken rule? Something that is signalled to you by the seats being too small or the seatbelts being insufficient or every person sitting next to you sighing and rolling their eyes. There is no sign you can point to and say, 'Look! I am being excluded here,' because if there were, then maybe people would react.

I still do not know how to explain all of this to a person – even my best friends – because how do I answer the inevitable follow-up question: then how can you still be smiling?

Resilience? I have no other choice. You do what you have to do to survive. Because regardless of how far society will go to let you know that you are not welcome – that you are a disease to be cured, that you are unworthy, that you have fewer rights than others – you do exist. You learn how to take precautions.

There is a loneliness to being fat, but it can also make you strong. Because by attempting to exclude us, they make us more resourceful. We learn how to get by, we become resilient, and we will figure out how to create a space for ourselves. I have not met a single fat person who I would not consider strong. Even if we never realise it, I think we all are. How can we not be?

You create Facebook groups which guide fat people to airplane seats, you buy all the accessories that straight-sized shops have, and you smile to your thin friends so that they do not feel sad. Because they are not as resilient as you. You learn how to protect them from your reality, because they are not ready for it.

You are fat and you are resilient.

Now, go back to your stomach again. Hold it. Cuddle it. Say nice things to it. By this point in the book, the end, I hope this feels easier to do than it did when you started reading. Your stomach is squishy, round, soft and lovely. Draw some eyes and a nose over the navel and see if you can make your stomach smile. Then take a photo and tweet it to me. It never fails to make me happy. It's difficult to fully dislike a smiling squishy stomach. Say to your stomach, 'We got this.'

Because you do.

They told you that you didn't, but you do.

Practise self-care

Uncover your strength

Never give up

Cry unapologetically

Hug yourself whole

Nourish your body

Always keep fighting

Zoom in on your worth

I believe in you

Start believing in you too

FAT LIBERATION MANIFESTO
by Judy Freespirit and Aldebaran
November, 1973[1]

1. **WE** believe that fat people are fully entitled to human respect and recognition.

2. **WE** are angry at mistreatment by commercial and sexist interests. These have exploited our bodies as objects of ridicule, thereby creating an immensely profitable market selling the false promise of avoidance of, or relief from, that ridicule.

3. **WE** see our struggle as allied with the struggles of other oppressed groups against classism, racism, sexism, ageism, financial exploitation, imperialism and the like.

4. **WE** demand equal rights for fat people in all aspects of life, as promised in the Constitution of the United States. We demand equal access to goods and services in the public domain, and an end to discrimination against us in the areas of employment, education, public facilities and health services.

5. **WE** single out as our special enemies the so-called 'reducing' industries. These include diet clubs, reducing salons, fat farms, diet doctors, diet books, diet foods and food supplements, surgical procedures, appetite suppressants, drugs and gadgetry such as wraps and 'reducing machines'.

WE demand that they take responsibility for their false claims, acknowledge that their products are harmful to the public health, and publish long-term studies proving any statistical efficacy of their products. We make this demand knowing that over 99 per cent of all weight-loss programs, when evaluated over a five-year period, fail utterly, and also knowing the extreme proven harmfulness of frequent large changes in weight.

6. **WE** repudiate the mystified 'science' which falsely claims that we are unfit. It has both caused and upheld discrimination against us, in collusion with the financial interests of insurance companies, the fashion and garment industries, reducing industries, the food and drug industries, and the medical and psychiatric establishment.

7. **WE** refuse to be subjugated to the interests of our enemies. We fully intend to reclaim power over our bodies and our lives. We commit ourselves to pursue these goals together.

FAT PEOPLE OF THE WORLD, UNITE! YOU HAVE NOTHING TO LOSE . . .

Thank you

To the **fat activists** in this world who endure attacks and abuse from all angles and yet who do their important work selflessly. They are fighting for me and you and the little fat babies being born today. They are making it easier for us to exist. For that, I am endlessly grateful.

To **Mark Watson** – For pushing me to write this book, for helping me to gather my thoughts surrounding it, for helping me to write it, for being there throughout the entire process, for being my dictionary, my thesaurus, my mentor, my (secret and unpaid) sort-of editor, my rock, for teaching me about hyphens and apostrophes and the word 'epitome'. Thank you. There are a lot of things which I could not have done without you and this book is one of them.

To **Andrea Storgaard Brok** – Thank you for feedback and criticism on the book. Thank you for deciding to study Russian almost a decade ago. You didn't just make me a better person, you made me a happier person, and you continue to inspire me on a daily basis. I would not be who I am today if it wasn't for you – and I really fucking love myself, actually. And you. I love you a lot, Andrea.

To **my mother** – for laying the groundwork and showing me that it's better to be different. When I said to my mother, 'You know, I'm glad you always took my side when I was arguing with teachers at school,' she said, 'Well, of course. I wouldn't raise you to be someone who respected authority!' and for that I am incredibly grateful. To **my sister** – for making me proud and for making me laugh. To **my best friend, Ina** – without whom I am half.

To my much-needed and much-appreciated therapist, **Claudia C.**, thank you for forcing me to talk about the book even when I deemed it unnecessary ('I'm FINE, I SWEAR!'), when it turned out that it wasn't.

To my editor **Sarah Thickett** and everyone at **4th Estate** for believing in me and making this book possible. And to **Charlotte Atyeo** for helping me over the finish line.

To **Political Fatties/Πολιτικα Χοντρελεζ** for letting me read a tiny part of my book at their *Fatties: Politics of Volume 2018* conference to a bunch of hardcore fat activists – one of the most terrifying things I've ever had to do.

To **Mollie Cronin** – also known as @art.brat.comics on Instagram – thank you for your wonderful illustrations throughout this book. A little dream come true for me.

To **Dawn Elizabeth Williams** – for the title *Happy Fat*.

To **Cat Pausé**, for understanding when I needed you to understand. For being my friend.

To **Chris Quaile**, my manager, for fighting my corner, even though I'm incredibly high maintenance, I don't do budgets and make ludicrous demands all the time.

Thank you

To **Matilda Ibini** and **Stephanie Yeboah** for sharing your experiences with me for this book and for enduring my long, rambling WhatsApp messages.

Thank you to **Dina Amlund** for sharing your knowledge with me so I could put it in this book, and thank you for helping me out when all my words scrambled together and I didn't know right from wrong.

And a very special thank you to **Kivan Bay**. My highly efficient, super-intelligent, hard-working, hilarious, thorough researcher: someone I am proud to call my friend. Thank you for being there when it felt like no one else understood and thank you for still being around. Thank you for researching for this book. Thank you for sharing your findings with me. Thank you for educating me and for making sure I was always going in the right direction. I am lucky to know you and the world is lucky to have you.

Recommendations

Just a few of the many people you should know:

Substantia Jones
Shoog McDaniel
J. Aprileo of *Comfy Fat*
Kivan Bay
Da'Shaun L. Harrison
Corissa Enneking
Linda Bacon
Haley Morris-Cafiero
FedFront Danmark
Cat Pausé
Charlotte Cooper
Marilyn Wann
Jessamyn Stanley
Lindy West
Stacy Bias
Smashlyn Monroe
Roxane Gay
Andrea Storgaard Brok
Ragen Chastain
Miranda Kane

Sarah Hollowell
Gabrielle Deydier
Virgie Tovar
Jes Baker
Scottee
Stephanie Yeboah
Melissa Fabello
YrFatFriend
Sonya Renee Taylor

And for representing:

Beth Ditto
Chrissy Metz
Keala Settle
Jo Brand
Rebel Wilson
Joy Nash
Adele
Nicole Byer
Tess Holliday
Gabourey Sidibe
Alison Spittle
Maddie Baillio
Lizzo
Bridget Everett
Danielle Macdonald
Aidy Bryant
Melissa McCarthy
Amy Lamé
Desiree Burch

Podcasts:

The Fat Lip
She's All Fat
Fat Club Podcast
Two Whole Cakes FatCast
Bad Fat Broads!
Woman of Size
The Belly Love Podcast
Friend of Marilyn Podcast

Books About Fatness:

Bacon, Linda and Aphramor, Lucy, *Body Respect: What Conventional Health Books Get Wrong, Leave Out, and Just Plain Fail to Understand about Weight* (BenBella Books, 2014).

Bacon, Linda, *Health At Every Size: The Surprising Truth About Your Weight* (BenBella Books, 2010).

Baker, Jes, *Landwhale: On Turning Insults Into Nicknames: Why Body Image Is Hard, and How Diets Can Kiss My Ass* (Seal Press, 2018).

Baker, Jes, *Things No One Will Tell Fat Girls: A Handbook for Unapologetic Living* (Seal Press, 2015).

Blank, Hanne, *The Unapologetic Fat Girl's Guide to Exercise and Other Incendiary Acts* (Ten Speed Press, 2013).

Campos, Paul, *The Obesity Myth: Why America's Obsession with Weight is Hazardous to Your Health* (Gotham Books, 2004).

Chastain, Ragen, *Fat: The Owner's Manual* (Sized For Success Multimedia, 2012).

Cooper, Charlotte, *Fat Activism – A Radical Social Movement* (HammerOn Press, 2016).

Cooper, Charlotte, *Fat and Proud: The Politics of Size* (The Women's Press Ltd, 1998).

Farrell, Amy Erdman, *Fat Shame: Stigma and the Fat Body in American Culture* (NYU Press, 2011).

Gay, Roxane, *Hunger: A Memoir of (My) Body* (Corsair, 2018).

Harding, Kate, *Lessons From The Fat-O-Sphere: Quit Dieting and Declare a Truce with Your Body* (Tarcherperigee, 2009).

Holliday, Tess, *The Not So Subtle Art of Being A Fat Girl: Loving The Skin You're In* (Blink Publishing, 2017).

Kinzel, Lesley, *Two Whole Cakes: How to Stop Dieting and Learn to Love Your Body* (The Feminist Press at CUNY, 2012).

LeBesco, Kathleen, *Revolting Bodies: The Struggle to Redefine Fat Identity* (University of Massachusetts Press, 2004).

Miller, Kelsey, *Big Girl: How I Gave Up Dieting And Got A Life* (Grand Central Publishing, 2016).

Murphy, Julie, *Dumplin'* (HarperCollins, 2017).

Murphy, Julie, *Puddin'* (HarperCollins, 2019).

Orbach, Susie, *Fat Is A Feminist Issue* (Arrow, 2016).

Pausé, Cat, Wykes, Jackie and Murray, Samantha, *Queering Fat Embodiment: Queer Interventions* (Routledge, 2014).

Rothblum, Esther and Solovay, Sondra, *The Fat Studies Reader* (NYU Press, 2009).

Schoenfielder, Lisa and Wieser, Barb, *Shadow on a Tightrope* (Rotunda Press, 1983).

Stanley, Jessamyn, *Every Body Yoga: Let Go of Fear, Get on the Mat, Love Your Body* (Workman Publishing Company, 2017).

Taylor, Sonya Renee, *The Body Is Not An Apology: The Power of Radical Self-Love* (Berrett-Koehler Publishers, 2018).

Tovar, Virgie, ed., *Hot & Heavy: Fierce Fat Girls on Life, Love & Fashion* (Seal Press, 2012).

Tovar, Virgie, *You Have The Right To Remain Fat* (Melville House UK, 2018).

Walker, Sarai, *Dietland* (Atlantic Books, 2015).

Wann, Marilyn, *Fat!So?: Because You Don't Have To Apologise For Your Size* (Ten Speed Press, 1998).

West, Linda, *Shrill* (Quercus, 2016).

If you want to know more:

HAES – Health at Every Size. www.healthateverysize.org.uk

Association for Size Diversity and Health – their website has a really good resources list, full of scientific evidence for fat acceptance, more books about fatness and where to find HAES experts to work with. www.sizediversityandhealth.org

Militant baker – www.themilitantbaker.com/2017/04/diversify-your-instagram-feed.html

End notes

Introduction

1 http://www.traveller.com.au/thai-airways-ban-fat-passengers-and-young-parents-from-business-class-seats-on-their-new-boeing-dreamliner-7879-h0xpsg
2 https://www.machins.co.uk/news/the-full-weight-of-the-law-can-you-discriminate-against-overweight-workers.html
3 https://www.naafaonline.com/dev2/education/laws.html
4 https://www.theguardian.com/inequality/2017/aug/30/demoted-dismissed-weight-size-ceiling-work-discrimination
5 https://web.archive.org/web/20021226042434/http://www.largesse.net/Archives/FU/index.html

Chapter 1

1 https://www.commonsensemedia.org/research/children-teens-media-and-body-image
2 https://www.sciencedirect.com/science/article/pii/S019339739800495
3 Rand, C.S, Macgregor, A.M., 'Successful weight loss following obesity surgery and the perceived liability of morbid obesity.' *Int J Obes. 1991* Sep;15(9):577-9.
4 https://news.yale.edu/2006/05/16/some-people-would-give-life-or-limb-not-be-fat

Chapter 2

1 https://www.huffingtonpost.co.uk/entry/26-times-white-actors-played-people-of-color-and-no-one-really-gave-a-sht_us_56cf57e2e4b0bf0dab313ffc

2 http://journals.sagepub.com/doi/abs/10.1177/0093650211401376? journalCode=crxa

3 http://www.telegraph.co.uk/culture/books/children_sbookreviews/11055696/Malorie-Blackman-deserves-our-support.html

4 The book I'm referring to is *Eleven* by comedian and author Mark Watson (Simon & Schuster, 2010). It's a bit awkward because if you've followed me online anywhere, it'll be quite obvious that Mark is a really close friend of mine, and I didn't want it to look like I was advertising his book in my book. Nor did I want it to look like I read his book and then adecided to stalk him because he seemed to like fat people – and now I've nailed him down as a friend. Ideally, you'll assume he wrote me INTO HIS BOOK, but if you do the maths you'll see that he didn't even know me at the time of writing it. But now that I've mentioned it in these end notes, maybe he'll be forced to write me into one of his future books. That's the dream. And I think he should. Especially now that I've written him into (the end notes of) my book.

Chapter 3

1 https://www.telegraph.co.uk/travel/comment/plane-seats-legroom-shrunk-worst-airline/

Interview: Kivan

1 https://medium.com/@kivabay/the-intersection-of-fatmisia-and-transmisia-78fb10f90551

2 https://www.pinknews.co.uk/2016/12/11/study-finds-40-of-transgender-people-have-attempted-suicide/

3 https://www.sciencedirect.com/science/article/pii/S1054139X15000877?via%3Dihub

4 https://www.nationaleatingdisorders.org/blog/shining-a-light-on-gender-identity-and-eating-disorders

End notes

Chapter 6

1 https://bmcpublichealth.biomedcentral.com/articles/10.1186/1471-2458-8-128#CR31

2 https://news.yale.edu/2006/05/16/some-people-would-give-life-or-limb-not-be-fat

3 https://onlinelibrary.wiley.com/doi/full/10.1002/oby.21538

4 https://www.nytimes.com/2016/05/02/health/biggest-loser-weight-loss.html

5 https://highline.huffingtonpost.com/articles/en/everything-you-know-about-obesity-is-wrong/

6 *American Journal of Public Health*, 2015

7 https://www.ncbi.nlm.nih.gov/pmc/articles/PMC4510944/

8 http://www.pharmacytimes.com/publications/issue/2014/july2014/complications-of-bariatric-surgery-dumping-syndrome-and-drug-disposition

9 http://www.pharmacytimes.com/publications/issue/2014/july2014/complications-of-bariatric-surgery-dumping-syndrome-and-drug-disposition

10 https://jamanetwork.com/journals/jamasurgery/fullarticle/1379763

11 https://jamanetwork.com/journals/jamasurgery/fullarticle/2448916

12 https://www.cbsnews.com/news/the-sanofi-suicides-who-knew-what-about-failed-diet-drug/

13 https://www.sciencedirect.com/science/article/pii/S0140673607617218, https://www.ncbi.nlm.nih.gov/pmc/articles/PMC3136184/

14 https://www.independent.co.uk/news/world/americas/playboy-playmate-dani-mathers-body-shame-woman-gym-naked-photo-snapchat-sentence-graffiti-remove-a7755771.html

Chapter 7

1 https://www.nytimes.com/1992/04/12/us/a-growing-movement-fights-diets-instead-of-fat.html *(quote on page 185)*

2 https://jamanetwork.com/journals/jama/article-abstract/409171

3 Conus F, Rabasa-Lhoret R, Péronnet F., 'Characteristics of metabolically obese normal-weight (MONW) subjects', Appl Physiol Nutr Metab. 2007 Feb;32(1):4-12

4 Velho S, Paccaud F, Waeber G, Vollenweider P, Marques-Vidal P, 'Metabolically healthy obesity: different prevalences', Eur J Clin Nutr. 2010 Oct;64(10):1043-51

5 https://www.nature.com/articles/ejcn2010114

6 https://www.ncbi.nlm.nih.gov/pmc/articles/PMC4731253/

7 Vaughan B, Baruth M, Beets M, Durstine J, Liu J, Blair S, 'Fitness vs. Fatness on All-Cause Mortality: A Meta-Analysis', *Progress in Cardiovascular Diseases, Vol. 56*, Issue 4, Jan–Feb 2014:392–390

8 https://www.jabfm.org/content/25/1/9.long

9 Read about the Obesity Paradox in this review: McAuley PA, Blair SN. 'Obesity Paradoxes', J Sports Sci. 2011 May;29(8):773-82

10 https://jamanetwork.com/journals/jama/fullarticle/192032

11 https://www.consumerfreedom.com/articles/162-history-of-a-great-unraveling/

12 http://www.scientificamerican.com/article/obesity-an-overblown-epidemic-2006-12/

13 https://www.obesitymyths.com/myth2.9.htm

14 http://www.scientificamerican.com/article/obesity-an-overblown-epidemic-2006-12/

15 https://onlinelibrary.wiley.com/doi/full/10.1038/oby.2001.108

16 https://www.nejm.org/doi/10.1056/NEJMsa021721?url_ver=Z39.88-2003&rfr_id=ori%3Arid%3Acrossref.org&rfr_dat=cr_pub%3D www.ncbi.nlm.nih.gov

17 https://www.nj.com/hudson/index.ssf/2018/03/hoboken_mans_pot_belly_was_actually_a_30-pound_tum.html

18 https://metro.co.uk/2017/02/07/man-told-by-doctors-that-he-was-just-fat-has-130lb-tumour-removed-6432034/

19 https://www.standard.co.uk/news/overweight-man-had-55lb-tumour-7199358.html

20 https://www.sciencedirect.com/science/article/abs/pii/S1740144517303790

21 https://www.legacy.com/obituaries/timescolonist/obituary.aspx?pid=189588876

22 https://fluffykittenparty.com/2018/07/13/unhealthy/

23 http://www.bbc.com/capital/story/20161130-fat-people-earn-less-and-have-a-harder-time-finding-work

24 https://www.cnbc.com/2017/11/03/study-finds-youre-less-likely-to-get-hired-if-youre-overweight.html
25 http://time.com/4883176/weight-discrimination-workplace-laws/
26 https://media.utoronto.ca/media-releases/university-of-toronto-scarborough/stereotyping-has-a-lasting-negative-impact/
27 https://ajph.aphapublications.org/doi/full/10.2105/AJPH.2011.300620
28 https://www.ncbi.nlm.nih.gov/pmc/articles/PMC1447722/
29 https://www.ncbi.nlm.nih.gov/pmc/articles/PMC1447722/
30 https://www.ncbi.nlm.nih.gov/pmc/articles/PMC2594553/
31 Williams DR, Neighbors H, 'Racism, discrimination and hypertension: evidence and needed research, Ethn Dis. 2001 Fall;11(4):800-16
32 https://journals.lww.com/psychosomaticmedicine/Abstract/2006/05000/Chronic_Exposure_to_Everyday_Discrimination_and.2.aspx
33 https://academic.oup.com/aje/article/166/1/46/135692
34 https://www.ncbi.nlm.nih.gov/pmc/articles/PMC2424090/
35 https://ajph.aphapublications.org/doi/10.2105/AJPH.2007.114769
36 https://ajph.aphapublications.org/doi/10.2105/AJPH.2007.114769
37 https://www.hindawi.com/journals/jobe/2013/291371/
38 https://www.ncbi.nlm.nih.gov/pmc/articles/PMC4115022/
39 Gruenwald T, Kemeny M, Aziz N, Fahey J, 'Acute Threat to the Social Self: Shame, Social Self-esteem, and Cortisol Activity', *Psychosomatic Medicine: November-December 2004*, Vol. 66, Issue 6:915-924
40 https://onlinelibrary.wiley.com/doi/abs/10.1111/1467-8624.00455
41 https://everydayfeminism.com/2014/09/classism-of-eating-healthy/
42 https://www.equalitytrust.org.uk/scale-economic-inequality-uk

Fat Liberation Manifesto

1 Originally published by the Fat Underground, Los Angeles, California, USA.